RESPONSIVE SCHOOLS, RENEWED COMMUNITIES

A publication of the
Center for Self-Governance

RESPONSIVE SCHOOLS, RENEWED COMMUNITIES

CLIFFORD W. COBB

 PRESS

San Francisco, California

This book is a publication of the Center for Self-Governance, dedicated to the study of self-governing institutions. The Center is
affiliated with the Institute for Contemporary Studies, a nonpartisan,
nonprofit, public policy research organization. The analyses, conclusions, and opinions expressed in ICS Press publications are those
of the authors and not necessarily those of the Institute, or of its
officers, directors, or others associated with, or funding, its work.

Inquiries, book orders, and catalog requests should be addressed
to ICS Press, 243 Kearny Street, San Francisco, CA 94108. (415)
981-5353. Fax (415) 986-4878. To order, call toll free in the contiguous
United States: (800) 326-0263. Distributed to the trade by National
Book Network, Lanham, Maryland.

Cover design: Ben Santora
Cover illustration: Jordan Santora (student)

Copyeditor: Linda Press Wulf
Production editor: Tracy Clagett
Indexer: Linda Gregonis

0 9 8 7 6 5 4 3 2 1

Library of Congress Cataloging-in-Publication Data

Cobb, Clifford W.
    Responsive schools, renewed communities / Clifford W. Cobb.
        p.   cm.
    Includes bibliographical references and index.
    ISBN 1-55815-205-9. — ISBN 1-55815-216-4 (paper)
    1. Educational vouchers—United States. 2. School, Choice of—
United States. 3. Minorities—Education—United States. 4. Poor
children—Education—United States. I. Title.
LB2825.C53 1992
379.1′3—dc20   92-18357
                                                              CIP

Contents

PART IV
Answering Criticism of Vouchers

A Note from the Publisher

With the publication of this volume, the Institute for Contemporary Studies, through its Center for Self-Governance, begins a new series of books on the schools. Let me explain why our schools, and what Clifford W. Cobb has to say about them, are so important to the self-governing way of life.

Good schools are more than the efficient utilization of inputs. Good schools are morally and intellectually productive communities. The question is, Do we know how to create these communities? Can we, to paraphrase Hamilton in *The Federalist*, create them through reflection and choice; or must we depend on accident and force to determine what our schools will be? This is a fundamental question that we Americans must address. In a time when citizens seek greater control over their institutions, should schools be exempt from accountability? The answer is no. But again—how do we go about creating schools that are productive communities?

Cobb contends that choice is critical to the process by which parents, students, and teachers can start to build the kind of consensus that allows a community of learning to emerge. Choice is the social glue that can unite the key producers of education into a purposeful team. It can also allow us to transform our government schools into true public schools. For without the exercise of an authentic mandate by those the education system is meant to serve, our schools are nothing more than bureaucratic extensions of government, driven by accident and force.

As Cobb's argument and case studies show, it is people who produce education—and when education can fairly be called public, it is because people have the right and the means to make it work. Sharing a common purpose and acting with real authority generates a reciprocity of needs that creates a genuinely public good.

Cobb recounts a number of attempts by parents and community leaders to initiate school choice plans involving nongovernment schools. These accounts reveal a consistent pattern of opposition from teachers' unions and district administrators. That the unions and professional administrators can rail against choice as destroying public schools merely demonstrates how impoverished our concept of publicness and our language of political discourse have become. The moral imperative for a self-governing society was articulated two centuries ago: that men and women, through reflection and choice, have the capacity, right, and responsibility to make the fundamental decisions that affect them and their communities. It is through the making of these decisions that they develop and refine their capacity to be self-governing. To say that a government monopoly that arrogates all decision-making authority to itself is somehow "public" and a moral force in the society is to employ a form of newspeak, bankrupt of meaning.

Schools have always been one of the key institutions through which young people learn the fundamental values that animate their society. We also know that one of the important ways children learn is by modeling their behavior on what they observe. If students see their parents and teachers working to manage a self-governing enterprise, they will learn the basic lessons of what it means to embrace the self-governing way of life. If, by contrast, what they see in school is bureaucracy run rampant, their experience will provide no model for the conduct and values critical to our country's well-being.

Cobb movingly describes the plight of young people in the impersonal environment of a bureaucratic school system, where, he tells us, each student faces the system alone. Because of their divisive and isolating treatment of students, government schools have given individualism a bad name among those concerned with school reform. But advocates of self-governance make a powerful and important argument that the distinction between individualism and community is a false one. Strong individuals come from strong communities. And strong, caring communities are the product of individuals who have come together to shape their own institutions.

Real reform of America's schools will occur only when we recognize that our institutions must empower people and offer incentives for change. Until then we will continue to pour money into government schools that are spiritually dead. But allowing the entrepreneurial and self-governing spirit to infuse the schools can make them truly public.

Fundamental to the kind of change I have been describing is the right of the people to reflect and choose. Cobb believes that the key to meaningful choice is a system of tuition vouchers involving nongovernment schools, together with deregulation to allow government schools to respond effectively to the challenge. He presents the rationale for such a system and shows how it would work. There are surprises in this book for anyone with preconceived ideas of what vouchers and choice in education mean. Here we learn that where they have actually been tried, voucher plans—often criticized as subsidies for the affluent—have fostered education that is nonelitist, pluralistic, and empowering.

This book affirms the potential of school choice not only to build true communities of learning within our schools but to renew the intermediate associations that sustain a self-governing society.

Robert B. Hawkins, Jr., President
Institute for Contemporary Studies

Foreword

When we consider how our schools may be made responsive to the real needs of students, families, and communities, it can be difficult to separate the effect of introducing choice from the effects of other pressures to reform. There seem to be indications that the fear of losing students, and with them community support, has had results in some school districts. Public schools in cities or states where choice plans have been—or may be—introduced seem more receptive to change than schools in other places (or than the *same* schools before choice became a possibility).

At the same time, there are dangers in the simplistic introduction of competition into areas of human services. In these areas the consumer's knowledge is usually limited; it is more difficult for parents to evaluate education than, say, a can of beans. If vouchers are proposed as the vehicle for choice, proponents must recognize that the qualitative values in education are as important as statistically quantifiable achievement. Voucher systems can tend to focus on results that can be measured, to the neglect of the subtler, deeper aspects of education. Additional evidence shows that emphasis on competition can entail the danger of fabricating results (it may become profitable for a school to coach students for forthcoming tests).

As this important book shows, however, a conclusion that there is no room for competition among schools would be mistaken. Some competition has always existed—that based on prestige, for instance. What is important is to acknowledge the value of community—to recognize specifically that competition takes place within societal capsules and that these set some of the conditions for competitive integrity. This means that sociological structures must be found that will guard against the potential pitfalls of competition.

Giving more information to the education "consumers" is a necessary but not sufficient step. Consumers typically have a hard time evaluating copious statistics and complex information. Already overwhelmed by the much simpler but overabundant information on cereal boxes and soft-drink cans, they do not have a lot of energy for proper comparison shopping. Thus, providing numerical scores to show how schools compare on a multitude of measures is likely to have little beneficial effect. Education consumers—students and their families—need indexed or summary information. An example from another sector illustrates how this need might be dealt with. Some restaurants now provide menus marked with heart-shaped symbols. These symbols attest that the dishes so marked have favorable scores in certain areas: few calories, low salt, low cholesterol, and the like. Thus, instead of having to compare dishes on several scales, a diner concerned about cardiovascular health can tell at a glance which dishes, in toto, are appropriate. Schools will have to offer similar summary evaluations if choice is to work.

Neoclassicists may argue that if consumers want such a service the market will respond with a profit-making evaluation agency that will charge its customers a fee. The profit motive does not guarantee integrity, however. Hence, we find a need for an extra-market force to provide evaluations of integrity (one that will be at least generally reliable, if not always beyond reproach). Here not-for-profit consumers' unions can play a role.

The first requirement, then, to make a school choice plan work is a system of condensed evaluation. Second, the examiners must be public officials—or private agencies scrutinized by public officials—to minimize incidents of test-result fabrication or the slanting of test content toward subjects that a specific school is good at teaching.

Third, educators will need to define the terms of competition, to ensure that instructional goals encompass not just higher math scores but also comprehension of literature, that tests include essay-writing requirements as well as vocabulary lists, and that transmission of skills and knowledge does not drive out education in the broader and deeper sense of human development and character formation. To the extent that these attributes cannot be readily measured, provisions may have to be mandated rather than left purely to choice. For instance, competing schools should not be allowed to provide more hours of home economics or basketball than of civics, on the presumption that these are the subjects the clients want to "buy."

Finally, the pure market never provides for the weaker members, because it does not adhere to the principle of one person one vote but responds to the vote of purchasing power. Hence, unless it is externally affected, the market tends to cater to the rich and neglect the poor. As I see it, the essence of public education is an effort to overcome this market bias. The more market forces are relied upon, the greater the danger that the poor will receive less than the rich. Hence, choice should be combined with efforts to increase the resources available to public schools in poorer areas.

Other mechanisms surely can be devised. This discussion seeks only to illustrate the point that we cannot turn a human service entirely over to the market and leave it to its own devices. As the book that follows shows very well indeed, in a system of competitive school choice, market forces need to be continually guided, directed, channeled, and improved.

Amitai Etzioni
The George Washington University
Editor, *The Responsive Community:*
Rights and Responsibilities,
a communitarian quarterly

Preface

For some advocates of education vouchers, the case is simple: parents should be able to choose where their children go to school, and the government should be impartial in making education available at either government or private schools. Choice is good, and compulsion is bad. End of discussion.

This book is for those who are not so easily persuaded and who understand that there are some ambiguities in the idea of "choice." Although I have used the term in this book, I believe it can give a misleading image of the nature of a voucher system, if those who use the word ignore the group loyalties that families may already have, loyalties around which new schools may arise. Focusing solely on choice implies that one is addressing a calculating "economic man," who makes decisions as an isolated individual rather than as a member of one of more groups with sustaining interrelationships and common interests. Even if choice plays a role, what ultimately matters and will give life to a voucher system is how people form the communities that build institutions.

My interest in this subject arose originally during a five-year period when I worked as a substitute teacher—handling both short- and long-term assignments—in a public-school district in a predominantly upper-middle-class city in California. I was convinced that something was profoundly wrong with the way schools function, but in the midst of the fray I could not pinpoint what it was.

Two books were instrumental in clarifying for me the nature of the problem with American education, at least at the secondary level. The first was *Public and Private High Schools: The Impact of Communities,* by James Coleman and Thomas Hoffer. Their thesis, that students perform better academically in the midst of a functional community, made sense to me intuitively. The second book was *The Shopping Mall High School*, by Arthur Powell, Eleanor Farrar, and David Cohen. In contrast to the statistical evidence presented by Coleman and Hoffer, this book consists of anecdotal information and stories based on in-depth observation of both public and private schools. *Shopping Mall* provides a rich picture of the significance of community as a resource for children and youth and the social costs incurred when a school fails to function as a community. There are other books that take this perspective, but few of them recognize the institutional obstacles to overcoming the bureaucratic mindset of schools.

I have come to the conclusion that vouchers present the best chance of creating the necessary, but not sufficient, conditions for recapturing the benefits of community in education. Theoretically, public schools could provide those benefits—but only if their bureaucracies and unions were defanged and declawed, and that would be as politically arduous a task as passing voucher legislation. Unless the powerful interests that control the schools can be dethroned, the gains from school reform will be trivial.

In an effort to be as comprehensive as possible in treating the subject of vouchers and deregulation of government schools, this book attempts to answer most of the objections that are raised to vouchers. Since readers will have differing interests, I recommend that everyone read the Introduction, Chapters 1–4, and Chapter 7. Other chapters cover topics of more specific interest and may be read selectively.

The element of the book that diverges most from other writing on education reform is Chapter 14. The latter part of it deals with the transition from school to work and the problems that are developing from the changing nature of work in the "information age." My discussion of those topics is far from complete. My purpose was simply to avoid a common gap in education analysis, which often conveys the sense that schools are divorced from the labor market and other economic realities. Most discussions of vouchers also ignore the issue of how schools can prepare students for an uncertain future. Chapter 14 is my gesture to the need for more analysis of that subject.

Acknowledgments

This book would not have been possible without the help of a number of people. Above all, I wish to thank John and Marilyn Coons for their ideas, encouragement, and assistance. I especially appreciate Professor Coons's patience in allowing me to imagine that ideas he had developed more than a decade ago were my original thoughts. His concepts are present in some way on almost every page, even where I have not explicitly referred to him. His wit and sense of humor have sustained me through this project, as they have sustained many other voucher advocates around the country. His lifelong advocacy for empowering the poor through vouchers served as living witness that this issue is not "conservative" or "elitist" and that liberal Democrats can espouse vouchers without shame.

The support of R. Terry Taft, Richard Mushegain, and John Cummins through the Institute for Educational Choice was instrumental in enabling me to complete this book.

Conversations with Janet Jamieson, Marcia Prenguber, Arlene Mayerson, and Wayne Miyamoto have helped me understand more clearly the difficulty of combining vouchers with existing special education laws. Mike Ricci and Roger Magyar also provided useful advice on specific topics.

Participants in a conference entitled "Schooling for the Postmodern World" at the School of Theology at Claremont (California) in the spring of 1991 gave me valuable feedback on a paper that I presented on vouchers. I especially thank Frank Rogers, Kathi Breazeale, Linda Perkins, Ignacio Castuera, Mary Elizabeth Moore, Malcolm Evans, and Donald Oliver for their comments. Oliver's book *Education and*

Community, which I discovered only much later, has been instructive to me as well.

The staff of the California State Library and the library of the California Department of Education were extremely kind in helping me find materials. Special thanks are due to the staff of the Government Documents department of the State Library and to Delia Chandra, Kathleen Smeltzer, and John Church of the Department of Education.

In a book devoted to the importance of communities in education, I would like to express appreciation to the members of the educational and ecclesiastical communities in which I have participated and learned. I was fortunate to experience a public-school education in the 1960s in a setting where a sense of community still prevailed.

Finally, I wish to thank my parents for their support and for reading and commenting on an earlier draft of this book.

RESPONSIVE SCHOOLS, RENEWED COMMUNITIES

Introduction

C hoosing schools isn't like choosing among cars or restaurants or even among lawyers or doctors. It is more like joining a church, a political association, or a social group that is based on shared values. The choice of schools involves a commitment to ongoing relationships that are sometimes as intense as those within a family. Indeed, if schools were functioning as they should, they would constitute a diffuse, extended family in which children, parents, teachers, and members of a larger community would engage in mutual support.

The marketplace metaphors of competition and efficiency have their place in discussions of school choice. Nevertheless, those features are only part of the story, perhaps no more than a footnote. The image of competition connotes entrepreneurial schools vying for a share of the education market. For parents who want a neutral, training-oriented education without moral content, those schools may be appealing; however, many Americans want schools that stand for something more than technical efficiency. A choice plan based on education vouchers and deregulation of government schools would provide parents, teachers, and children a chance to form community-based schools with clear values and goals.

Under a voucher system, tuition certificates would be distributed to families for all children between the ages of six and eighteen, enabling each child to attend the school of the family's choice. Government and nongovernment schools would receive state funds for each student with a voucher. Deregulation, on the other hand, involves giving government schools more autonomy so they are able to operate as effectively as nongovernment schools.

Both policies could improve education by renewing community in schools. In addition, by facilitating the development of schools based on

1

mutual responsibility and active engagement, vouchers and deregulation can strengthen democracy.

Rekindling Community

In a community, people take responsibility for collective activity and are loyal to each other beyond immediate self-interest. They work together on the basis of shared values. They hold each other accountable for commitments. In earlier centuries, a person was born into a community and a set of reciprocal obligations. Now, those who seek an identity as part of a larger whole must invent community by voluntarily committing themselves to institutions or groups.

At one time local schools served as the focal point of a fairly homogeneous community life in small towns and some urban neighborhoods. The same school now acts as a meeting ground of various communities, each vying for control of some element of the curriculum. In the process, the overarching sense of community has been lost. The school is now a neutral, value-free zone in which students and teachers function as individuals with little collective identity. In many urban neighborhoods, the school is the complete opposite of community. It is an outside institution with little hold on the loyalty of anyone.

Yet if community is dying or dead in some schools, it is flourishing in others. Inner-city ethnic and church-affiliated schools are islands of hope in a sea of despair. While public schools around them are failing, they are succeeding because they form communities defined by their values and distinctive character. Children learn more, gain more self-confidence, and take more intellectual risks in a community-centered school. The members of the community, both children and adults, share a commitment to the school and its purposes. This cohesion makes possible remarkable achievement.

Vouchers and deregulation would create the conditions in which community-based schools could become more widespread in both poor urban neighborhoods and middle-class suburbs. There is no guarantee the opportunity will be accepted. Nevertheless, the history of efforts to establish new schools suggests that a stable financing mechanism could generate an enthusiastic response from idealists and visionaries eager to see their dreams given practical reality.

Rebuilding Democracy

As Americans, we have always insisted that schools should do more than teach cognitive skills to children. We have asked that schools prepare democratic citizens as well as competent workers. This has generally been understood as a mandate to teach civics courses, which amounts to a rather simplistic and mechanistic conception of the duties of citizenship. A superficial knowledge of the Constitution and the legislative process does not promote democracy any more than knowing the rules of baseball makes a good player. Democracy requires active, informed, and at least partially selfless participation, not merely passive observation.

Unfortunately, few schools foster constructive engagement in public life. Although a few energetic teachers may try to encourage independent thought, most schools contribute to widespread apathy and dull-minded acceptance of orthodox opinion. By functioning as impersonal, bureaucratic structures beyond the influence of their participants, government schools add to people's sense of powerlessness and resignation. Students learn to become citizens who wait for government to provide services and to solve problems for them. Schools instill in students the belief that public institutions are resources to be exploited rather than communities worthy of loyalty and support. Lacking any clear purposes themselves, schools cannot bind the nation together.

By their actions, schools teach that democracy consists of a majority imposing its will on a minority. They ignore the principle set forth by James Madison in *Federalist* 10 that majority rule can become tyrannous and that protecting minority dissent is an equal part of democracy. Only institutions that encourage dissent and the development of unorthodox opinions can keep democracy alive.

The problem is fundamentally that public schools are creatures of the state, and the state can set only minimum standards of behavior. The government cannot impose a sense of civic duty, a spirit of skepticism about those in power, or any of the other prerequisites of democracy. Political leaders occasionally inspire public-spiritedness and a willingness to sacrifice personal goals for collective purposes. Most of a nation's capacity for devotion to a higher good, however, stems from the habit among its citizens of participation in local community activities.

Relying on central government to provide the basic elements of democratic life leaves a society open to a loss of vitality and competence among its members. If we lose the habit of personal involvement in efforts to solve common problems, we will gradually lose the power to govern ourselves.

Mass Society or Local Community

Government schools have become the antithesis of democracy because they represent mass society instead of local community. Democracy, at least American democracy, depends on the communities of interest that arise out of free association. As Alexis de Tocqueville pointed out 150 years ago, the separation of citizens from each other is the basis of despotism: "Equality places [people] side by side, unconnected by any common tie; despotism raises barriers to keep them asunder; the former predisposes them not to consider their fellow creatures, the latter makes general indifference a sort of public virtue."[1] His observations apply even more strongly today than when they were written. Community has declined in a variety of ways: mobility has destroyed neighborhoods, secularism has dissipated religious communities, and television has displaced local leadership with a "star" system in both culture and politics. Public opinion polls have replaced public debate. The national "community" exists as an electronic abstraction, a passive audience that is partially activated every two years. Yet the majority of citizens feel left out of this process. Mere voting is not sufficiently engaging to create a sense of community.

The existence of communities or associations independent of central control lies at the heart of democracy. Nations and other mass organizations can remain internally democratic only if members associate with each other in small social units that are independent of the governing body. Otherwise the members operate as isolated individuals in a mass society, and the central authority of the organization acts as an oligarchy. In a 1956 study by Lipset, Trow, and Coleman of the way unions are governed internally, they found a thriving democracy within the International Typographical Union (ITU), which was in sharp contrast to the undemocratic governance of most trade unions.[2] At least part of the explanation for this internal democracy was the prevalence of social clubs and recreational groups in which the members of ITU locals associated with each other outside of the work environment. In other words, subgroups were bound by personal loyalties that ran deeper than union politics.

The basis for democracy within the nation as a whole is no different from the basis for democracy in a union.[3] A mass society without secondary organizations to offset the power of government leaves individuals relatively powerless. Individuals can exercise power effectively in nations or in large organizations only through independent, mediating institutions. As Lipset, Trow, and Coleman explained:

> Democratic politics necessarily rests on a multitude of independent organizations, the manifest functions of which need not be political. Such organizations serve in society as a whole or in unions (1) as arenas within which new ideas are generated, (2) as communications networks through which people may learn and form attitudes about

politics, (3) as means of training potential opposition leaders in the skills of politics, and as places in which they can attain the status necessary to become political leaders, (4) as one of the principal means of getting individuals to participate in the larger political arena, and (5) as bases of opposition to central authority.[4]

The principle is simple. If individuals do not have a community rooted in personal relations within which to test ideas and develop political skills, involvement in public life will decline, and democracy will suffer. A society without strong communities will ultimately become a society that cannot sustain open debate, public-spiritedness, and all of the other elements that make democracy possible.

One well-known example of this principle is the importance of black religious institutions in fostering political strength among African Americans. It is no accident that most of the black leaders who have risen to prominence in American public life in recent decades—Adam Clayton Powell, Martin Luther King, Jr., Malcolm X, and Jesse Jackson—have been ministers. The church for over a century (and the Nation of Islam in more recent decades) has given African Americans a community within which to practice politics, a place to learn leadership skills, and a platform from which to launch ideas. Although some black lawyers and entrepreneurs have gained political office by relying on other sources of power, the enduring strength of black leaders has derived from the religious communities from which they have arisen. Other groups based on ethnicity or national origin have similar support communities. However, none are as politically effective as black churches.

What happens within these communities affects not just their members' relative power in national or state politics. The quality of democracy for all of us is connected with the capacity of diverse groups to maintain an independent voice in public life. Yet that is precisely what we have been losing as community life has dissipated. This is occurring throughout the world. Increasing mobility, individualism, and communication through mass media are leading to a decline of community in every society.

True democratization means rejecting domination by mass organizations and embracing local participatory institutions. Returning the power to ordinary citizens to create community-level schools and other organizations does not mean withdrawal from the larger society. It means reengaging the capacity for community self-reliance, disengaging from the "cargo cult" mentality that waits for help to come from outside, and undermining the control of government and corporate elites. In education, it means overthrowing an establishment that denies everyone, and especially the poor, the opportunity to govern themselves. Two hundred years ago, a democracy in which ordinary folk participated in government was a novel idea. Apparently consent of the governed still seems radical in education.

Restoring Diverse Communities

Historians can debate whether there was once a time in American history when strong local communities threatened the integrity of the nation. For example, some might argue that nineteenth-century voluntary schools that were rooted in particularistic community groups needed to be supplanted by common schools operated under increasing state domination. It may once have been true that building a new nation required an educational system that overcame the parochialism of distinctive schools. Even at the time, however, critics charged that the common schools were being used for the authoritarian purpose of trying to force dissenting groups to bow to the will of the majority.

Whatever the merits of the state-control argument may have been a century and a half ago, continuing to support centralization and uniformity now is sheer folly. If diversity was once a problem, we now face precisely the opposite condition. If uniformity was once part of the cure for the illness of disintegration, it has now become part of the disease.

Our culture has become increasingly homogenized. Television has unified us by making all of us passive consumers of popular culture. Thus, we have developed an electronic national identity, but at the cost of losing distinctive subcultural identities. Instead of being too deeply rooted in parochial traditions, most of us lack any roots at all. We have become an atomized society in which all differences are minimized.

That is simply another way of saying that we have lost communities in the quest for the national community. If we once felt uncertain about our identity as Americans, we are now lost souls on a deeper level. The lack of roots and attachments has led to a widespread condition: "the homeless mind."[5] Instead of having a sense of connection to a neighborhood and its long-term residents, or to other local institutions in which people are judged by their character, an increasing number of Americans live in a network of casual and impermanent relationships. Many have no identity other than through work, and that connection is fragile and insecure.

Restoring democracy depends on deepening the involvement of people in face-to-face organizations. Simply belonging to an association of like-minded people and contributing money to support its staff is no substitute for active participation. We learn about democracy by practicing it on a scale which allows the contesting factions to be visible. We learn about public responsibility by becoming involved in community activities.

Small-scale organizations give people the opportunity to know each other on a personal level and to learn to negotiate with each other. Community activity can serve as a training ground for politics by enabling people to learn how to engage in conflict. Constructive dissent and debate become possible only when people first agree on some values. A group that is too diverse has no language to define the issues on which there is disagreement. Within a group that has a common vision, conflicts can be resolved by appealing to the group's traditions and values, rather than to formal rules. This context provides the basis for learning how to accommodate dissent without disintegration.

Thus a group need not be internally democratic in the sense of "one person, one vote" for the people in it to develop democratic skills. Most organizations would quickly fall apart if they had to spend all of their time ensuring procedural fairness. Instead, intermediate institutions teach democracy by serving as a forum for cooperation and conflict among factions. Learning to build consensus among competing interests is the fundamental lesson in democratic politics. If no one has the capacity to bring people together around common goals, then a city, a state, or a nation will become ungovernable. We are already beginning to see signs of that condition in this country.

A mass society always runs the risk of achieving consensus at the price of silencing the voice of dissent. If we are to maintain a tradition of openness to dissent at the level of the national "community," our citizens need situations in which to experience the tension between orthodoxy and heterodoxy at close range. At the national level, these issues are often too abstract for the average citizen. Unless we have firsthand knowledge of political conflict and of the skills and emotional capacity for compromise, the tolerance of differences within society is likely to fade.

Policies that strengthen devotion to national unity can be profoundly dangerous. The desire to shift allegiance from primary communities to the nation as a whole increases the risk of generating enthusiasm for war as a concrete expression of the collective spirit. A nation that tries to function as an all-encompassing community with one will and one common purpose rather than as a community of diverse communities is liable to become both bellicose and tyrannical.[6] The image of the nation as a seamless web, without division by parochial concerns, has been a seductive ideal. But the quest for that ideal has taken a tremendous toll by sapping the vitality of local communities of affiliation that make participatory self-governance possible.

Preserving primary, immediate communities is important in order to instill a sense of duty toward the public good. Practically speaking, we develop the habit of bending our self-interest to the common good in the context of local activity. Unless citizens devote time and attention to community building at the local level, the capacity for public service simply withers and dies.

In most schools today, children and parents are unlikely to experience a sense of community that asks much of them in terms of responsibility to the group. Personal loyalty to individual teachers persists, but the sense of belonging to a community that has a moral claim on its members has diminished. This is both a symbol and an example of the loss of the glue that holds society together.

Schools as Communities

Instead of allowing schools to continue to contribute to individualism and the loss of group identity, we could enable schools formed by voluntary affiliation to serve as the catalyst for new sources of identity. That will not be an easy task since individualism is so pervasive in our culture. But parents, particularly single parents, have an incentive to create or strengthen communities. They need support from each other and from the rest of society in raising children. Living in isolation from each other, nuclear families are subject to tremendous stresses. A sense of belonging to a larger community is essential to the process of child rearing. Family-centered and community-based schools could help to fill a void in the lives of parents as well as children.

I do not mean that schools alone can fill the void and avert the continuing drift toward a mass society that has fewer and weaker communities with the capacity for independent thought and action. Continued mobility and impersonal economic relationships may overwhelm any efforts to alter the momentum toward isolated individualism. Even the most limited community—the family—has been weakened by all of the forces that undermine the authority of local institutions. However, trying to preserve families without considering the conditions of community life is futile.

Although other methods of strengthening local communities might be found, nonbureaucratic schooling constitutes a potentially important institution with which to begin restoring frayed social ties. Donald Oliver proposes that schools must have several characteristics if they are to form genuine communities. Above all, their activities must be oriented toward a common life instead of being segregated from other facets of society. Thus, a community involves the sharing of honest work [including manual labor, such as gardening and carpentry], a broad mix of people of all ages and temperaments . . . to allow for the natural evolution of interdependent coalitions [among age groups] as well as leadership, . . . [and] the sharing of a common religion or cultural tradition. A voluntary noncoerced community requires that there be meaningful senses of work, celebration, decision making, suffering, and the like which can be shared by all. In a society in which many of these relationships are either invisible or trivial, meaningful culture and hence meaningful schooling cannot exist without coercion or extrinsic rewards.[7]

According to Oliver, schools have been operated predominantly on behalf of technical efficiency, with a few nurturing elements that superficially humanize them. Nevertheless, public schools deliberately undermine community by drawing "the individual away from the parochialness and the specialness of family, social background, religion, dialect— anything that might make one seem odd or unusual in the mainstream of cosmopolitan life."[8] In addition, these schools disrupt community by furthering the separation of people by age, and by prolonging childhood and making it an object of custodial care. Schools cannot become communities simply by adding accessory, therapeutic programs to compensate for their dispassionate and detached atmosphere.

Only schools that engage the full range of their participants' experiences can truly be said to function as communities. The school can function in this way only if parents and local groups are given an opportunity to establish schools that serve as supportive networks. Vouchers and deregulation of public schools would provide that opportunity, creating the conditions of self-governance that would enable schools to become communities. Still, the state assistance that would provide the freedom to form voluntary educational associations does not *guarantee* a transformation in the nature of schools. A voucher system would create potential; how it was fulfilled would depend on deeper cultural forces over which government has little influence.

The reestablishment of community-based schools by means of vouchers could not only provide a source of personal resilience in society, it could also help reverse the erosion of public-spiritedness. For example, as children and parents participate in religion-based schools that promote service to others, they develop a sense of social responsibility that carries over into other activities. When families identify with a school that espouses a group-centered philosophy, they do not simply exploit the school for personal gain.

By contrast, government schools are currently plagued by indifference, as evidenced by both low morale and high levels of vandalism. A teacher who sacrifices free time to work with students is regarded as slightly naive (or in violation of union rules). In far too many cases, public schools have developed an impersonal character that undermines caring. As a result, teachers, administrators, parents, and students calculate how to take from the school without giving anything in return. They spend its social capital without building it up. Reversing that downward slide is difficult. Civic responsibility is not a virtue that can be learned in the abstract. Only institutions that inspire people to live responsibly and that create a climate that reinforces mutual aid and service can overcome the national trend toward unmitigated individualism.

Vouchers will prod the painful process of rebuilding community within government schools because the loss of students to nongovernment schools will force school leaders to consider a new charter or structure that can inspire public confidence. Government schools will need to be freed from the thousands of burdensome rules that destroy the potential for inspired leadership and teamwork.

Strengthening the Social Foundations of Learning

By promoting community-based schools, vouchers will do more than contribute to the renewal of democracy. They will also produce direct educational benefits by strengthening the social fabric that makes learning possible. Some gains may be achieved by virtue of competition among schools, which will require school officials to become more client oriented and less concerned with bureaucratic empire building. But the deeper reason why vouchers will enhance educational quality has to do with the way in which voluntary association is essential to the central relationship among teacher, student, and parent.

Despite a great deal of writing to the contrary, education is not primarily a technical enterprise. To be effective, it requires motivation on the part of both teacher and student and a relationship of trust and respect. If the core relationship between teacher and student degenerates to a mechanistic legal contract, as is so often the case in schools today, only the barest minimum of learning will occur. The kind of relationship that inspires excellence can only be encouraged, never coerced. Compulsory attendance at an assigned school is thus a recipe for failure. By contrast, voluntary association under a voucher system makes possible the development of schools with purpose, intensity, and common vision. Both government and nongovernment schools can participate in the process of developing voluntary relationships in community and indirectly raising the level of academic achievement.

This process of building upon personal relationships is likely to be especially successful among the lowest-achieving students. Equity will be served more effectively by making voluntary association possible than by treating the poor as educational charity cases in need of treatment. Those who feel invisible and unconnected in impersonal school settings could benefit by participating in a caring community in which they are also asked to contribute to others. Moreover, the emotional health of children is likely to improve in schools that are initiated by churches and other community agencies that provide a range of programs for families under stress. Instead of trying to turn government schools into social service centers, it would be more effective to establish schools in institutions where families already participate in the life of the community.

The stakes in education policy are high. Lack of participation by ordinary citizens in the processes of democracy has led to apathy and despair. Economic productivity is stagnant. Families are falling apart because of the inordinate burdens placed on them, and children are faltering because they lack social support networks. We have a chance to change these conditions through the way we organize the transmission of culture to the next generation.

Some argue that we must hang on to the education system we have. They believe that the state must exercise control over education in order to guarantee results for all students. If the state could live up to that promise, there would be no public demand for reform; indeed, non-government schools would have no constituency. But the system that worked well for close-knit communities in the past does not respond to the needs of diverse urban populations. Shifting power from a school bureaucracy to parents and independent schools does not ensure success, but perhaps it is time to recognize that education cannot be guaranteed. The state can provide the means of financing education, but it cannot coerce inspiration and commitment.

Conclusion

If families and communities were largely intact, changing the way schools operate would not be an urgent issue. But with the web of social relations disintegrating around us, we need to look for fundamental changes in the institutions that guide us.

Since the New Deal, we have been looking for large-scale solutions to overcome the problems in our society. In the process, the neighborhood, the church, the community center, the service club, and other local self-help organizations have been neglected. Now we are in trouble. Neither national nor state governments can jump-start a stalled educational system, because we have allowed its social foundations to erode.

A voucher system cannot force better schools into being, nor can it coerce the renewal of communities. It can only create the conditions under which people can take charge of their lives. Paternalistic skeptics argue that ordinary people cannot handle that responsibility. Pointing to child abuse and neglect by parents, drug abuse among adults and kids, and other evidence of dysfunctional family life, they recommend keeping education in the hands of professionals. Yet reliance on professionals stifles our trust in ourselves and each other. We cannot survive long in that atmosphere of distrust.

We must take the risk of trusting parents to find or form schools that better serve their needs and the needs of their children. Those parents who initially fail are likely to grow into their responsibilities, particularly if the new circumstances provide a forum for parents to learn from one another. That is the strength of self-governance within a community: it encourages a life-long process of recognizing one's debt to others. Ordinary people can learn from mistakes and change course if need be. Granting parents control over the education of their children would force them to become more conscious of education and allow them to learn from their mistakes.

This book is divided into four parts.

Part 1 deals with general issues in education and with the need for choice, particularly through vouchers. Chapter 1 is an overview of the conditions of education today and the reasons that government schools are no longer able to meet the needs of a changing society. Chapter 2 describes some of the paradoxes and ideological factors that surround the debate about vouchers. Chapter 3 looks at how the controlled and limited choice among public schools functions at present, and explains why the absence of incentives to expand the supply of alternative schools undermines the success of this approach. Chapter 4 considers an opportunity for choice that involves both government and nongovernment schools and describes some of the features that would be included in a voucher system.

Part 2 focuses on the failure of efforts by government schools to improve the education of minorities and the poor. Chapter 5 examines the ways in which government schools have historically exacerbated class and racial stratification at the same time that they have claimed to promote equal opportunity. Chapter 6 considers the history of African-American and Hispanic attitudes toward school integration, as well as the effects of choice on desegregation and the quality of education for minority groups. Chapter 7 examines the positive characteristics of nongovernment schools that are seldom found in government schools, particularly those characteristics positively affecting the poor. These features can be replicated by providing vouchers to enable the poor to attend nongovernment schools and by deregulating government schools to give them greater autonomy.

Part 3 examines empirical evidence about the effects of nongovernment schools on the poor and the effects of voucher-like policies in higher education and in systems of primary and secondary education around the world. Chapter 8 is devoted to the experience of poor children in nongovernment schools and to case studies of schools (primarily nongovernment schools) that are functioning effectively with students from low-income households. Chapter 9 considers the history of the GI Bill and other scholarship programs for higher education. It also examines the role of proprietary (profit-making) schools that have arisen under these programs. Chapter 10 describes voucher-like systems of education by which public funds are used for independent and sectarian education in Europe, Canada, Australia, and the United States.

Part 4 responds to criticism of vouchers and examines the larger social issues involved in permitting choice. Chapter 11 addresses three common critiques of vouchers: the problem of providing information equitably, the difficulty of attracting investment to schools in poverty areas, and the presumed dangers of failing to socialize all children in a common culture. Chapter 12 considers whether selectivity by nongovernment schools is the same as elitism and why a system of choice should not have regulations requiring open admissions. Chapter 13 shows why promoting distinctive communities with particular loyalties will also foster a sense of national community. Chapter 14 examines the issue of accountability from several angles: the accountability of schools to parents, voters, and employers, and the reciprocal accountability of businesses to prospective employees. Regardless of whether vouchers are adopted, the question will persist of whether employment trends will encourage the belief that hard work pays off. Diversity in education, however, will make this issue more visible.

The conclusion, Chapter 15, reviews issues raised throughout the book and examines some of the political motivations that will sustain ongoing conflict over vouchers in the ensuing decade.

PART I

THE FUNDAMENTAL ISSUE: BUREAUCRACY OR COMMUNITIES OF CHOICE

Government schools come under attack year after year for their failure to teach children adequately to meet the changing demands of our society. Experts dispute whether schools are worse now than in previous decades, although gradual declines in SAT scores since the late 1960s are generally regarded as a sign of deterioration.

I have not made any attempt to demonstrate statistically that America's schools are in trouble or getting worse. Instead, I have presumed that most readers will begin with the assumption that some type of school reform is needed. It is not well known, however, how structural pathologies undermine the purposes of schools.

Chapter 1 begins with an analysis of the reasons that public schools are unhealthy or dysfunctional systems. The underlying problem is that schools have become large, impersonal bureaucracies in which children's needs are displaced by the imperatives of the system. The renewal of education depends not on a series of technical fixes but on a return to a community-based pattern of organization. Vouchers could make that transition possible.

In Chapter 2, I examine some of the ironies and ideological conflicts in debates over vouchers. Part of the difficulty in trying to fashion a new orientation toward education policy is confusion in the language that is commonly used to discuss controversial issues, particularly in the use of the terms *public* and *private*. The ideologies that guide policy can be self-defeating. Somewhere between the conservatism of leaving people to lift themselves entirely by their own bootstraps and the liberalism of benign paternalism that saps personal effort, a communitarian ideology promotes individual empowerment in the context of mutual responsibility. My defense of vouchers rests on that communitarian concept.

If it is accepted that choice is essential for empowering communities of people, it is also true that not all choice systems are created equal. Chapter 3 is a discussion of what happens when educational choice is limited to government schools. When schools lack autonomy, they cannot offer distinctive options. Consequently, choice among government schools has generally amounted to a set of vacuous options. The one counter-example to that tendency, District 4 in New York City, was able to offer genuine choices only because it arose in unusual circumstances that are unlikely to be duplicated elsewhere. Controlled-choice or magnet schools, which were developed for purposes of integration, are not intended to give choices to most families. Nor is there any evidence that magnet schools are academically superior to zoned schools for students who are not doing well in school.

Choice plans that include nongovernment schools are the subject of Chapter 4. Tuition tax credits and vouchers are the two major options that allow parents to choose among all schools in an area. Because tax credits are more prone to financial inequities than vouchers, I have considered them only briefly. The bulk of this chapter is thus devoted to the financial and administrative requirements of a voucher system.

1

Decline and Renewal in Education

Schools are failing to fill in the gaps left by the declining strength of other social institutions in American life. Although teachers and administrators can reasonably say, "We're doing what we have always done," that is no longer sufficient. By not addressing new conditions, schools are indeed failing.

Children are different now from the way they were twenty or forty years ago, because they are not getting what they need from parents, relatives, neighbors, religious leaders, and the other adults who used to provide guidance and stability in children's lives. Children are more likely than in previous generations to grow up in single-parent households. They are more likely to be confused and insecure about whom to trust. Their parents are likely to be more mobile than previous generations. As a result, the kids are less likely to have a resilient network of adults beyond their parents from whom to seek help and advice. They are more likely to resort to casual sex, drugs, or suicide to overcome their sense of isolation.

This seems to confirm the school officials' refrain: "It's not our fault. We're doing as good a job as ever. The kids and their parents are the problem." Yet that kind of excuse has merit only if one assumes that the purposes of school are fixed. If we ask how schools could best be organized to help children, we might imagine a very different set of relationships between adults and children and among children themselves.

The current school system came into existence during a period when the United States was rapidly industrializing. The schools were formed in the image of the factory: bells dividing the day into units, work stations dividing labor into specialized sections, and the organizational structure dividing management from workers (that is, college prep from general education). One can debate whether this social regimentation was ever useful, but certainly in the late twentieth century, rigid bureaucracy has overstayed its welcome.

The people who work inside schools are understandably defensive when they come under attack. The public blames teachers for not doing more to help children learn, which seems unfair to those working long hours in the presence of emotionally demanding children. Almost any adult, teaching under the constraints of the existing system, would achieve approximately the same level of success. Instead, we should be looking at how the existing depersonalized system has established incentives for both teachers and students to accept the average rather than strive for the best.

That does not mean, however, that we should accept the excuse that the problems of schools derive from divorce, poverty, drug addiction, or any of the other home situations with which kids have to contend. Nor should we accept the idea that adding to schools another layer of expensive professional services in the form of social workers and psychologists will make a difference. What kids (and adults) need is a sense of belonging to a caring community, not an endless array of therapeutic relationships. In Japan, the key to academic success has been the supportive family and a strong sense of group identity. In America the decline of family and community loyalty has left individuals on their own.

Unfortunately, schools have failed to respond adaptively to the changing conditions in the surrounding society. Instead of becoming more like an extended family, schools have grown in size and become more alienating and bureaucratic. Although some kids may value the chance to be "invisible," most find the anonymity and impersonal conditions isolating.

The academic effects of this subtle shift in the culture of schools have been the most obvious consequence. Textbook difficulty (and interest level) is lowered a bit more each year. Declining test scores, high dropout rates, and the limited skills of high school graduates have made newspaper headlines for a decade. The tragic specter of millions of kids leaving high school each year unprepared for work or college encompasses not only inner-city minorities, but also many white, middle-class graduates of supposedly good schools. When teacher, student, and parent no longer feel responsible for one another, schools do not provide kids with a healthy environment. As the social fabric has come unravelled, teachers are forced to negotiate treaties with students to gain a minimum level of cooperation.[1]

Who Suffers?

Children are the most obvious victims of bureaucratic indifference at school. In theory, schools exist to serve children. In practice, schools have become like every other large organization: they serve their own internal purposes.

In his recent book, *Childhood's Future,* Richard Louv describes the way society approaches childhood. He likens the way children are treated in our society to a "child production industry." Although he does not draw the parallel to schools, his description fits them with painful accuracy: "This industry is staffed with distracted, stressed out workers and poorly trained managers. It emphasizes production quotas, not quality. The industry's one-size-fits-all approach ignores market needs. As a result, the industry is spending more and more on recalls. . . ."[2] The "recalls" in this case are children in psychiatric hospitals (with the number of patients under the age of eighteen quadrupling since the early 1970s); youth in prison (with more young black men behind bars than in college); and teenage mothers on welfare (with 60 percent of the nation's welfare budget going to women who had a first child as a teenager).[3] Some of the failures are more permanent: the rate of suicide among kids aged ten to fourteen doubled between 1980 and 1985.[4]

Teachers are as much victims of this situation as the students. Many who enter the teaching profession join for idealistic reasons: they want to help children. When they start teaching, however, they are faced with the grim reality that schools are bureaucracies designed to warehouse large numbers of young people. Teachers are rewarded for control, not for sharpening young minds. Those who stay in this corrosive environment must make internal adjustments to the conditions of the school system. Above all, to maintain their own equanimity, teachers learn to accept that they cannot change the elements of the system that destroy children.

One indication of how public-school teachers feel about the schools in which they work is the high proportion who send their own children to nongovernment schools. Between one-fourth and one-third of the teachers in urban public schools send their own children to independent schools (as compared with only about one-sixth of the general population in urban areas). In the Los Angeles–Long Beach metro area, 29 percent of public-school teachers send their kids to private schools, while only 17 percent of the general population does. In San Francisco, the figures are 28 percent and 19 percent; in Atlanta, 25 percent and 14 percent; in Albuquerque, 30 percent and 14 percent.[5] Individual teachers are not to blame for choosing to provide their children with a decent education. They should be criticized only when they hypocritically support their unions in blocking state programs to help poor families exercise the same choices they have had.

Parents also suffer from the conditions their children are forced to endure. They are forced to move, lie about the child's place of residence, negotiate interdistrict transfers, connive ways to place their children in magnet schools, or pay the cost of sending their children to nongovernment schools. Many parents agonize over these moral dilemmas, yet they want decent schools for their children.

Adults without school-aged children also have reason to be concerned if the majority of children are not learning to function as adults. Prisons are already burgeoning with illiterate or alienated youth, as are welfare rolls. Our social fabric is damaged by the corrosive atmosphere of apathy and indifference that breeds in schools; everyone suffers from it.

Meanwhile, businesses are moving operations overseas in search of low-cost labor. Only those workers who can write well, speak well, and reason effectively will be adaptable enough to compete for highly skilled jobs outside the unskilled service sector in America. Despite higher graduation requirements, a large number of high school graduates lack the basic reading and math skills necessary to fulfill the requirements of entry-level jobs. (About one-half of the applicants for jobs such as telephone operator are rejected because they cannot read at the eighth-grade level.)[6] Only 10 percent of high school graduates and half of all college graduates can perform such basic operations as understanding a newspaper editorial, reading a bus schedule, or calculating a tip in a restaurant.[7] Many youths are disillusioned when they discover that their so-called education has inadequately prepared them for the future.

Reforms That Have Not Worked

Public school officials say they could improve the system if they had more money. But providing extra money does not alter the structures that debilitate the education process. Regardless of whether funds come from taxes or from school-business partnerships, money cannot overcome the structural problems facing schools.

Public school officials talk about "getting parents involved." Yet in most schools programs for parent involvement have nothing to do with building ties to the community in ways that help children. These programs might more appropriately be called "parent management." Black parents in New York and other cities tried to gain some real power over the way their children were taught through the community control movement of the late 1960s and early 1970s. Their efforts ultimately failed, however, in large part because of the dramatic rise of teachers' unions at that time. Thus, the connection between school and community remained a mere formality.[8]

Compensatory programs such as Head Start, Chapter I, and dropout-prevention programs may have had some beneficial effects on low-achieving youth. Yet they have not been sufficient to make up for the general failure of schools to teach adequately. They are part of a larger, bureaucratic system that is failing not merely "disadvantaged" students but average students as well. Michael Timpane of Columbia University observes, in connection with various successful dropout prevention programs:

> All these processes can work, and there seem to be instances described in the literature where they all do. But . . . many of these [processes] start late in the game. And, in aggregate, the situation does not seem to improve much. . . . We must look beyond all special programs and projects for dropouts and begin to correct how the system as a whole works. . . . Look at the system itself rather than concentrating on improving this, that, or the other aspect of the system.[9]

Although Timpane is specifically referring to dropout-prevention programs, the same principle applies to all of the special, add-on programs that schools have tried. Those add-ons cannot compensate for the failure of basic educational programs.

The fundamental problem with school reform in the past several decades has been unwillingness to limit the power of high-level administrators and union officials. The "school effectiveness" and "site-based management" programs of the 1980s might have been steps in the right direction—toward better management and greater autonomy. Ultimately, however, these reforms, like hundreds before them, were too timid to challenge the powerful interests (unions and administrators) that vie for control of the schools. Only a genuine power shift within schools will benefit children and teachers and contribute to the renewal of community within schools.

By maintaining the pretense that the defects of schools can be remedied with a bit of finetuning, those with the power to make changes hide the depth of the problem. Yet those who are tired of the old patterns of denial know that only a willingness to face some unpleasant truths about the education system can offer hope for schools.

Chronic Lies and Painful Truth

The crisis in America's schools is described in terms of their failure. The problem is precisely the opposite: the public-school system has not been *allowed* to fail.

Failure, like pain, is not purely negative. Pain is the body's way of signaling a threat to itself, a threat that could end in death if ignored. Likewise, failure indicates that a mistake has been made that needs to be corrected. Failure, per se, is not negative. (The fact that adults in general and schools in particular convey to children a fear of failure is a major flaw.) The inability or unwillingness to learn from failure, however, is a sign of an unhealthy organization.

Economist Joseph Schumpeter argued that capitalism's genius lies not so much in the innovation produced by competition as in its capacity for creative destruction.[10] Just as personal maturity involves accepting our limitations and mortality, a healthy society must learn to accept the failure or death of institutions and enable others to take their place. This frees people to take risks, innovate, and let go of past mistakes.

The failure of schools is thus paradoxically their inability to fail. They suffer from denial: schools actively avoid knowing the damage they inflict. This is a form of social pain that never reaches the nerve center of the educational organization. As a result, a charade continues that prevents schools from honestly responding to their weaknesses.

In an environment in which no distinctions are made between success and failure, positive recognition has a hollow ring. Schools are so shy of confronting teachers, administrators, and students with their failure that they create no incentives for moral and intellectual development. By avoiding the pain of honesty, schools have increased the pain that students ultimately bear when they leave school unprepared for the future.

Denying their alarming shortcomings has meant that schools have settled for weak managers and ignored leaders with vision. Instead of accepting blame, those who control the schools treat those advocating radical reform as scapegoats.

The dynamics of this pathology are portrayed in the film *Lean on Me*, which tells the story of Joe Clark, an authoritarian principal who changes an inner-city high school by directly confronting the denial system that previously allowed the school to drift in apathy and chaos.[11] Instead of keeping alive the illusion that the school is basically healthy, Clark declares the school educationally bankrupt and proceeds to clean house. He breaks all the rules. He steps on people. He is ruthless in his determination to make the school a place of learning.

Clark has intense convictions and a willingness to fly in the face of a system that prefers business as usual to effectiveness. The enduring image of the film is of a man who cares enough to rip open the facade of a school that has failed to provide a decent education. The lie he exposes is the great American myth: "We provide an education for all children." Instead, as he knows, the dropout rate in inner-city schools is between 40 and 60 percent, and most of those kids are forced out inconspicuously by schools that refuse to educate them.

What Joe Clark did was not unusual, except for the fact that he did it suddenly and without playing by the rules. He was attacked, not because he was unjust, but because he hung out the dirty laundry of the school in public. He openly said and did what other school officials say and do behind closed doors.

As a society with the power to change the way in which schooling is structured, we have options Joe Clark did not have. We can give kids better choices than prison-like schools or a life without decent employment. In particular, we can find ways to create communities in which those who feel alienated from the existing schools can experience a positive learning environment.

The Need for Community-centered Education

An effective school has to be a community in which personal relationships based on trust outweigh impersonal rules. A community based on shared vision and close personal interaction is not a frill; it is a necessity.

When public or common schools were first started in the middle of the nineteenth century, they could make a legitimate claim to serve as community institutions. (In the nineteenth century the overwhelming majority of people still lived in towns of fewer than 2,500 people.) The connection between school and community was never as close in big cities as in small towns, but even urban neighborhoods were genuine social units based on ethnicity, not random assortments of individuals.

Changes in the nature of schools accompanied urbanization and industrialization. During the early part of this century, as part of the general reforms of city government by the Progressive movement, school administration was rationalized. The explicit aim was to make schools act with the same attention to efficiency as businesses. Objective criteria were established for hiring teachers. Textbooks and curriculum became more standardized. Power was removed from neighborhood politicians and centralized in the hands of professional administrators.

Yet these reforms, largely positive at the time, sowed the seeds of many of today's problems. The rational school bureaucracy eventually became a rigid mechanism that thwarted new reforms. Uniform rules for hiring and promotion reduced the pool of potential teachers to those who took teacher-training courses of dubious value. Increasing control by centralized authorities robbed teachers of a sense of professional dignity and led to the countervailing pressure to unionize. Uniformly acceptable textbooks became platitudinous and devoid of any intellectual content. The social distance between parents and school officials increased as the connection between school and community was severed. In cities, the school became an institution in the neighborhood that was nevertheless controlled by outsiders.

In this century, as an increasing proportion of the population moved into metropolitan areas in this century, the school as a factory with knowledge-crammed graduates as its endproduct gradually displaced the school as an extension of the community. Enrolling children in school amounted to relinquishing control over their upbringing and turning them over to the state.

Reversing a process that has been steadily displacing the power of families and neighborhoods for over a century and a half will require a broad public recognition of the importance of community-based institutions. As Richard Louv argues, "The most important school reform has less to do with curriculum than with community—with strengthening the invisible web that connects the school and its children to parents and other adults in the surrounding community.[12] The problem is not so much changing the "text" (what the school teaches) as the "context" (the organizational setting within which it operates).

The shift from bureaucratic to community-centered schools can occur on a broad scale only by providing people with the means to form their own communities. In some small districts, in which schools still serve as an extended family and parents are able to play an active role in shaping policy, the need for change is perhaps modest. (Even in those cases, dissenting groups should have the right to form their own schools with the same tax funds as the majority.) In most larger districts, however, schools represent pseudo-communities brought together only by arbitrary lines drawn on a map and compulsory attendance laws. The importance of making it possible for people to form schools around genuine communities is especially obvious in those circumstances.

Community-centered schools can provide a nurturing environment for children, but only by providing a support network for adults as well. There is no reason to conceive of schools as institutions that are purely for children. Since children model their behavior on their parents more than on anyone else, providing parents with new sources of caring and peer support would have tremendous benefits for their children. If parents have no local institutions from which to draw inspiration, their ability to pass on the wisdom of the community will be lost.

Creating communities with positive peer relationships that encourage competence and responsibility is the only way to prepare kids for constructive involvement in public life. As long as a school seems an

The Highlander School:
An Example of a Radical Education Community

We could expect many of the schools initiated under a voucher system to be modeled on existing schools, with only minor changes in structure and curriculum. But a voucher system gives people with new visions a chance to put them into practice. Believers in radical social and educational reform should be especially interested in vouchers as a way to foster education communities that could make a profound difference.

The Highlander Folk School of Tennessee is one of the most interesting education programs in the country. Highlander was founded as an adult school in the 1930s by Myles Horton to help oppressed people in Appalachia find their own voice.

In addition to regular academic classes, the school conducted seminars on social change in which discussion was based on actual labor conditions in the mining and timber industries. Horton was in the vanguard of reform, providing a community institution that enabled the workers of Appalachia to challenge the mine owners and other industrial interests. Highlander included black community organizers in the 1930s and 1940s, frequently in direct violation of the Jim Crow laws that required racial separation of schools; and throughout the civil rights era, Highlander played a role as a catalyst.

A significant measure of Highlander's success is that it has survived arson, arrests, and the confiscation of its property. It has been a source of inspiration and leadership for decades because it empowers ordinary people to act in their own interest. As Frank Adams wrote in 1972:

> Through Highlander's programs, many people have been encouraged to find beauty and pride in their own ways . . . and to learn of their own power to accomplish self-defined goals through social movements built from the bottom up.
>
> People learn of unity by acting in unity. They learn of democracy by acting democratically. And each time they do these things as a result of experiences at Highlander they both renew their capacity to act in these ways again and demonstrate the process of education in action.*

Vouchers could help people found more such schools.

---

* Frank Adams, "Highlander Folk School: Getting Information, Going Back and Teaching It," *Harvard Education Review* 42, no. 4 (November 1972), p. 519.

alien environment to a child, the peer culture will undermine the school's formal educational purposes. If that happens, the child will resist the school's values and concepts, including the rudimentary social skills that a potential employer will consider essential. By contrast, if a school fosters a peer culture that encourages responsibility, it can develop capacities in students for effective citizenship and work.

Religion: Binding Community Together

Caring. Community. Inspiration. Isn't this the language of religion rather than education? Perhaps, but religious language should not be divorced from education. As the philosopher Alfred North Whitehead once noted, "The essence of education is that it be religious."[13] Worthwhile education is imbued with excitement, or what Whitehead called romance: "a ferment already stirring in the mind," from which stem ideals and imagination. He also recognized the importance of precision, but technical education without religious imagination is barren. This applies to all fields of endeavor, even to business. Whitehead observed that the mere pursuit of money does not generate an enterprising spirit. Instead, people educated to see work as being "transfused with intellectual and moral vision" are more likely to become successful entrepreneurs.[14] Perhaps the depletion of America's spiritual capital has something to do with its weakening economy. Forging schools that function as communities of shared belief could restore some of that capital.

The trouble with government-run schools (and, incidentally, with large corporations) is that they have taken on the characteristics of a state church that has no vision and no purpose other than self-perpetuation. Part of the problem is sheer size. In the past, in small, locally controlled schools, the teacher was part of the same community as the students. Moral or spiritual instruction was never entirely divorced from the broad range of subject matter. Whether or not the schools engaged in pious rituals (for example, Bible reading), they were religious in the larger sense of coalescing a community (from the Latin root, *religare,* meaning "bind together"). The glue that binds most schools together now is the rulebook; seldom does a common spirit infuse the life of a public school.

Public schools are hamstrung on the question of values by the conflicting visions of citizens, teachers, and parents. In theory they could unite parents and staff behind a common secular vision. But in practice, government schools lack the autonomy to give themselves a distinctive identity. By contrast, a school that represents a well-defined philosophy can bind people together in a common spirit.

The Importance of Traditions

The hallmark of a community is that it both draws on traditions and creates new ones that are shared by its members. Education is a process by which children, with the help of their parents, choose mentors who will teach them skills and the meaning of those skills within a particular tradition that provides a history, an identity, and a set of values. In other words, education involves both knowledge (the skills) and wisdom (the traditions). Examples of traditions are liberal arts, science, humanism, specific academic disciplines, trades and crafts, religious faiths, political ideologies, and clan or ethnic group histories. In a sense, there are thousands of traditions that could provide the framework for the mentor relationship between teacher and student or community and family. Some traditions are thin, and a child will quickly outgrow them if given the chance to explore them and to move on. Other traditions are so dense and rich that a lifetime would not suffice to comprehend them.

There is little in the current curriculum of elementary and secondary schools that enables a child to participate deeply in any tradition. Even a great deal of higher education has lost touch with the sustaining tradition of liberal arts, largely because the professors themselves often have such shallow roots that they do not see how their work is connected to disciplines outside their own. Unfortunately, just as shallow roots mean stunted plants, raising children in shallow traditions means their minds will be stunted. Yet if we can provide the climate in which children can grow, their unseen roots will burrow deeply into the soil of tradition. Adults do not need to do all of the work for the kids: we merely need to provide the inspiration for them and sufficiently fertile ground in which they can seek insights.

Few people in our society have the opportunity to experience that kind of deep participation in any tradition. The educational freedom offered by vouchers is one means by which that experience could become more widespread. Establishing a voucher system is not the final word in that process. The freedom to choose among alternative traditions does not guarantee that citizens will choose wisely. Many will continue to be influenced by the dead hand of the bureaucratic tradition, in which one receives a diploma as a reward for passively enduring long hours of repetitious work devoid of intellectual value. Yet, over time, the mold will be broken by those who value educational depth.

New Types of Schools

If we want children to receive a rich education, not a barren and uninspired set of technical lessons, we must be prepared to transfer much of the responsibility for education away from the institutions we now call schools. Asking children to come to learn in settings that are alien, bureaucratic, violent, and uninspiring is a sure recipe for failure. Why should we expect kids to work hard if schools bore and humiliate them? We must imagine ways to take education to them in settings that seem more natural to them, more integrated with their daily lives. Instead of bringing kids to school and asking them to trust strangers who have no prior connection with them, we should find people and institutions that kids and parents trust already and build on those relationships. Instead of forcing kids to fit inside a predetermined institution, we should be giving them a chance to learn in organizations in which they feel a sense of ownership.

In contrast to the limited creative power of government, people joining forces to accomplish a goal can create a new context or weave a new social fabric. They create new institutions out of imagination and hard work. They start daycare centers, storefront churches, youth clubs, sports associations, small businesses, and hundreds of organizations that simultaneously bind a community of caring people together and accomplish a social purpose. These are the kinds of events that occur because of citizen, not government, initiative.

All of that skill and energy and creativity could be unleashed to invent new schools and to reform old ones if rules were changed to encourage innovation. Real reform involves disrupting old patterns, removing power from people who are used to running the show, and taking risks with new forms of school organization.

It is not necessary to start from scratch. A preschool or a community center or a church school could expand its programs. Older children and retired adults can teach small groups of children at very little cost. Cross-age tutoring programs, in which teenagers with reading problems teach young children to read, can be of immense value. Not only does this provide the younger children with tutors; more importantly, it motivates the older ones to learn to read better. Feeling needed can be a great spur to being productive.

Education rooted in communities of interest could gradually transform the way we conceive of schools. With a number of adults working with children in different roles and in different settings, education could be integrated into the life of the adult world, instead of taking place in complete isolation. Learning networks could utilize adults (and children) who can teach particular skills (photography, word processing, music, journalism). For children whose parents are illiterate, joint schooling for both age groups could bring families closer together and help parents participate in the teaching process. If we think of education as community-based, rather than site-specific, the potential for learning at dispersed sites, including private homes, commercial offices, and churches, becomes a more feasible alternative. Once we get past the image of schools as factories, an image reflected in their physical structures, we can begin to conceive of a range of new relationships.

Who Can Teach?

Turning over education to people who understand kids and work well with them, regardless of whether they have credentials, cuts against the prevailing wisdom on the subject. The education establishment has convinced the public that the only people who can teach are state-certified teachers. There is no evidence to substantiate this claim. As Samuel Peavey, professor emeritus of education at the University of Louisville, who worked for many years certifying teachers and who is now a consultant on home schools, notes, "After fifty years of research, we've found no significant relationship between teacher certification and pupil achievement. It's just nil."[15] Donald Erickson, professor of education at the University of California at Los Angeles is even harsher: "Some of the worst teachers I've ever seen are highly certified. Look at our public schools. They're full of certified teachers. What kind of magic is that accomplishing? But I can take you to the best teachers I've ever seen, and most of them are uncertified."[16] Although it seems unlikely that certification has a direct negative effect on the teachers who pass through the system, the indirect effect of excluding potentially good teachers who refuse to spend time on methods courses may be damaging.

Saying that credentials don't count for much is not the same as saying that ability is unimportant or that anyone can be a good teacher. On the contrary. As school officials and those involved in teacher training are fond of saying, just knowing subject matter does not make a person a good teacher. Even many of the people who have been forced to take methods courses in teacher-training programs still think of teaching as standing in front of the classroom and talking. Finding ways to engage students in the learning process and to inspire students to overcome obstacles depends on ingenuity that can be acquired in many ways, in or out of school.

Conclusion

A century and a half of government-controlled education has led to an untenable situation. Governments do not weave the fabric of society. They only work within it. Creating new social contexts for schools is not something that can be decreed from on high. Propaganda can be imposed; education cannot. Furthermore, government programs, including schools, are invariably patchwork compromises among competing interests, each pulling in its own direction. This tends to generate outcomes at the lowest common denominator of what is deemed acceptable, not an inspiring vision of excellence.

With the flexibility offered by vouchers, no longer would there be "one best system" governed by a few for the supposed benefit of many. Custom would continue to lead most people to put children in boxes called classrooms with credentialed teachers and grades and report cards and assemblies and all of the features of school that most of us grew up with. Yet once the imagination has been set free and everyone has the chance to experiment with new forms of education, convention will give way to new models.

As I try to conceive of how education might appear fifty years after responsibility for it has been returned to families and chosen communities, I am reminded of something I once heard the novelist and essayist Wendell Berry say: "Education is free." Clearly, he did not mean that schooling costs nothing. State and local governments spend up to one-fourth of their budgets on schools. I take it that what he meant was that schooling is an elaborate Rube Goldberg device. It achieves at great expense what an inquisitive and diligent person can achieve for only the cost of a few books. Education existed before schools came into being, and most of the curiosity and intensity that makes education possible within schools is still generated outside the walls of those institutions.

Now, however, our educational system largely ignores the reservoir of experience and insight beyond the confines of formal schooling. Every community includes adults whose ideas and guidance could help children develop mature minds. Instead of denying that potential resource, education policy should be geared to make use of it. Each child has a desire to understand the world. Instead of stifling that interest for the sake of a predetermined curriculum, a nurturing community could sustain that excitement and give it focus.

A voucher system, in conjunction with the deregulation and scaling down of all schools, could enable both government and nongovernment schools to become creative educational centers. By providing the basis for widening the scope of schools, vouchers could give America an education system that would be both effective and exciting for kids.

2

The Ideological Context
of Vouchers

T he merits and drawbacks of education vouchers have been debated
  extensively since the early 1970s. Subsidizing choice among
public and private schools has been proposed as a way to increase
diversity; raise the satisfaction of parents, students, and teachers;
improve academic achievement; and provide low-income families with
the same opportunities to attend nongovernment schools that wealthier
families have had. Vouchers have also slowly come to be seen as a means
of strengthening local communities, which give moral support to both
parents and kids.

Most Americans like the idea of permitting parents to choose the
school their children attend. Most of those who favor choice believe
that the options available to parents should include independent schools.
Yet for a significant minority of citizens, the idea of a voucher system
is troubling.[1]

Those who feel uncomfortable with the voucher concept do not like
the thought of state money enabling a child to attend a school that is
not controlled by an elected school board and a state legislature. "How
can we control quality and equity if parents can send their children to
any school they choose?" is the sort of question they ask. "Control" is
the key word. The question reflects a philosophy that the government
owns its citizens, not vice versa. This view unwittingly reveals the intellectual origins of modern schools in the military states of ancient Sparta
and eighteenth-century Prussia. These were the examples from which
Horace Mann and his colleagues drew inspiration when they began the
common-school movement in the middle of the nineteenth century.[2]

Many who question the wisdom of vouchers parrot the propaganda they have heard: that it will lead to inequities between blacks and whites, rich and poor. They argue that since the rich will supplement their vouchers, they will continue to be able to buy better education than the poor. Above a certain level (perhaps $4,000 per year per student), however, the connection between spending and educational quality is highly questionable. High-quality inner-city schools, heavily attended by children from poor families of all races, are successful not because they spend a lot of money, but because they are devoted to learning. Nevertheless, the question of how vouchers could enhance equity is complex, and much of this book is devoted to discussing it.

Others regard the present school system as sacred; it serves for them as a quasi religion or church. Its doctrines emphasize liberal Protestant values such as progress, tolerance, and individualism. In a society honey-combed with religious sects, the school system is expected to function as a kind of "mother church" that binds us all together despite our differences. Criticism of the state church is acceptable, but anything that threatens to reduce its power amounts to heresy. Vouchers have thus been portrayed as enemies of public education because they would allow a schism in the established school system.

The Ironies

The national debate over vouchers is comparable in many ways to the sixteenth-century conflict in Europe over the question of church authority. The central issue is the same: must everyone swear loyalty to a unifying institution, or will individuals and groups be free to discover the truth in the institutions of their choice? Ironically, the Protestants and Catholics have reversed their positions. The Protestants defend the School Universal, while the Catholics believe in the con-science of the individual. Actually, many Protestants (including myself, a liberal Protestant) favor vouchers, and some Catholics oppose them, but the irony holds.

The lineup of political parties on the subject of vouchers is also ironic. At the turn of the century, Republican reformers created the existing bureaucratic urban school systems in order to remove schools from the patronage system of big-city bosses (Democrats). Until that time, teachers were hired on the basis of political connections, not qualifica-tions. Almost a century later, Republican reformers are trying to decen-tralize power and undo the damage caused by bureaucracy. This time around, they want to give the power to families. Therein lies the greater historical incongruity. The Whigs, the ideological predecessors of the

Republicans, were the nineteenth-century founders of the common school, which set the stage for state control of education. The Democrats, who were partially represented by immigrants and Catholics in northern states, comprised much of the opposition to the destruction of family-supported schools by tax-supported public schools. Now those roles are reversed: the modern-day Whigs favor family choice, while the Democrats favor state control.

A final irony lies in the liberal support for compulsory attendance at a government-run school. From the start, one justification for state-run schools advanced by liberal reformers was the importance of inculcating tolerance in young minds. Yet in order to teach all children the value of tolerance, the actual toleration of distinctive traditions was denied. Only families that could afford to pay taxes for government school plus tuition at an independent school had (and have) the luxury of being afforded true tolerance.

In fact, all of these ironies disappear if one ignores these labels and considers instead the relative power of various groups. Within the arena of educational politics, liberal Protestants have had more power than Catholics or evangelical Protestants, Democrats more than Republicans (in recent years), and liberals more than conservatives. Vouchers offer a way to redistribute power, but not by simply reversing the situation and giving conservatives, Republicans, and Catholics power over liberals, Democrats, and Protestants. Instead, vouchers would take power politics out of education altogether so that powerful groups could no longer dictate terms to weaker groups. The majority could no longer impose its views on a minority. The Bill of Rights attests to the idea that protecting the minority from abuse of power by the majority is a central feature of a democratic society. Yet government schools are founded on the opposite view: namely, that majorities have the right to impose their will and their brand of truth on minorities.

The Misuse of "Public" and "Private"

Many people have been inculcated with a mental image of private schools as elite academies of rich, white Yuppies. The hundreds of schools run by African Americans, struggling to survive on tiny tuition payments, have not entered public consciousness. Multiracial schools operated by evangelical Christians are neither elitist nor exclusive, although the religious character of these schools offends the taste of many secularists. Catholic schools offer the only decent source of education for many inner-city children, and without the dogma that middle-aged people associate with Catholic schools prior to Vatican II. Nevertheless, the power of suggestion in the propaganda against nongovernment schools is strong. By calling these schools elitist and exclusive often enough, the lie has stuck.

The use of the word "public" to characterize government schools is part of the propaganda that has been internalized by most Americans. It is highly misleading. If public means nonexclusive, then 80 to 90 percent of nongovernment schools are more public than the government schools in elite suburbs where the price of admission is the downpayment on an expensive house. If public means paid for out of public revenues, then vouchers would make almost all schools public (the exceptions being some elitist schools for the very rich that probably would not accept vouchers). If public means accessible to the public or serving a public purpose (as in the case of a privately owned but publicly accessible restroom within a department store, a privately owned intercity bus line, or a privately owned "public" golf course), then most nongovernment schools already qualify as public.

Before the common school movement of the 1840s, no one would have imposed the terms public or private on schools.[3] The schools were simply voluntary. The rich attended academies and the poor attended either the same schools on scholarship or "free schools" operated by charitable agencies. When tax support for schools expanded in the 1830s in Massachusetts (the most urbanized state at the time), voluntarism could have been maintained by providing state support for attendance at any school. Instead, reformers such as Horace Mann, the first secretary of the State Board of Education, insisted on channeling taxes into government-run schools over which the state had authority. Rather than increasing total school enrollment, the common schools displaced most of the voluntary schools.

As a result of the policy, only the rich could afford to attend a voluntary school by paying a double price: a school tax plus tuition. Mann then set about attacking the remaining institutions as elitist. He repeatedly insinuated that there was a *moral* distinction between public and private schools.

Yet what was really at stake was a political power struggle over who would control the schools. Mann pitted state compulsion against voluntarism and parental control. Since the contest was over elementary schools where children learned only the bare rudiments of literacy, and since most employment at the time was not dependent on education, it is important not to read modern concerns about equal educational opportunity into the debates of that time.

When Mann complained that some students attended schools outside the state's control, this reflected less a concern for the quality of instruction than his desire to inculcate a uniform set of ideas and nonsectarian religious beliefs. For Mann and many other reformers, public school was a conscious means of removing children from the influence of their parents. Their attacks on independent schools were a disguised attack on religious diversity and working-class solidarity. Because history has been written by the winners, compulsory government schools came to be viewed as guardians of the moral order, whereas nongovernment education is still regarded with suspicion by millions of Americans.

The question before us now in the debate over vouchers is whether private institutions can serve public ends better than government institutions can. We should judge the institutions in each sector on the basis of their actual performance rather than experiencing a Pavlovian reaction to the words "public" and "private." The question of whether vouchers or a government school monopoly will better serve the public interest is one that should be decided by debate, not according to terminology.

The Confusion of Liberalism

Despite the authoritarian roots of government schools and the bad faith of those who verbally support public schools and send their children to private schools, educators perpetuate an image of holiness surrounding public schools.

Yet why do liberals trust school bureaucrats so wholeheartedly even when they are skeptical of government officials on other subjects? The answer seems to be that liberals regard public schools with quasi-religious sentiments. Government schools are defined as serving the public good, no matter how poorly they function. In this haze of blind acceptance, liberals defy any efforts to define the purpose of schools clearly enough to hold them accountable. If schools are criticized for not teaching basic skills, the defenders of the faith assert that other, larger goals are nonetheless being achieved. Government schools promise to bring together children from different backgrounds and to promote social cohesion, economic equality, tolerance, and the capacity for critical reflection.

When the public school is judged by its accomplishments even according to these nonacademic criteria, the results are not impressive. Public schools do not foster cohesion: mere physical proximity to those who are different breeds contempt as often as respect. They do not promote equality: the organization of government schools is as likely to reinforce economic inequality as to overcome it. Government schools do not further the liberal values of tolerance and critical reflection by which they justify their protected, noncompetitive existence. Instead, by failing to provide children with any clear identity, they breed mistrust, insecurity, intolerance, and conformity.

Religious beliefs are generally judged more by their expressive value than by their results, however. Faith in quasi-religious government schools is based on the powerful symbolism in St. Paul's metaphor of the church as the body of Christ: many parts, one mystical body. Although common schools were initially established on a congregational or local governance model, one of Horace Mann's ulterior motives was to establish a unifying Protestantism as the civil religion of the common schools. This religion would bind together what was otherwise separate. The common school, as he envisaged it, would rise above the sectarian rivalries and denominationalism of nineteenth century Massachusetts and represent a universal set of moral principles on which everyone could agree. Mann did not perceive then, and many liberal Protestants still do not perceive, that his Enlightenment-based faith was merely one religious vision among many. Not everyone shared his belief that reason, as opposed to revelation or ecclesiastical authority, should be the sole foundation of religious conviction.

The cultural image of schools as a secularized church that unites us in our differences is the oldest and most powerful source of inspiration for those who oppose changes in the structure of schooling in the United States. The fact that unity under one banner has always meant the suppression of dissenting voices has never troubled liberal Protestants too deeply, for the simple reason that the schools have reflected their biases. It is all too easy for those whose truth is represented officially as a universal truth to regard dissenters as mere troublemakers.

Liberalism and White Guilt

One chink in the psychological armor surrounding public schools was the perception among white liberals that the school as secular church had failed in its missionary duty to ethnic minorities. This was a dull perception at first, and it has never come into sharp focus. For centuries, whites had been debating what to do about the "Negro problem." In fact, the problem from the start had been a "white problem," because it was built upon white concepts of racial supremacy and racial purity plus a history of slavery and exploitation. Segregated African-American schools in both the North and the South (and segregated Hispanic schools in the Southwest) were an embarrassment to the liberal faith. In fact, as Derrick Bell, a black civil rights lawyer, reminds us, one important factor in the landmark *Brown v. Board of Education* decision declaring segregated schools unconstitutional was the political concern that racial discrimination in the United States gave communism a propaganda asset in the world.[4] Although the desegregation decision may have seemed radical at the time, it was seen as necessary to maintain a larger system of economic and political power.

Desegregation policy was, from the start, founded upon white guilt rather than a consideration of the interests of African Americans. The logic went something like this: "Those poor people want something that we have. We will let them come to our schools and be blessed by association with our children." Many black leaders were disturbed by the implicit racism in this idea. They objected to the assumption that black schools were inherently inferior. They wanted power, not handouts from white liberals. In effect, desegregation became a means of buying black support for the existing school system rather than giving African Americans the same power to control their children's fate that whites had had. The white liberal Protestant establishment has continued to control most school boards and all of the state legislatures.

As a consequence, the curriculum has been circumscribed by the "melting pot" ideology that defines nonwhite, non-Anglo contributions to American society exclusively in terms of the values acceptable to the dominant culture. The European heritage is treated as more nearly universal than others and thus on a higher plane. As children from other cultures grow up, some begin to realize that they are being forced to attend a paternalistic school that does not belong to them or their parents in any meaningful sense. At least a few students in these circumstances become resistant and challenge the authority of their teachers. Although this may be disruptive for the school, a worse scenario is that if those students do not resist, they will passively lose their identities in a system that denies their value.

White guilt has promoted only limited changes in the schools, including the expenditure of extra money for "compensatory education"; it has yet to lead to any real transfer of power to nonwhites. Until ethnic minorities have gained sufficient economic and political power through their own institutions, white America will not provide anything more than lip service to the goal of equality. The white liberal establishment has opposed vouchers and other methods of community control of education on essentially paternalistic grounds. This group, which has controlled social policy for decades, refuses to recognize that "help" that denies people control of their own destinies "for their own good" is the least bearable form of domination. (On the other hand, conservatives have often been content to let the poor suffer in order that workers would be more docile on farms and in factories.)

The school system and the welfare system, both operated by a professional class, have created a population of dependent adults. The claim that the poor require professional help has thus become a self-fulfilling prophecy. Dependence breeds dependence. A patronizing school system and a demeaning welfare system both teach people to see themselves as powerless. Rather than looking for ways to end this pathology, the middle class has used it as a way to control the poor.

Unfortunately, this use of the poor to build the power of the middle class has not been limited to whites. Summarizing an argument by black sociologist William Julius Williams (from *The Declining Significance of Race*), Joel Spring describes the rise of an educated black middle class, then observes:

> The irony is that the advancement of many middle-class blacks has been in government and educational programs designed to serve the poor. In other words, part of the black middle-class population is building its careers on the backs of a poor black underclass and depends on the continued existence of that class.[5]

Thus, ironically some of the people who were previously objects of paternalistic concern have joined the ranks of the paternalists. Now they hypocritically profess concern for the oppressed yet fight programs that would directly empower the supposed subjects of their concern. The issue is not whether the professional educator or social worker provides a valuable service to the poor: the question is whether the poor would willingly pay for that service if given the power to choose among alternatives.

Unfortunately, the paternalists do not ask that sort of question. Instead they are obsessed by whether the "disadvantaged" would be responsible in using vouchers or similar forms of empowerment. This is simply "the Negro problem" in a new guise: a new way of defining the need for control on the basis of some group's supposed inadequacy.

The Social Costs of Individualism

Unquestioning liberal support of public schools has also overlooked the damaging effects of individualism in education. Schools intentionally separate children and encourage personal achievement rather than collective success. Instead of fostering community, they promote competition. This is disturbing to all students, but especially students from cultural backgrounds that are not so individualistic.

High school students, even more than their teachers, have a powerful intuitive sense of the importance of community. Teenagers resent having to make their way through school as individuals when they most need reinforcement and a supportive structure. They recognize the lack of "school spirit," but they do not have a vision of how to create it. They know when teacher morale is low and no one is willing to make the extra effort to help them. The kids know that cliques (groups formed on the basis of social status) can interfere with education in subtle ways by making some students feel like second-class citizens in a school, but they are also resigned to the fact that teachers and administrators will ignore this situation.

What most adult observers of schools fail to recognize is how divisive and demeaning the entire system is for those who are trapped inside it. Each student faces the system alone. The effect of being treated like drones in a beehive at school is duplicated in adult life only when we are "processed" by a large bureaucracy—the IRS, a motor vehicle department, an insurance company, or a credit bureau. When we adults come face to face with any bureaucratic system, we quickly discover how insignificant our own case is considered, and we are grateful if our encounter is brief. The difference is that we ask children to endure that kind of Kafkaesque treatment in impersonal institutions for twelve years.

Bureaucracy is the inevitable corollary of individualism, but this is not the only way to run a school. The alternative to operating a school on impersonal rules is to rely on community expectations. Discipline, high academic standards, and policies that encourage students to engage in hard work can all be attained more effectively by means of loyalty to a common ideal than by elaborate standards and procedures.

Ultimately, however, the regimentation resulting from individualism and the absence of community is not the worst form of abuse. The more enduring damage to kids working in isolation in impersonal environments stems from the experience of neglect. From a teacher's perspective, this feature of children's lives is obvious. The craving by some kids for attention is almost palpable. Others are completely withdrawn—the other side of neglect. This emotionally destructive condition cannot be overcome by providing more school psychologists or more sympathetic teachers. The problem is built into the structure of schools because it stems from the ideology of individualism. Only schools organized around natural communities can improve the situation for children.

Teachers are also in need of schools that are based on community rather than individualism and impersonal rules. When teachers face administrators as separate individuals in a closed, bureaucratic system, they lack power and are subject to paternalism. The tendency of administrators to be patronizing is reinforced by the fact that administrators have historically been men, and teachers have generally been women, particularly in elementary schools. Thus it is understandable that teachers have banded together to try to protect their professional status and their dignity.

Unionization has not resolved the underlying problem of paternalism, however. Collective bargaining has heightened tensions. It has also given power to the (predominantly male) professional union negotiators who now have a vested interest in maintaining conflict. There is little evidence at the level of an individual school site that unionization has given teachers the desired feeling of empowerment. Because unions have only the power to negate, but not the power to create, collective bargaining has not improved working conditions for teachers. The collective bargaining process unites teachers only in a superficial sense: as individual members of a group over which they have little control. Finally, the rule-governed school environment that results from negotiated contracts is not conducive to a collegial atmosphere in which teachers would work together with enthusiasm and a sense of common purpose. Instead of helping teachers overcome the isolation caused by individualism, unionization has created one more hierarchy in which teachers are at the bottom.

Teachers might benefit if they could join together and negotiate at the site level, where the issues are clear and teachers are directly involved. That sort of bargaining occurs in many nongovernment schools, without the overlay of a giant state and national union structure, and at much less expense to everyone concerned. Negotiations within a single school have the potential to enhance the sense of community and collegiality of the teachers because the discussions are based on concrete conditions, not merely on abstract rules and procedures.

Vouchers would create schools with this sense of community. Small schools, each with lower administrative overhead than in the government system, would provide more collegial teaching opportunities. Since that sort of empowerment is not compatible with the interests of the unions that supposedly speak for teachers, however, we cannot expect to see many vocal proponents of vouchers emerging from their ranks.

Competing Ideologies

If I am critical of liberalism, it is as an admirer not an enemy. I am not suggesting a rejection of liberalism but of the corrupted form of it that enables power and privilege to disguise themselves as humanitarian concern. Liberalism makes a crucial contribution to American life by reminding us of the importance of social capital or the willingness to set aside personal interest for the common good. Liberal Democrats have also sought to avoid extremes of power and wealth in society. But they have done so by creating large government programs that have reduced the public perception of the need to take responsibility for ourselves and our neighbors. In the process of accepting the demise of community, liberals have settled for the paternalism of the welfare state. In the name of protecting the poor, the Democrats have created programs that have kept the poor in a state of dependence—in their place, so to speak.

The great value of conservatism, by contrast, lies in its recognition of the ways in which self-interest can be constructively channeled. Yet if conservative Republicans have avoided paternalistic policies, they have not necessarily practiced a more benign form of compassion. They have simply ignored the suffering of the poor, assuming that economic growth would solve any existing problems of resource distribution. Thus, conservatism has falsely presumed that the common good can be fulfilled solely by the universal pursuit of private ambition. It has promoted individual freedom and private gain at the expense of social obligations.

The problem of both liberalism and conservatism is their willingness to embrace both individualism and large, impersonal institutions that stifle local empowerment: liberals for the sake of justice and equality, and conservatives for the sake of efficiency. That is to say, they are both willing to sacrifice the personal bonds of community for some higher social good. An example is found in the embrace of large schools and districts by both liberals and conservatives. Liberals hope to equalize the tax base that supports schools, and conservatives expect to save money through economies of scale. Schools have thus sacrificed community for equality and efficiency and achieved neither of those goals in the process.

In general, the liberal has been willing to endure big government for the sake of social goals; the conservative has promoted policies that favor large commercial enterprises for the sake of efficiency. Neither seems particularly concerned that in the modern world humans have been made to serve institutions rather than the other way around.

I am proposing that the real political debate should turn from the tired battles between conservatives and liberals and instead focus on the problems associated with large-scale operations. The fundamental question should be how communities can be organized and strengthened so that people need not feel powerless or dependent on large, distant institutions. National policy has permitted reliance on bureaucracy and impersonal markets to supplant mutual dependence and community empowerment based on personal relations. To reverse this, public policy should treat people as participants in social groups rather than as isolated individuals. The rejection of paternalism need not entail stinginess. Government can still play an important role in bringing about a transition to a less individualistic and less paternalistic order that fosters supportive communities.

Education vouchers provide an opportunity to develop an alternative, communitarian model of government policy: one that gives power back to ordinary people and community groups in tangible form. The communitarian ideology is based on the belief that large-scale bureaucracies and impersonal systems of exchange are frequently destructive of community and that the costs of being dominated by giant institutions outweigh the benefits. It offers a third way that balances individual freedom with social responsibility by limiting the scale of institutions and making them self-governing.

Some Republicans have begun to embrace a communitarian philosophy as part of their ideology of empowerment. In the context of that party's century-old history of empowering corporations at the expense of communities, this new-found interest rings somewhat hollow. At the same time, an increasing number of Democrats are looking for new methods of providing social services. In their search, they will have to overcome the tradition of paternalism and patronage within their party. If either party can change course sufficiently to embrace this new outlook, it may succeed in initiating a new era of social activism, while the other party is left wondering what happened.

Conclusion

The debate over vouchers has been overshadowed by the confusing and sometimes contradictory ideological language of liberal paternalism and conservative ideas of individual self-reliance. Although those arguments over ideology are frustrating to those who simply want better schools, we can never escape from ideology. At some level, we need a set of ideas that clarify the larger meaning of schooling and its relation to family, community, and nation. We cannot know what "better schools" are unless we have an ideology that defines the purposes of education.

A communitarian ideology has the potential to resolve some of the tensions that have arisen in American society. Individualism, in combination with big government and large-scale private enterprise, has left many people feeling powerless. We need to begin examining all aspects of life through a new lens.

The ideological context of education debates is extremely important because education is symbolic of the direction we want our society to take. Thus, the voucher question should be decided not merely according to the effect on the technical competence of students but also in terms of the kinds of social institutions we want to promote.

3

Choice among
Government Schools

C hoice in education does not necessarily contribute to the development of new schools or to communities in support of learning. Most of what currently passes for choice in education is nothing more than musical chairs. In other words, being allowed to choose among providers who offer exactly the same service in different neighborhoods is an empty promise. I fear that if choice policies are limited in that fashion, the public will tire of the concept before it is ever tried.

Choice in education is an empty container that can be filled in a variety of ways. The interesting questions arise when one begins to ask what kinds of choice should be available to parents and how the policy alternatives affect the range of schools available. If the education cartel maintains control of all the options, then choice will remain phony.

In this chapter, I examine two types of choice within the public sector, which I call limited choice and controlled choice. In the following chapter, I examine two policies—tuition tax credits and vouchers—that would include nongovernment schools.

Choice exists only when a consumer faces genuine options and can select freely among them. This occurs when four conditions are met: (1) new schools can come into being in response to perceived demand (overenrollment or waiting lists at popular schools), (2) schools that do not attract students are allowed to fail, thereby relinquishing the space to another school or set of schools, (3) each school has sufficient autonomy to allow it to be different from others, and (4) parents and students are provided with a means of choosing among alternatives. In other words, only a policy that includes a method of expanding the variety of distinctive options should legitimately be called a choice plan.

In practice, any plan that excludes nongovernment schools probably cannot meet these conditions. In theory, a state could eliminate the statutory elements that require uniformity in government schools: curriculum, textbooks, teacher certification, tenure, and mandatory collective bargaining. If this were combined with parental choice rights and a provision allowing individual schools the right to opt out of district control, it would enable public schools to operate on the same flexible basis as private schools. If a state were to give government schools the same ground rules under which nongovernment schools operate, however, there would be little reason to exclude the latter. Ideally, a choice plan would include both nongovernment schools and deregulated government schools.

Most so-called choice plans around the country have not included either nongovernment schools or reduction of state regulations. Consequently, they have not been effective.

Limited Choice

By the term "limited choice," I am referring to what is sometimes known as "public schools of choice." I call this limited choice because it is limited to schools that are directly controlled by the government. Independent or nongovernment schools are excluded.

Controlled choice, as I use the term in the next section, is distinguished by its emphasis on integration. Most of the actual choice plans around the country are of the controlled-choice variety. Nevertheless, for the sake of conceptual clarity, I will start with the simpler idea of limited choice among government schools without consideration of integration, then add the racial factor in the discussion of controlled choice.

Limited choice involves two possible options: open enrollment among schools within a district or enrollment across district lines as well. In states where property taxes continue to provide the majority of school support, interdistrict choice adds the complexity of determining how the sending district should compensate the receiving district. The more important question, though, is why anyone would want to send their child to a neighboring district or to a school outside one's attendance area within a district. (I am assuming that a neighborhood school is closer. In fact, however, district lines may be drawn in such a way that a particular household is closer to a school in an adjacent district.)

The Key Paradox: Different but Similar

Limited choice is stymied from the start by a logical contradiction. Choice among public schools can have meaning only if there is variation among schools, yet the entire rationale of the government school system is to provide a standardized form of instruction. At its root, the system is set up to make choice unnecessary. Each public school provides a diverse program that is supposed to meet the needs of every child. Each school claims to aspire to the same vague goal of excellence, employing teachers with equivalent credentials and similar textbooks, and following a uniform state curriculum. Can they all be the same and yet different, too?

In fact, in terms of the formal activities in classrooms, public schools are remarkably similar. Choosing among them would be exceedingly difficult if one were to judge them purely on the basis of what they teach. But parents don't accept the notion that the school in Snobsville is the same as the school in Plainville. Schools are distinguished in parents' minds less by their programmatic features than by the neighborhoods they are in. Parents want their children to attend school with classmates who are motivated to work hard. Since public schools are designed to be fairly similar in the way they approach their task, parents have little to choose from other than the composition of the student body. (Private schools can distinguish themselves along lines other than social class, which is why they are generally less socially segregated than public schools, contrary to the mythology on this subject.)

Once the district or the state permits parents to choose, many who are in the Plainville district will try to send their child to Snobsville, and few will want to transfer from Snobsville to Plainville. (The exception is when the state or district pumps money into special programs in Plainville, in which case it may draw some students from Snobsville. But that scenario is more likely to occur with magnet schools or controlled-choice plans, to be discussed below.) How can the system accommodate this imbalance in the choices made by parents? It cannot— that is why I call this limited choice. Only a few families are allowed to make a choice.

In Minnesota, where intradistrict and interdistrict open enrollment has operated since 1987, less than 0.5 percent of students (3,218) in the state took advantage of the option in 1989–90.[1] Most of the large-scale transfers under the program have taken place in rural areas where enrollment decline, district consolidation, and the configuration of district boundaries make enrollment in a neighboring district more convenient. In St. Paul, only 201 students left the district for neighboring suburban districts. All of this suggests that there is not enough difference between districts to make transfers worthwhile. Presumably transportation poses some barrier. (The state has offered to reimburse low-income parents for transportation costs, but thus far none of the appropriation has been used, either because parents are unaware of it or because the inconvenience of interdistrict transportation has limited interest in transfers to suburban districts.)

No Flexibility of Supply

Faced with changes in demand, independent schools can respond over time by expanding or opening new schools in some locations and contracting or closing schools in others. A small school can even move to a new site. More important, nongovernment schools appeal to different families on the basis of distinctive educational features. By contrast, government schools are committed to providing all students with a uniform education (in theory, at least). Without the ability to make qualitative distinctions, shifting the location and quantity of service would not help greatly.

If the response to higher demand for the schools in Snobsville district is to add new school facilities there and reduce the supply in Plainville, this would simply move students and teachers to a new location at considerable expense. Even if the people of Snobsville were willing to construct extra schools for the transferring Plainville students (and that is highly unlikely), there is no reason to believe that there would be any significant improvement in any student's education. If Plainville students transferred en masse to Snobsville, they would bring whatever strengths and weaknesses they had before. The schools themselves would not be very different.

Thus, the first and biggest problem with a choice plan that is confined to public schools is that the limits on supply automatically set boundaries on the availability of high-quality schools for which families will compete. There is no incentive to increase the supply of good programs because the government schools form a closed system. Interdistrict choice systems might appear to remedy this problem to a limited extent, but districts have no reason to try to attract students from other districts. In fact, if the plan imposes new construction costs on the receiving district, there are powerful reasons to avoid bringing in students from outside.

Since government schools cannot redirect resources to any great extent, they deal with excess demand by rationing it. Some districts create waiting lists or they offer space in schools on a first-come, first-served basis, opening a campground in front of the district office for parents who are forced to line up days in advance to enroll their children. Other districts ration good schools by setting entrance requirements that only a few children can meet. According to Donald Moore and Suzanne Davenport, open enrollment policies in New York, Chicago, Boston, and Philadelphia that are based on entrance examinations have tended to operate to the detriment of students who are at risk of dropping out or failing to achieve minimal levels of competence—thus adding to the elitism within the existing system.[2] Selective schools within a district, which choose students on the basis of academic achievement, not only remove the best students; they are also able to limit class size and obtain the most resources per student. This leaves the other schools in the district with larger classes and fewer resources. In effect, open enrollment based on selectivity increases segregation by race, class, and ability, producing *within* districts the same stratification as flight to the suburbs has produced between districts. Because a system that includes only a fixed number of schools is closed, a gain by one student is offset by another student's loss.

No Penalties for Failure

A second problem of a choice program limited to government schools is the absence of any rewards for success or penalties for failure. If a school attracts students, it becomes overcrowded. If a school loses students, either new students will be assigned to it, or teachers from the declining school will be reassigned to the growing schools. The whole concept of choice leading schools to become more accountable to parents is doomed in a system of guaranteed employment for teachers and administrators. Choice among government schools will only be genuine if teachers and administrators at schools that fail to attract students are subject to the same need to find a new job that educators face in the private sector. This is not cruelty; it is the basis of responsiveness to clients that is part of professionalism.

It would be unfair to teachers and administrators to allow their schools to fail, however, unless schools are allowed to become distinctive and to display their superior features to parents. Accountability only makes sense if people are allowed to act on the basis of their own judgment. If each school is forced to be basically the same as all of the others, holding the faculty of any given school accountable for the effects of parental choice is unfair.

Lack of Autonomy and Distinctiveness

A third feature of limited-choice plans that undercuts their effectiveness is the lack of the autonomy that would permit government schools to operate distinctive programs. Under existing plans, schools differentiate themselves on the basis of as little as one course: an added music or drama or social studies class. Mary Anne Raywid, an advocate of choice among government schools, notes with dismay that organizational differences, such as the degree of teacher autonomy and the sense of a clear school mission, are often lacking in public-school choice plans.

> [T]he focus in schools comprising choice systems (magnet schools) tends to be programmatic only, and not organizational. This is unfortunate in light of the mounting evidence of organizational impacts on the attitudes, behavior, and accomplishment of workers in all types of organizations. . . . [R]esearch into private schools and others is revealing powerful evidence that these organizational features may be precisely what most needs changing in public schools.[3]

Raywid is reluctant to admit the superior organizational climate of nongovernment schools because she opposes vouchers. Yet she recognizes that nongovernment schools are organized in more successful, less bureaucratic ways than government schools. She seems to imagine that government schools can simply copy the practices of nongovernment schools to improve themselves, but at present there are too many dissimilar features. In fact, only radical deregulation of government schools would give them the autonomy necessary to compare favorably with nongovernment schools.

Government schools have great difficulty developing distinctive identities (other than by labeling themselves as different) for two reasons. First, public schools are asked to be all things to all people. They must avoid offending any constituency. For the same reason that politicians resist saying anything controversial during a campaign, politically controlled schools avoid identifying themselves with any clear values in terms of academic quality, discipline, or personal character. In contrast to a nongovernment school, which can identify itself with a particular philosophy, a government school must remain a generic blob. Consequently, public schools differentiate themselves almost entirely by the family income of their neighborhoods, not by their pedagogical or philosophical characteristics.

The second reason government schools cannot establish distinctive characteristics is that the local bargaining unit of the teachers' union, which represents all of the teachers in a district, wants all teachers to be treated exactly alike. If each school were distinctive and were legally empowered to set its own personnel policies, the union would lose power. Unions would compete to represent each school and the power of any given union would thereby be dispersed. As long as a single union represents all teachers in a district, site administrators have little leverage with the teachers they supposedly manage and little chance of creating distinctive schools.

Two Case Studies

The best way to understand the problems inherent in limited choice is to compare the two most famous choice systems of the past twenty years: Alum Rock, a predominantly (55 percent) Hispanic elementary school district in San Jose, California, and District Four, a racially mixed elementary and junior high district in East Harlem, New York City. In both cases, choice was restricted to government schools. In both cases, the concept of choice was supported by the district superintendent. Yet the outcomes were quite different. The Alum Rock experiment yielded little change in the quality of schools, whereas East Harlem showed that choice can make a difference under the right conditions.

Alum Rock, San Jose   The program in Alum Rock began in 1972 as a demonstration project, funded by the federal Office of Economic Opportunity, to test the feasibility of an education voucher plan developed by Christopher Jencks and his associates. The original intent of the experiment was to test the effects of a voucher system that included nongovernment schools. But that possibility was eliminated when the California state legislature, in authorizing the Alum Rock district to carry out the program, gave the teachers in the district effective veto power over the entry of private schools into the program.[4]

Specifically, the GRO-Kids School, which had already signed up fifty students and had strong support from Hispanic parents, lost community backing when it was forced to meet the criteria set up by the union-dominated Certificated Employees Council. In order to participate in the voucher program, the Council required private schools to employ only California-certified teachers at the same salary and fringe-benefit rates, and the same staff to student ratios as applied in the Alum Rock district. In addition, any waivers of the Education Code had to be approved by the Council. Nongovernment schools had to become ensnared in the same bureaucratic requirements as government schools in order to compete. The purpose was to protect the teachers' union, not the families who had signed up to send their children to the GRO-Kids School.

Thus, from the very beginning, powerful groups within the district ensured that choice would not represent any threat to their interests. Some evaluations of the demonstration project have falsely implied that this was a test of vouchers. Not only did the exclusion of private schools prevent an evaluation of the voucher concept, but even within the boundaries of the public schools, choice was severely constrained. Only 14 of 24 schools in the district participated. Counselors were not able to offer independent advice about programs on other sites because they were administratively tied to a particular site. Again and again, the internal politics of the school bureaucracy stood in the way of offering real choices to parents. "Turf battles" could only be resolved by reallocating power within the district, because there was no outside competitive pressure to induce all schools to improve. With a captive clientele, no penalty for failure, and the limitations imposed by the teachers' union, there was no incentive to establish schools that would respond to parental objectives.

Since nongovernment schools had been excluded, the absence of distinctive alternatives was the single biggest problem in the program, although this fact is almost never mentioned in summaries of the project. According to an in-depth study of variations among classrooms in the district, the classes participating in the program were almost indistinguishable on a multidimensional scale from those that were not participating.[5] Despite the elaborate publicity about offering various educational options to parents, there was very little to choose from. The three truly distinct classrooms in the study appeared to be different only because of teacher characteristics, not because of the demonstration project.

If a true voucher system did encourage a diversity of schools, the experience of Alum Rock could help us understand how to provide information about options. In particular, the studies of parental choice in Alum Rock shed light on the ways in which families of different income levels and ethnic identities might respond to options. Chapter 11 examines the issue of access to information in more detail.

Given the narrow range of options available among the "mini-schools" within the system, it is not surprising that parents made choices on the basis of location and convenience rather than academic quality.[6] Nor is it surprising that there was no systematic increase in test scores among students in the demonstration project.[7] In this case, both the control group and the experimental group took the placebo. The flawed design of the program, due largely to the politics of the public school monopoly, undermined the usefulness of any conclusions drawn from the experience.

District 4, East Harlem   Another choice system that also began in the 1970s was the open enrollment system in District 4 in East Harlem.[8] The student population is approximately two-thirds Hispanic and one-third African American, with a tiny number of whites. In 1973, the schools in the district ranked at the bottom of New York City schools in reading. By 1982, the district ranked 15th out of 32 in the city, and it has remained in that position. In math, the district rose from 23rd out of 32 in 1983 to 19th in 1988. Presumably the math ranking was even lower before 1983, the year of the first city-wide test. Admission to selective high schools throughout New York City rose from almost zero to around 10 percent of the graduating class of 1987, almost double the average rate for the city.[9]

These figures are especially impressive when one considers that about one-third of the District 4 population receives public assistance, and over one-fourth of the households are headed by single parents, three times the rate for New York County. Nearly one-third of the population of East Harlem is adolescent, twice the rate of Manhattan as a whole. As Sy Fliegel, deputy superintendent of the district during the program's early years, noted, "Conventional wisdom and demography suggest District No. 4 would be a difficult place to produce any significant educational change."[10]

The achievement of District 4 shows that kids from poor or limited English households can do well in school if the conditions are right. Based on the complaints of Howard Hurwitz, a New York City principal from outside District 4, however, Myron Lieberman has suggested that much of the improvement in the district may have resulted from the influx of 1,500 students from other parts of New York City.[11] Yet only 51.6 percent of transfer students were reading at or above grade level, which by 1983 was below the proportion for District 4 as a whole.[12] (By 1988, 64.9 percent in District 4 had reached that level.) Instead of regarding transfers as a way of raising test scores, one should view them as a positive sign that school improvement in response to choice among genuine alternatives leads to voluntary integration.

The success of District 4 has a great deal to do with the administrators who believed in reform. Rather than treating District 4 as a hopeless war zone, the non-paternalistic leadership of the district decided to give teachers and principals a chance to take risks and to experiment. Teachers were allowed to initiate schools with distinctive philosophies and goals. The power to initiate was conditional upon district approval (unlike schools started by innovators in the private sector), but the district office encouraged teachers by taking their ideas seriously and by backing them with funds. (One of the features of District 4 that has not received a lot of publicity is that it has served as a showcase program and has thus been able to attract outside funding to reduce class size and purchase equipment.)[13]

Yet the authority to revoke the license to innovate rested with the district. It still determined policy, and the central administration of the New York schools still appoints district superintendents. Much of what happened in District 4 depended on a fortuitous confluence of events: lack of meddling by the Central Board or by the teachers' union (United Federation of Teachers); a decentralization policy that had resulted from a protracted struggle in the late 1960s between minority groups and the white bureaucracy of New York City schools; and dynamic leadership in District 4. The fact that this was an idiosyncratic experience that was spurred by a particular group of personalities is underscored by the fact that no other district in New York City has sought to institute a similar program. Choice has not been institutionalized, and many of the obstacles to differentiation and choice (laws and collective bargaining agreements) persist. Even Sy Fliegel, one of the planners of the system, calls the process of innovation "creative non-compliance." Since educational administrators in the government schools tend to be career bureaucrats rather than entrepreneurs, the idea that many of them will engage in sustained bending of rules for the sake of children is wishful thinking.

Nevertheless, something of importance did take place in District 4. Beginning in 1974, the district allowed innovators to create three "alternative" programs, one specifically for hard-to-handle students whom other schools were happy to remove. In almost every year since then, more alternative schools have opened. Only one-fourth (5 out of 20) of the elementary schools are subject to choice. However, by 1988, almost all junior high students were able to enroll in a school of choice. Around 60 percent received their first choice, 30 percent their second choice, and 5 percent their third choice; the remainder (fewer than 5 percent) went to a lower choice or were assigned to a school without regard to their choice. This compares favorably with controlled-choice programs that permit only around 20 percent to choose an alternative school.[14]

Since students are screened for entrance to many schools with tests or interviews, it is significant that 90 percent of first and second choices were honored. This shows that selectivity by schools does not necessarily mean exclusivity. Instead, the idea that one must do well to gain admission to the next level of school may give students some motivation to try harder. Myron Lieberman notes that the improvement of test scores in East Harlem may be due more to selectivity than to choice.[15] That is, however, a specious distinction. Genuine choice requires differentiation, and the only way in which schools can maintain their differences is by screening prospective applicants to be sure their interests and the school's program match. The fact that part of the achievement gains are due to students striving to gain admission to selective schools means that choice is effective in several ways.

One important and unusual feature of the leadership of District 4 was its responsiveness to consumer demands and its willingness to grant considerable autonomy to individual schools. When one school is in high demand, the effect is to encourage the opening of new schools with similar orientations to satisfy the demand. Thus the highly popular Central Park East (CPE) was followed six years later by CPE II and two years later by River East, all patterned on the same format. Moreover, the district has permitted failing schools to go out of business and to reopen under new management. This contrasts with most choice systems among government schools in which success is not repeated and in which failure does not result in closure.

In fact, as Sy Fliegel, an architect of the East Harlem plan, observes, most school systems reward failure, not success:

> If you're failing, you qualify for aid. If you're doing well, then you lose the aid. That doesn't make any sense to me. It doesn't work that way anywhere else. If you go into business and fail—so long. Nobody's going to say, "Oh you're failing? Here's some more money." It doesn't work that way anywhere else, so somewhere along the line the government has to say, "Let's support what works and stop supporting what fails." I think we ought to close failing schools and let them open up as new and different schools. Let's fund places that succeed. That makes sense to me.[16]

Nevertheless, the district is not entirely free to reward success and remove failure in the area of school personnel. It has been governed by the rules of its contract with the teachers' union and other requirements that limit its flexibility in selecting teachers, an important aspect of autonomy. Yet some teachers have voluntarily transferred to other districts and others who liked the idea of choice have moved in. In fact, part of the explanation of the district's success may lie in the exit of intransigent teachers and the entry of innovative teachers. This flexibility is much easier to achieve when only one part of a larger system changes. If all of the districts in New York became "choice" districts, the capacity to transfer teachers who disagreed with the concept would be much lower.

Ultimately, the schools in District 4 have improved because they foster a sense of ownership among both teachers and students. They have created a supportive climate or ethos that is often found in nongovernment schools but seldom in government schools. It appears likely that the leadership of Sy Fliegel explains the distinctly inspirational character of the District 4 program. He stressed the need for each school to have a distinct purpose: "Without a dream, vision, or mission for a school, the school will go nowhere. A school is an idea, a vision, not a building."[17] Students compare the schools of choice favorably with other schools because the former are small and because students and teachers all know each other. Part of the sense of ownership derives from the small size and the belief that the school constitutes a family.

If the magic of District 4 could be packaged and sold, one could be optimistic that this plan could simply be transplanted to other districts around the country. Yet sixteen years after the program was established in East Harlem, no other system of choice within public schools has copied it. The problem, as Fliegel himself commented, is that the way in which public schools are governed means that failure is more often rewarded than success. Consequently, achieving the circumstances in which government schools will be given the freedom to innovate and rewarded for attracting students is not to be taken for granted. Speaking of the uniqueness of the District 4 success story, John Chubb and Terry Moe note:

> The East Harlem reforms have been driven by a small group of visionaries who used district authority not only to provide parents and students with choice, but also to liberate the supply and governance of schools from district control. The freeing up of the supply side is what makes the East Harlem system so bold and unique. But its creation is entirely dependent on the visionaries themselves and their hold on power. The structures of democratic authority remain in place, and, if they become occupied by people with different beliefs or constituencies, the same public authority that liberated the schools could then be used to regain control over them.[18]

In the wake of a recent scandal and a replacement of some district personnel, the district appears to be entering a phase of retrenchment that may slowly erode the choice system built up over a decade and a half. In the absence of a larger legal and political framework that supports genuine choice (a voucher system or deregulated, autonomous public schools), one district with charismatic leadership cannot serve as a model for other districts.

In summary, both District 4 in East Harlem and Alum Rock demonstrated that districts that are not wealthy, with predominantly Hispanic households, could take advantage of systems of choice in education. Despite widespread poverty, East Harlem was able to raise its test scores in both reading and math. The personal energy and leadership of Sy Fliegel, the willingness to allow failing schools to go under, and the autonomy and distinctiveness of alternative schools in East Harlem all contributed to its success. Alternative schools continue to operate in District 4, but future innovation is in doubt.

The exclusion of nongovernment schools limited the range of alternatives available and left both districts vulnerable to a return to a more traditional system as those who favored choice in the public schools faded from the scene. Only a system that gives individual government schools autonomy and that includes nongovernment schools can release the energy available when a school functions as a community rather than a bureaucracy.

Controlled Choice:
Magnet Schools for Desegregation

Most of the choice plans that have come into existence in the past decade or so have not been primarily aimed at expanding choice for all families. Instead they have used alternative schools as bait to catch a different fish: by creating magnet schools that are visibly better than neighborhood schools, or by allowing interdistrict transfers from city to suburb and vice versa, integration can be achieved without forced busing. Although magnet schools are technically distinct from the systems called controlled choice in Boston, Cambridge, Lowell, Little Rock, and Seattle where a larger portion of the population is provided with choice, I am lumping them together by the common characteristic that they are designed to promote integration.

It is important to recognize that the original intent of magnets and other controlled-choice programs had nothing to do with giving more opportunities to low-achieving students who are neglected in government schools. Rolf Blank, the director of a major national study of magnet schools, notes that the purpose of these programs was simply to create heterogeneous student populations, not to help the students who most needed options:

> The magnet school arose as a practical solution for local school leaders' efforts to meet goals for school desegregation while at the same time trying to reduce the conflict and the draining effect on education that has often accompanied mandatory assignment plans. . . . Few, if any, magnet schools were conceived as a major solution for the problems of at-risk students, and magnet schools have often been viewed as a program to retain middle class students.[19]

Given those aims, it should come as no surprise that magnet schools have shown no consistent educational advantage relative to other schools, except that they may attract the best students and teachers and more money.[20] There is not even any evidence that the racial mixing, which is the paramount goal, leads to any beneficial social effects, such as greater racial tolerance and understanding.

The typical magnet program allows some choice, but sets aside a block of spaces for white or black children in the most desirable programs in order to achieve voluntary integration. As a result of limiting the number of desirable schools, most districts permit only 20 percent of students to exercise choice, and the remainder are simply assigned to a neighborhood school. Many of the magnet schools are distinguished from one another more by their programmatic interest than their academic effectiveness. They may enable parents to enroll their children in a school that offers special art classes, but only a few schools are likely to offer choices based on the organizational features that make schools effective. Thus, on the whole, there is no reason to expect students to learn more in a magnet school than elsewhere.

The exceptions to that rule are magnet schools that have highly selective entrance requirements. Often these schools are exempted from the rules governing other schools in the district. They may be able to select the best teachers instead of having teachers assigned on the basis of seniority.

Whether assignment to magnet schools is by lottery among students of each race or by selective entrance requirements, magnet schools amount to private (that is, exclusive) schools within the public system. In an effort to bribe white families to remain within government schools, some urban districts have designed schools aimed at bringing whites to black neighborhoods, or else they bus black children to predominantly white schools. As Polly Williams, a black state legislator in Wisconsin who established a state-funded voucher program in Milwaukee, describes the situation under controlled choice in that city:

> They [district officials] have destroyed or failed to build new schools in the inner city. If busing ended tomorrow, there would be 40,000 kids downtown and 20,000 places in school for them. They have built new, fancy magnet schools next to the suburbs to entice white kids from across the city line in buses. They are busing kids from one black elementary district in this area to 104 different schools. A group of African-American parents is going to propose we modify this busing madness and start building schools kids can walk to again. Even if [the magnet schools] are in African-American neighborhoods they are largely filled with whites from the suburbs. People attack my plan for subsidizing private schools. Well, these magnet schools are private education at public expense. I simply say that my black parents want the same choice they [white parents] do. None of the people who oppose my plan lack choice in education themselves. They have no idea what the lack of choice in education means, the damage it does when you have to go to an inferior school that will trap you for life.[21]

Although she is speaking specifically about the negative results of the controlled-choice system in Milwaukee, the experience there is not unique. African Americans are supposedly being helped by controlled choice because it promotes integration. Yet, if the experience of Milwaukee is any guide, they are being controlled, while whites are being given choice.

One underlying assumption of controlled choice is that educational quality is a scarce commodity. In other words, it is based on a zero-sum philosophy: the notion that one child's good school experience necessarily implies that some child elsewhere must have a negative experience. If the size of the pie is fixed, then the best the state can do is to devise fair rules to fight over the pieces. Controlled choice suffers from the general problems of limited choice. It is distinguished by the single characteristic of trying to achieve racial balance. In the process, both choice and quality are sacrificed for most students.

In fact, controlled choice is even more likely than limited choice to create inequities as a result of "creaming," the process of removing the best students from neighborhood schools. In the case of limited choice, all students in a district can apply to other schools, and in East Harlem, 90 percent receive either their first or second choice. If, however, choice is constrained by elaborate rules to ensure racial mixing, far fewer students will have choice, as in the situation described above by Polly Williams.

Nevertheless, controlled-choice plans do provide valuable information about one issue: the effects of choice on integration. We now have conclusive evidence that whites will go out of their way to attend multiracial schools, if those schools are of high quality. From that evidence we should draw the conclusion that the task of education is to increase the autonomy and diversity of schools and to allow families to decide for themselves what constitutes a good school. A decade or more of experience with voluntary integration indicates that making schools attractive will bring about continued integration. Thus, instead of concentrating on busing students between one deteriorating school and another, we should be creating education communities that are exciting enough to attract families of all races.

Conclusion

Much of the criticism that has been directed at school choice is appropriate and well deserved. Limited and controlled forms of choice are either elitist or ineffective or both. Even the effort to achieve integration with choice has worked to the detriment of African Americans by setting aside the best schools as magnets to attract middle-class whites.

The fundamental problems with most of the choice plans developed thus far are their lack of boldness in promoting new schools, their reluctance to allow inadequate schools to go out of business, and their failure to create community within schools. They have been tied to the fortunes of government schools, which have become increasingly bogged down in bureaucratic and political contests. Unless government schools have enough autonomy to establish a clear identity and respond to changes in the demands of parents and students, family choice will remain a mere slogan. The one apparent exception to the general rule that public-school choice is ineffective, District 4 in New York City, has not been replicated in other districts of New York or in the rest of the country.

The educational system is designed to reproduce itself, not to encourage imagination and innovation. Those who are waiting for public-school choice to achieve significant improvements in education will be vindicated only if their patience is unlimited. For the rest of us, who want to see improvements in our lifetime, the only hope for genuine change is to open the system to the fresh air of alternative, nongovernment schools, organized without the heavy hand of bureaucracy.

4

Choice Plans That Include Nongovernment Schools

In Chapter 3, I considered the problems created by limiting educational choice to government schools. Lacking autonomy, those schools cannot differentiate themselves. Thus choosing among them has little to do with their educational qualities. Instead, the distinguishing feature of public schools is primarily the social class of the student body.

By contrast, nongovernment schools are free to organize themselves around ideas or principles that appeal to distinctive groups of parents and students. Students attending these schools do not receive a government subsidy, however. Their parents must pay the full cost of tuition (often with the assistance of charitable organizations). The absence of a subsidy limits the range of families that can use nongovernment schools and the number of schools that can afford to operate.

The second type of educational choice would provide families with the financial means of attending either nongovernment or government schools. There are two categories of assistance to make that wider choice possible: tuition tax credits and vouchers. The impact on families is considerably different. I examine those differences in the discussion of tax credits, and discuss the more general features of subsidizing nongovernment schools under the category of vouchers.

Tax Credits

While the effect of choice limited to public schools has created confusion about the likely consequences of a voucher system, proposed tuition tax credits have muddied the waters even more. Tax credits would allow a taxpayer to deduct the cost of qualified educational expenditures from federal or state taxes. Usually this would apply to the income tax, but in states where education is financed primarily by property tax, deductions from that bill would be allowed instead. Generally, the credit would be available only to those who already pay a tax, thus excluding low-income families. The initiative placed on the Oregon ballot in November 1990, however, included a complex provision for refunding money to low-income families that had no tax liability. Still, families would have to go to far greater lengths to take advantage of the credit than they would if vouchers were distributed to everyone.

Some of the most ardent proponents of tax credits are libertarians who believe in the abolition of taxation for schools altogether. They want to make reponsibility for financing education a purely private matter. They view tax credits as simply a way of reducing the amount of tax that a family would pay. They argue that parents are entitled only to that amount of the educational tax that they themselves have contributed. This would mean that those too poor to pay taxes would not be able to provide their children with an education. Since libertarians do not believe that citizens have a social duty to provide education for all children, they would leave the education of the poor to private charity.

Many proponents of tax credits naively imagine that the use of the tax mechanism (rather than a voucher system) would prevent government involvement in the operation of nongovernment schools. But a state legislature would still be able to impose its chosen restrictions by narrowly or broadly defining the nature of expenditures eligible for the credit. Nor is there any evidence that courts would distinguish between tax credits and vouchers on the subject of church-state relations. The Supreme Court will allow a system of funding for nongovernment schools if the system is neutral among public and private schools, including sectarian schools, and if it provides aid to sectarian schools "only as a result of decisions of individual parents rather than directly from the State to the schools themselves."[1] In fact, since the Court held that any acceptable scheme must provide for all children, not merely those in nongovernment schools, tax credits could face more constitutional difficulty than vouchers.

The primary similarity between vouchers and tax credits is that both would enable parents to choose nongovernment schools at partial or full state expense. As a result, for almost twenty years, tax credits and vouchers have been lumped together by opponents as "aid to private schools" or "subsidies of the rich at the expense of the poor." Estelle James arrives at a false conclusion, based on this fuzzy thinking:

> In the United States, one of the arguments against privatization is that the rich and middle classes would vote for low-cost, low-quality

public schools, thereby saving on taxes, and would send their own children to high-quality private schools. We would therefore get a segmentation of education along class lines and a perpetuation of class differentials.[2]

She has confused the issue by grouping all policies together under the term "privatization." The situation she describes is precisely what happens in the *absence* of aid to families that choose to send their children to nongovernment schools. At present, the people who have opted out of government schools have no reason to vote for school taxes. If, however, the state provided a full-tuition voucher to each child, all parents would have an incentive to vote for *higher* education taxes since schools receiving vouchers would become tax-supported or public.

Nevertheless, there are two conditions under which this charge of "privatization" has some validity. Those conditions are: (1) providing credits (or vouchers) in amounts below that necessary for full tuition, and (2) providing credits at the national rather than the state level.

If a tuition tax credit of only $250 had been enacted, the number of families making use of nongovernment schools would probably not have increased substantially.[3] That small amount certainly would have given no incentive to establish new schools, because the demand would have been only marginally higher. That means the credit would have assisted rich families already sending their children to private schools far more than it would have benefitted poor families that had not been able to afford that option. Thus it was legitimately criticized as inequitable and a form of privatization.

Moreover, because the tax credits would have been offered at the national level, they might have had the effect of encouraging families with children in private school to reduce support for *local* school taxes. This problem, stemming from the difference between federal and state or local taxes, would arise with tax credits but not vouchers (since no one has seriously proposed a national voucher system). This emphasizes the value of keeping any school financing scheme at the state or local level where money for education has traditionally originated.

Intellectual honesty has suffered as reasonable arguments against partial tuition tax credits at the national level have been transferred wholesale to full-tuition vouchers at the state level. Whereas a $250 nonrefundable tax credit would induce few poor families to look at alternative schools, a $4,000 or $5,000 voucher would open a variety of new options to those families. A national system that undermines support for local school taxes might reasonably be called privatization, but vouchers issued at the state or local level should avoid that problem.

Vouchers

The weaknesses of the choice policies described above and in the previous chapter give an undeservedly bad name to vouchers. In contrast to limited or controlled choice, vouchers would create new educational options instead of shuffling people among existing schools. In contrast to tax credits, vouchers or direct scholarship aid would permit *all* families to participate, not just those who pay high taxes.

I am assuming in what follows that the amount of the voucher would be close to the level of per-pupil spending in government schools, say 80 or 90 percent of the state and local expenditures. If the amount of the voucher falls below the minimum amount necessary to provide a full school program (including rent or amortization of a building), the system would suffer from the inequitable features of a small tax credit plan: only the wealthy would make use of it.[4]

This understanding of vouchers is not universally shared. Some libertarians bring with them to this issue the psychology and politics of stinginess—the idea that the poor should gnaw on education bones while the rich provide their own children with education meat. Thus they propose vouchers at levels below that necessary to start a school today. Well-to-do parents could make up the difference, but the poor could not. By trying to force some of the costs of education back on the shoulders of low-income families, they push individualism to a reductio ad absurdum. They would undermine the guarantee that all children will have access to education, and thereby unravel the social fabric within which their vaunted individualism can operate.

Financing Vouchers

The initial question in establishing a voucher system is who would provide the funds for it. In most states, education finance derives from a combination of local property taxes and state revenues. To provide funds directly to families a state could either contribute the per-pupil share of state education funds or require local taxes to be contributed to the voucher pool. If the state took over school finance altogether, it could equalize per-pupil spending by providing all students with vouchers. To avoid raising state taxes, it would have to require local governments to take over financing of programs the state now pays for. (Tax credits solve the budgetary problem only by engaging in "backdoor" spending; that is, by losing revenues. As a result, either other programs have to be cut or taxes have to be raised. Although tax credits superficially look like a "free lunch," the bill must come due in some form.)

A significant percentage of education funds are now channeled through categorical grants or specialized programs: various forms of compensatory education, special education, school lunches, and dozens or hundreds of others. A voucher system could leave some of these intact and eliminate the rest, although federally funded programs would presumably be continued, at least for students in government schools. There might also be a need to set aside more money at the state level for special education, as I will explain below.

Another complicating factor in the financing of vouchers is whether to include in the calculations the cost of construction of new buildings and the use of existing facilities. This issue arises if the amount of the voucher is set in relation to per-pupil spending. The amortized cost of facilities is a considerable segment of the total cost of government schools. Whereas the annual operating costs of a government school are generally in the range of $4,000 to $7,000 per pupil in 1992 (with wide variation between states), the amortized cost of buildings runs from $1,000 to $1,500 per pupil per year. (These numbers are rough estimates because they vary considerably according to land prices, building costs, school size, and other factors, such as whether the buildings are for elementary or secondary schools.) In other words, the cost per pupil of building and maintaining facilities is around 20 percent of the true cost of schooling.

This capital cost remains hidden in most discussions of school finance, including debates over vouchers. States have assumed a growing portion of school operating costs, but capital costs are generally borne by local districts. Unless the state wants to assume responsibility for construction of all schools and exacerbate conflicts between districts vying for state funds, it is probably wise to leave the capital subsidy out of the voucher discussion. The absence of tax-financed facilities will place an unequal burden on nongovernment schools, but that is an inequity that may simply have to remain. To the extent that enrollment in government schools declines however, leaving empty spaces, nongovernment schools should have first priority in leasing the buildings from the school district.

The Value of a Voucher

Since the core of the voucher concept is the distribution of scholarship certificates to all families, determining the value assigned to each voucher is of great significance. As long as the amount of the voucher is set below the average amount spent per pupil in government schools, most districts will gain slightly for every child who transfers to a nongovernment school.[5] Of course, total district revenue will fall. If overhead costs are high, top-heavy districts will have to cut the positions or reduce the salaries of administrators, maintenance workers, teachers on special assignment, and other noninstructional staff. Otherwise the district will have to lay off teaching staff faster than the rate of decline of the student enrollment. Predictably, school officials never admit that their opposition to vouchers stems from a desire to preserve a bloated administrative structure.

Vouchers would also put pressure on school districts by increasing the student population that would receive government-funded schooling. Approximately 10 percent of children are currently enrolled in non-government schools. Money that is now being spent on students in government schools would have to be spent on students from nongovernment schools as well. The effect of a voucher system is financially the same as closing all nongovernment schools and sending their students to government schools. If four hundred private-school students transferred to a public school district of four thousand students, public funds would be as diluted as if vouchers were provided for the four hundred students to remain in independent schools. Yet opponents of vouchers accept one prospect and complain about the other, even though the per-pupil spending in public schools would be spread over an extra 10 percent in both cases. They have not bemoaned the dilution of public school funds when Catholic parishes have had to close some of their urban schools, thereby forcing some of their students to attend public schools. If providing children from rich families with public money to attend a nongovernment school is inequitable, why is paying for their education in a government school not inequitable? A voucher system does not spend public money for private purposes; it provides for the education of all students in the state, regardless of which school they attend.

Another issue is whether to give different categories of students different grant levels. John Coons and Stephen Sugarman propose four basic alternative grants: uniform, varying according to family income, varying according to differences in cost of schooling, and "power equalized" in such a way that additional spending by poor families costs them less than add-ons by richer families.[6] There is a trade-off between simplicity and equity in these options. Attempts to equalize grant amounts according to need quickly arouse difficult questions regarding place of residence, size of family, stability of income, and costs of local schools. Far simpler would be a provision in the authorizing legislation that prohibits discrimination on the basis of ability to pay. Schools charging more than the voucher amount (and not many cost as much as that now) would be required to offer scholarships to low-income applicants to make up the difference between the voucher and the tuition charge. One way to encourage high-cost schools to accept low-income students would be to require them to set aside 10 percent of each voucher for a scholarship pool, to be used only to subsidize low-income voucher holders.[7]

Special Education

A far more difficult problem for vouchers (or tax credits) is posed by special education. According to federal law (Public Law 94-142), a teacher, a school representative, and a parent must jointly adopt an individualized education program (IEP) for each special education student. The IEP specifies (among other things) the services to be provided to the student. At present, if a school believes it can serve the needs of a student adequately, it does so. Otherwise, it must find an alternate placement. The federal law allows parents to appeal the placement decision through the courts and provides that parents will receive legal fees to accomplish this. A parent who chose to use a voucher to make a unilateral placement of his or her child could lose the rights guaranteed by the federal law.

The placement procedure dictated by federal law has the effect of determining the amount of money that will be spent on a given child. The concept of "appropriate" education, without consideration of cost, determines the entire process. In the case of alternate placement, the receiving school charges for the service specified in the IEP. The courts can decide the placement ultimately, but the school district and the state jointly share the cost. The existing system has no financial accountability.

Making this procedure the norm for setting voucher levels for special education students could be very complicated. It would require the IEP to specify not only the type of services to be provided, but also the amount of the voucher to achieve predetermined goals for each child. Since the type and severity of handicapping conditions varies so greatly, it would probably be necessary to calculate the value of vouchers for special education students on a case-by-case basis. Since the dollar amount of the voucher could determine the quality of the service a child would receive, any procedure for determining that amount would be likely to lead to endless lawsuits.

Another element of the federal law is the requirement that special education students be placed in the "least restrictive environment." Historically, handicapped children were frequently either excluded from school or placed in rooms where the only service they received was baby-sitting. Now they are entitled to participate in normal classes to the extent that their handicaps allow. The extent to which any particular child should be mainstreamed and the specific classes that are appropriate are an ongoing controversy in every school.

The creation of separate schools for the handicapped is not an acceptable alternative for most special education students. Even if agreement can be reached about how to set the voucher amount for disabled children, parents will still have a problem finding nongovernment schools in which disabled students can be mainstreamed. At present, nongovernment schools that provide services for the handicapped are rare, except for the schools that specialize in those services. Nongovernment schools cannot afford the additional costs of admitting disabled students without government assistance. They would have to modify their physical structures and hire special teachers.

Under a voucher system, if handicapped students were eligible for vouchers worth more than regular vouchers, there would be an incentive for nongovernment schools to accommodate special-needs students. Nevertheless, when one considers the history of neglect of the handicapped, it becomes clear that incentives alone might not be sufficient. Accommodating disabled children raises a host of issues that administrators might prefer to ignore. It might be necessary to prohibit schools from discriminating against potential students on the basis of their handicaps.

Nongovernment schools will still need to be able to practice some form of selectivity. Not every school could afford to accept students with every type of handicap: speech impaired, orthopedically handicapped, learning disabled, and retarded, to name a few groups of these students. A reasonable expectation would be for nongovernment schools to provide services for one or two special-needs populations. If schools are to be required to design their structures to accommodate physically handicapped students, perhaps schools under a certain size (one hundred or two hundred students, for example) might be exempted. It would certainly be unfair to expect a school opened in a private home for five or ten students to comply with the same physical requirements as a school with a thousand students. Perfectionism in the name of equity could easily destroy the viability of a voucher system.

The problem, therefore, is how to preserve the rights that the handicapped have won thus far while providing more choice to those who want it. For the most severely disabled who are currently in residential or other specialized facilities, there seems little likelihood that their choices can be expanded with vouchers. The cost of establishing such facilities is sufficiently great that vouchers would not be likely to induce an increased supply.

For the majority of learning-disabled children, though, vouchers would represent a potential for improved education. Even among those who received only the base voucher amount for the nondisabled, most would be able to find schools serving their needs as well as or better than government schools. Some of them might attend ordinary nongovernment schools. Others might choose schools that included special classes for children with learning handicaps. Judging by tuition at existing nongovernment schools, the base voucher amount would exceed the cost of attending most of them. If a particular student qualified for extra money, the extra funds could be used to purchase special assistance, either at the chosen school or from an outside tutor.

Because of the problems that a centralized administration would have in determining the appropriate voucher amount for each handicapped student, separate categorical funds might need to be maintained for special education. Those funds would be allocated to school districts (or multidistrict consortia) on the basis of population. At present, approximately 10 to 12 percent of students are classified as handicapped or disabled in some form, and the services they receive cost approximately twice as much per pupil as for nondisabled students.[8] The state would therefore provide around 80 percent of the total education budget for nondisabled students and 20 percent for disabled students. Districts would then decide how to parcel out the special education funds among the competing claimants, with the proviso that none could receive less than a nonhandicapped student. A district would be obligated to determine the amount of voucher funds for which any given handicapped student was eligible, recognizing the overall limit within the district. It could distribute vouchers to parents of handicapped children on the basis of a formula of the district's own devising. The district (or local education agency) would be required to provide an appropriate education for the amount of the voucher, but the parents would be able to choose an alternate placement using the voucher as the basis of their choice. The budgetary limit would force a district to make hard decisions about the amount to provide for various handicapping conditions. This is not presently the case. Currently, if a district increases spending on handicapped children, the funds come from either the state or the district's general fund; that is, from the nonhandicapped.

Another special category of children are those who are currently institutionalized under the direct supervision of a state agency or who are living alone without parental supervision. Whatever educational choices are made on behalf of institutionalized children will presumably continue to be made by their legal trustees. For teenagers who are runaways or, more often, "throw aways" whose parents have expelled them from home, alternative, community-based schools could provide a group that would function as a surrogate family. These youths should be allowed to participate in the voucher system directly, perhaps with some community agency serving as a legal trustee. Vouchers could thus indirectly provide support for agencies that are giving sanctuary to teenagers living on the street.

Creative social workers might also find ways to use vouchers to help children in distressed families. If local zoning laws permit, a large house might serve as a combination school and residence for several homeless families. Vouchers could pay at least part of the rent, as well as instructional costs. Although the school might be less than ideal, a child with a fixed residence is likely to learn more than one living in cars or temporary shelters.

The Machinery of the Voucher System

The key administrative tasks for the government under a voucher system would be distributing vouchers to families with school-aged children, ensuring access to information about schools, and reimbursing schools when they redeem vouchers. States and districts might also provide transportation, either as a direct service or through vouchers.

Vouchers and school information would be made available to parents through the district-office channels currently in place. The state should also inform parents about the availability of vouchers through radio, television, and newspapers, although word of mouth has generally proved the most widely used source of information about schools for people of all income levels.

Parent-information centers could be set up in district offices and in community-based organizations where citizens already expect to find other services. Whatever form a voucher system takes, making information available to parents about options is essential for its effective operation. At least initially, county education offices might be charged with the responsibility for compiling lists of schools in each district that accept vouchers. The lists would include the amount of tuition charged, the size of the school, the type of curriculum and after-school care offered, and other relevant information to help parents make an informed choice. Schools would have an incentive to provide adequate information in order to attract students. Many schools would choose to advertise independently.

With voucher in hand and a list of eligible schools, parents would apply to one or more schools on behalf of their children in much the same way they now apply to daycare centers. The state would need to provide a transportation subsidy, at least for poor and rural children to ensure their access to schools at a reasonable distance. Since vouchers might eventually replace integration plans in some cities, the huge amounts

Polly Williams:
The Woman Who Brought Vouchers to Milwaukee

When State Representative Annette "Polly" Williams convinced her colleagues in 1990 to pass legislation in Wisconsin establishing the first voucher program for low-income children, her intense desire to enact the program came from personal experience.

In the 1970s, Ms. Williams sent her own children to independent, nonsectarian elementary schools, even though she was on welfare for a time. When she wanted to find a good public high school for them, she discovered that Milwaukee's magnet-school program was closed to her children because they were black. Black children were assigned to schools and bused all over the city to achieve racial balance.

After her oldest child was not permitted to attend the school of Ms. Williams's choice, she wrote a letter of appeal to the district. The appeal was denied. Then she presented an oral argument before the school board. That request was also turned down. She explains what happened then:

> Now remember, I'm not your plain, average, every day parent. I'm a hard nose. I don't take "no" for an answer. You can imagine [what happens to] the other parents who don't fight. . . . [She explains how the district intimidates poor parents by threatening them with loss of food stamps or with imprisonment if they do not accept their children's assigned school.]
>
> I went up to the superintendent's office and left a note for him. . . . It said, "I'm taking my child. I'll be going home. Send your police; come and arrest me, because I'm not letting you send my child to a school that's against my will."
>
> When the superintendent came in and saw that note, the superintendent called me and said, "You can get the school that you want." So I got my kid into that school. . . . And all of my kids went to the same school because I believe in continuity and consistency.*

From that time, and as a member of the Wisconsin legislature since 1981, Ms. Williams has been fighting for better education for African-American families. She does not claim that nongovernment schools are the answer for every family. She merely wants to be sure that the poor have the same chance as the rich to make choices.

---

* From a speech by Polly Williams in San Francisco, June 10, 1991, sponsored by the Pacific Research Institute for Public Policy.

that have been spent for busing could be made available for transportation subsidies for those who need them.

Regulation of Nongovernment Schools

In contrast to its current role, the state would not be involved in the inspection, regulation, and evaluation of schools under a voucher system. (Local fire and safety regulations could be enforced, however, just as they are in any public building.) The state might require that certain academic subjects (particularly English) be taught, but it would not dictate the actual content or manner of teaching. The only limit on religious instruction should be a prohibition on requiring a nonbeliever to engage in activities that involve a violation of personal conscience. Nevertheless, Christian schools should be allowed to teach Christian doctrines and Moslem schools to inculcate Islamic values. As long as no child is required to go to any particular school, allowing schools to promote ideas and beliefs allows for diversity without infringing on the right to religious freedom.

Under the voucher system, the concept of graduation from high school might need to be modified. Instead of requiring that prescribed courses be covered, the state might accept the successful completion of a proficiency test. The more important question, however, is what colleges and employers would require as a demonstration of competency. Students seeking enrollment at state-run universities might be required to achieve minimum scores on a battery of achievement tests in various subjects. This would be as reliable an indicator of academic ability as completion of coursework, especially if the test scores were combined with written evaluations of a student's capacity to do academic research on an undergraduate level.

Although Americans have grown accustomed to intense government regulation of education, parental and community control can more effectively guarantee the well-being of children. In fact, without parental empowerment, schools face the perennial problem: "Who shall regulate the regulators?" In theory, school boards and state legislatures are responsive to citizens, but in fact, they are more responsive to concentrations of power and money. Teachers' unions play an inordinately large role in determining nominations and elections to public office. Parents are largely outside the circles of power. Vouchers would restore their power by ensuring direct oversight of the schools by those most concerned with their success.

Schools and other socializing institutions have tried to convince us that we and our neighbors are not competent to evaluate and regulate professional behavior. Yet comparison and evaluation of professionals goes on every day. Whenever clients choose to transfer to a new lawyer or doctor or psychotherapist, they are "regulating" the professional they leave behind. Of course, many incompetent and corrupt people continue to engage in those professions. When regulations are applied by the state to control an occupation, the purpose is not so much to protect the public as to protect the existing members of the guild from competition. Loss of public reputation may not be a perfect form of control, but it is better than the typical bureaucratic methods of requiring reams of paperwork. At any rate, bureaucratic regulation has never guaranteed quality in education. Parental oversight could only be an improvement.

A matter of considerable importance, therefore, in the wording of legislation for a voucher system should be a near total restriction on the power of the state to regulate schools receiving vouchers from families. Of course, the restriction would not permit a nongovernment school to engage in illegal activities such as fraud, child abuse, or actions endangering the life of children. Short of extremes such as those, however, the intent of voucher legislation should be to prevent well-meaning but misguided intervention by the state, particularly in matters of academic significance.

Divisibility and "Banking" of Vouchers

Most discussion of vouchers seems to presuppose that the entire amount of the voucher would necessarily be spent at one institution. For the sake of flexibility, however, a system of divisible vouchers would be preferable. Since the whole purpose of vouchers is to enhance the choices available to families, there is no reason to restrict those choices artificially by requiring that the entire voucher amount be spent at one place. Most of a voucher might be spent at a single school, but the remainder of the amount could be used for special tutoring, for payments on a personal computer, or for special classes offered through learning networks. A school need be no larger than a single instructor who has applied for that status in order to be eligible to receive students with vouchers. Many "schools" might be housed in one building to achieve administrative efficiency and to reduce transportation costs. This would be an ideal use for abandoned space in government schools that are losing students. Other schools might be in offices or private houses.

Permitting divisibility of vouchers among a variety of small programs and tutorials instead of a single institution might make the administrative costs of reimbursement excessive. That problem could be resolved by requiring individual tutors to seek reimbursement through schools, which could deduct a small administrative charge from each payment.

Divisibility could also lead to corruption. Individual tutors might engage in kickback schemes with parents. However, apart from the safeguard that could be provided by independent audits, vouchers have a built-in resistance to corruption of that sort by virtue of the desire of most parents to serve the best interests of their children. Recipients will not imagine that they are "ripping off" some faceless bureaucracy. A parent would also have to keep the fraud a secret from relatives and friends who might inquire about the child's education. Only a socially isolated family could sustain the pretense for long. Nevertheless, the state might inhibit simple kickbacks by requiring schools to enroll children from several unrelated families, thus ensuring that those engaged in fraud would have to obtain the collusion of several others. This would also eliminate payment for home schooling in individual families, but it would not prevent several families from joining together and forming a school. Thus, no one could be paid simply for teaching his or her own children.

If vouchers are divisible, then units might also be accumulated from year to year. "Banking" would create an incentive for parents to use low-cost options in the early grades (including no-cost home schooling) in order to save the voucher units for higher-cost secondary schooling. Conceivably, the accumulated units could even be transferred to pay for college tuition. A system allowing accumulation of voucher units would have the advantage of encouraging families to take a long-range view of education. The main disadvantage would be the necessity to check more carefully on the physical presence of children receiving vouchers. Otherwise a child who has left a particular state might continue to accumulate vouchers there. If this administrative cost is not too large, a system of accumulation would be beneficial.

Divisibility and flexibility in a voucher system would reduce the problem of selective admissions in nongovernment schools. Parents would have the option of buying specific tutorial services in subjects such as music, algebra, or writing from dozens of educational providers for a portion of a voucher, combining those services into an individually tailored program. With several math or reading programs plus numerous individual instructors in a given area, the problem of not gaining admission to any particular program would be relatively minor. This fragmentation might not be as rewarding as a comprehensive program, but it would guarantee that no student would be relegated to a "dumping ground" school, as voucher critics have claimed. Private companies already provide tutorial services to children from wealthy families in the suburbs, and community agencies provide similar services in inner-city neighborhoods.

In the event that vouchers are not divisible and parents are not allowed to allocate the voucher to more than one institution, however, parents would be limited to a choice among schools which offer a comprehensive program. Under those circumstances, children not accepted at an independent school would continue to attend a government school. In the first few years of a voucher program, before the supply of new schools had expanded, this limitation might cause some frustration.

Creating New Schools

The supply of independent schools will grow over time in response to increased demand, thereby reducing the initial problem that some parents would have in finding a suitable school. With the external funding provided by vouchers, teachers and parents dissatisfied with existing schools could work with one another and with community organizations to start new schools. Corporations would be likely to open schools, either for the children of employees or because they want to enhance the quality of the workforce with better education. Since most private colleges in the United States were founded by religious institutions, it is reasonable to expect that churches will establish some primary and secondary schools as well. Some denominations have already done so. The number of schools with a focus on black or Hispanic cultural heritage would probably grow. A variety of schools for those with special needs or with special interests such as art or music would undoubtedly emerge. There is no reason to expect the variety and quantity of schools for K-12 education to be more limited than the range and number of colleges and technical institutes today.

Vouchers create an open-ended system rather than the relatively closed system with which we are accustomed to dealing in education. Elementary schools, in particular, can be started without large overhead expenses. Existing preschools might offer to extend their programs through the primary grades (K-3), or parents might choose to start small neighborhood schools in their homes. For the creation of high schools, the impetus would probably need to come from churches, community groups, and learning exchanges which could provide meeting sites, some initial capital, and administrative expertise. In addition, entrepreneurs would establish proprietary schools at all grade levels, just as they have set up these schools at the postsecondary level. (The effectiveness of these schools will be discussed in Chapter 9.)

Conclusion

Choice in education is an abstract concept, not a policy. Favoring choice without specifying the form it would take is essentially meaningless. Except for fascist or communist nations, no modern society has attempted to deny its citizens some choice in schooling. If families are limited to government schools, the potential for nurturing schools with distinctive identities is weakened. Choice is empty if all schools are similar by design. Government schools are differentiated at present only by social class and race, because they are not supposed to develop educational or ideological differences.

The only means of providing genuine choice to all children is by providing enough resources to each family to enable them to generate new education communities. New schools will almost certainly come into being. Only a small percentage of parents or teachers or other citizens need take the initiative to start new schools. Communities depend on followers as well as leaders.

Simply providing choices among government schools is not sufficient. Even with complete autonomy, the range of options offered by government schools will be more limited than those which nongovernment schools will provide. In particular, government schools can never offer the distinctive religious traditions that many parents want their children to inherit.

The potential to participate in distinctive education communities should not be limited to the wealthy. In theory, tuition tax credits offer the resources necessary for all parents to enroll their children in nongovernment schools. Yet, since tax credits will primarily benefit the wealthy, they are not a general solution to the problem of educational renewal.

Vouchers, by contrast, are egalitarian or even possibly compensatory. If the amount of the voucher were made approximately equal to the total per-pupil spending on education in a state, that amount would be adequate to pay tuition at all but the most elite private schools. Even a flat-rate voucher could permit the poor to have almost the same range of choices as are now open to the well-off. Higher voucher amounts for the poor would go even further toward achieving equality.

The possibility of dividing and banking vouchers could alter the nature of education even within the private sector. In particular, the chance to apply vouchers toward college costs could create a tremendous incentive for parents to reduce spending on early education in order to increase the opportunity for their children to attend the institution that is most valued: college or university.

Above all, vouchers would create a system of education that encourages families to work together to gain the most effective results for the least amount of money. Until we have had experience with vouchers for a prolonged period, we will not know the full range of possibilities that may emerge as a result of innovations by thousands of schools and families. Only through that sort of challenge will we discover the true potential of local self-reliance and voluntary community enterprise.

PART II

WILL VOUCHERS EQUALIZE OPPORTUNITY OR WIDEN THE POVERTY GAP?

P art of the public-school mythology is the notion that government schools are moving to correct the inequities of society. Government schools have tried a variety of strategies to overcome the legacies of poverty and racism: desegregation, compensatory education, and consolidation, to name a few. None of these strategies has been especially successful. Nevertheless, when voucher proponents argue that families should be given the chance to regain control of education, the public-school lobby argues that vouchers will disrupt all of the attempts to create a society with more equality.

Instead of promoting communities that can empower the powerless, which ought to be the fundamental goal of a program of social justice, the existing schools produce the stigma of "disadvantaged" and "at-risk" students. Those students are then either shunted off to dull, repetitive classes where they learn only to hate school, or they are "compensated" with programs that further stigmatize them.

In the following three chapters, I shall focus on the ideal of equal opportunity and the reality in government schools. My aim here is to develop a basis for comparing the existing school system with the more flexible system that vouchers would allow. We cannot know in detail how vouchers will affect equity issues, but we can judge in a rough way whether or not vouchers will lead to an improvement over the present system. There is already some empirical evidence from inner-city nongovernment schools and from other choice programs (discussed in Part 3) demonstrating the equalizing effects of vouchers. The only fair comparison is between that limited set of empirical observations and an evaluation of how government schools now operate. Even though public schools *aspire* to promote equality and racial harmony, they should be judged by their achievements, not their goals.

There is considerable evidence, discussed in Chapter 5, that government schools throughout this century have reinforced barriers to social mobility by keeping students from lower-class families in classes with low expectations. Many students become "disadvantaged" by their experiences in school.

Since the 1960s, schools have been under pressure to improve educational opportunities by promoting integration, the topic of Chapter 6. Yet integration has turned out to be a double-edged sword. Since the white majority has continued to control most schools, absorbing ethnic minorities into white schools, integration has often led to disempowerment of African-American and Hispanic families.

The question of structural reform is taken up in Chapter 7. The problematic way in which government schools are organized is compared with the organization of nongovernment schools. Small size, autonomy, and a distinctive mission all contribute to relationships within a school that make an effective learning community. The absence of those features in most government schools could be remedied in part by allowing them to function beyond the constraints of state regulation. Yet that sort of change is only likely to occur in conjunction with a voucher system.

5

Disadvantaged at School, or by School?

Government schools, particularly high schools, were designed originally for white, middle-class boys with professional ambitions. Over time, government schools expanded their mission and included all children, but they did not take into account the differences in cultural background of entering students. Schools require everyone to conform. Those who don't fit in are simply treated as rejects or losers. As Rona Wilensky and D. M. Kline point out:

> The culture of American public schooling is most familiar and comfortable to those who already have succeeded in the economic system but often perceived as alien by those who are cut off from the economic and social mainstream. In general, schools actively promote this majority culture while *turning the strengths of minority and poor students and communities into problems that impede schooling*. The process of devaluing potentially legitimate skills, experiences, talents, energies, critiques and dreams that children bring to school from their homes and commmunities is what Fine describes as "pathologizing." Instead of building on a culture of cooperation, schools replace it with a culture of competition and individualism and even denigrate cooperation as cheating. Instead of praising and accommodating the student who must drop out of school to help take care of a sick family member or help support younger siblings, these actions are seen as part of the problems that schools must heroically overcome.[1]

For a large proportion of students, school is a colonial institution that they resist because it denies the value of their families and culture.

79

Whether or not a child comes to school with a "disadvantage," he or she is likely to become "disadvantaged" by the school if the label sticks.

Social Decay

I would not deny that some children come to school with prior handicaps. I am not referring here to linguistic or cultural differences. I have in mind rather the emotional instability that results from constant mobility or from violence or neglect. These conditions, which cut across lines of race and class, interfere with a child's success at school.

Yet the fact that a problem begins at home does not deny the possibility that school life may compound it. Children from dysfunctional families are often double victims: they are mistreated and neglected first at home and then again at school. In schools that lack community, these children will be either ignored (if they are withdrawn) or punished (if they act out). In schools that conceive of students as "cases," most children from dysfunctional households will simply flounder.

Unfortunately more and more families are dysfunctional and thus failing to meet the needs of children. Divorce and remarriage leave children uncertain about family relationships. Parents spend less time with their children than in previous generations. More and more kids are abused or neglected, largely because there are so few resources, such as extended families, available for parents under stress. Mobility has decreased neighborliness. The presence of a wide range of caring adults in children's lives has diminished.

The breakdown of social networks is placing pressures on families of all social classes. Middle-class families are able to buy extra professional services that the poor cannot afford, but professionals cannot solve the problems resulting from the decline of community. The important question should be, How can we provide the resources to enable all families to rely more on each other?

Defining Some Students as Losers

Rather than recognizing the importance of community in resolving the growing problems faced by schools, administrators continue to devise categories for "difficult" children who don't fit into the settings where they are placed. School officials persist in ignoring pathological social conditions and acting as if failure or misbehavior were simply a result of defects in the individuals concerned. As a result, schools treat the supposed defects in the character of particular students rather than the defects in the school system that exacerbate individual problems. This approach justifies the existence of a giant bureaucracy engaged in applying various forms of treatment. Beyond that, it enables the school system to avoid blame for the millions of children who fail to learn, attributing the success or failure of individuals to the fact that some are winners and others are losers.

The problem of labeling is compounded by the use of poverty as a shorthand characteristic to prejudge which children will fail in school. Schools have used the concept of a "culture of poverty" as an excuse for failing to teach millions of children. Poverty is not an inherent quality of certain individuals. Poverty stems from policies that erode community self-reliance and produce a fatalistic acceptance of being victimized.

Many of the programs designed to help poor children are self-defeating precisely because they reinforce the stigma of defeat. Multiplying special programs within schools that are designed for failure makes less sense than promoting schools in which everyone can succeed.

Dropouts and Push Outs

The most visible effect of the insidious campaign to sabotage the poor is the tremendous school attrition rate of lower-class children. In keeping with the mythology of individualism, school officials define dropping out as a purely individual choice, thus ignoring the central role that school organization and policies play in the decision. Although some students willingly leave school for purely personal reasons, a large percentage of early leavers are in fact "push outs" rather than dropouts.

Schools push out lower-class children as undesirables. This rejection is a cumulative process by which those children are made to feel that their presence is not wanted in school. As Bernard Lefkowitz notes in his study of low-income inner-city youths, the main factor is that no one intervenes when a lower-class student starts giving signs of dropping out. According to James Vasquez, a school superintendent to whom Lefkowitz spoke in Texas:

> My feelings tell me that a lot of kids who are labeled dropouts are really kick outs. . . . The attitude that prevails now in the schools is, If you don't want to stay in, then leave. What the schools are really saying to these kids is, You make our situation better by leaving. What really gets me is the deceit. Schools will never admit that they're encouraging the hard cases to leave. They pretend it's all the student's fault for dropping out.[2]

Thus even if a school does not actively encourage students to drop out, the impersonal structure sends them a message that no one cares. This is especially significant in the case of lower-class children who are less likely to have peer support to stay in school than their middle-class counterparts.

Statistical evidence indicates that school organization plays a large role in nudging kids out of school.[3] Dropping out is associated with schools having (a) low concentrations of students in academic programs, (b) conflicts between the principal and the teachers, (c) a high degree of tracking, (d) a high degree of social diversity, (e) a low level of discipline and order, and (f) large school size. The probability of dropping out of a Catholic school is lower than in public schools and is less affected by the social class of the students. Dropping out is not simply an individual act; it results from differences in school environments. Despite this evidence, public schools treat dropping out as a product of external forces over which they have no control. This absolves the school of responsibility and blames students for failure.

Tracking by Level

Most of the efforts to reduce inequality in education have been aimed at equalizing differences between school in spending or integrating racially segregated schools. The most important inequality, however, stems from intraschool separation of children into ability categories: the process known as tracking.

In theory, ability grouping enables teachers to provide lessons that are tailored to different students. The stated intent is to help all students: the brightest, the slowest, and those in between. According to common belief, putting less able students in the same class with top students will retard the progress of the latter and humiliate the former.

However, as Jeannie Oakes notes in *Keeping Track: How Schools Structure Inequality,* the one consistent conclusion to emerge from studies of ability grouping over the past sixty years is that "no group of students has been found to benefit consistently from being in a homogeneous group."[4] She points out that a few studies have shown that bright students learn more in groups of peers and that average or low-level students are not harmed by being put in homogeneous groups, but that the preponderance of studies contradict both of those conclusions. In general, according to the evidence of careful studies, students do not learn best in homogeneous groups. The reason is not hard to fathom: students have always learned as much from each other as they have from the teacher. In heterogeneous classes using cooperative learning, the slowest students learn from the brighter students, and the best students learn by teaching.

Ability grouping has an adverse effect on achievement levels over the school career of a child with low initial test scores. Within-school achievement differences are greater than between-school differences. Thus, the track in which a child is placed matters more than the school he or she attends, because tracking amplifies rather than narrows the gap between high-achieving and low-achieving students.[5] An initial gap of a few months in first grade becomes a gap of several years by the time children leave school, because tracking slows down some students and speeds up others.

Tracking is the primary form of resegregating African Americans in "integrated" schools. The most blatant form of this practice is the assignment of a disproportionate number of African Americans to "educable mentally retarded" classes (at twice the rate of enrollment) and the underrepresentation of African Americans in gifted and talented programs (at half the rate of enrollment).[6] Even though the academic effects of school integration are minimal, one study found that integration of individual classrooms (that is, a reduction in racially based tracking) does improve black test scores.[7] The U.S. Commission on Civil Rights noted that in-school segregation stigmatizes black students more obviously, because it is based on presumed tests of ability. It concluded that black students have been more harmed by within-school segregation than by between-school segregation.[8]

The damaging effect of tracking on the self-esteem and aspirations of students in the lower track has been confirmed in a number of studies.[9] Indeed, it is evident to even the casual observer that students in the lower-track classes internalize the derogatory labels placed upon them. The teachers and student peers in the low track expect them to perform poorly, and they learn to conform to that expectation. Since the studies cited by Oakes control for social class, ability, and self-assessment prior to tracking, it is clear that the low self-opinion of students in the bottom tracks derives directly from the tracking process itself.

Tracking stigmatizes the low-level students because it appears to be based on merit. Students are placed in bottom-track classes largely on the basis of standardized tests. As Oakes points out, the tests are designed to place half of the subjects below the average. Thus, standardized tests provide no information about absolute differences in achievement and even less about learning ability.

Worse than placement by testing is placement by the subjective judgment of teachers and counselors. The evidence reported by Oakes indicates that counselors are likely to assign students to groups on the basis of language, dress, and behavior, each of which are associated with social class or ethnicity.[10] Thus the presumption that racial minorities and the poor will perform poorly in school becomes a self-fulfilling prophecy when those groups are automatically assigned to the classes which are the least demanding and rigorous.

The difference in content between high-level and low-level classes in public schools is the crux of the discrimination against the poor and minorities. Oakes describes the content of high-track and middle-track English classes as

> "high-status" knowledge in that it would eventually be required knowledge for those going on to colleges and universities. These students studied standard works of literature, both classic and modern. . . . Students in these classes were expected to do a great deal of expository writing, both thematic essays and reports of library research. . . . Low-track English classes rarely, if ever, encountered these kinds of knowledge or were expected to learn these kinds of skills. . . . It is probably not surprising, given the differences in *what* they were learning, that the differences in the intellectual processes expected of students in classes at different levels were substantial. Teachers of the high-track classes reported far more often than others that they had students do activities that demanded critical thinking, problem solving, drawing conclusions, making generalizations, or evaluating or synthesizing knowledge. The learnings in low-track classes, in nearly all cases, required only simple memory tasks or comprehension.[11]

The same differences apply to mathematics and science instruction where the low-track classes emphasize repetitive computational exercises instead of logical, algebraic, and geometric concepts.

Nor is this nearly universal practice in the public schools an accident. A few reformers may complain about it because they recognize that tracking belies all of the ideals of equality of opportunity to which school leaders pay lip service. But tracking is built into the organization and self-definition of government schools.

The Roots of Tracking

Dividing students into categories that are associated with social class has been characteristic of public schools since the first decade of this century. (Racial divisions, until desegregation, were primarily between schools rather than within them.) That was the decade when the comprehensive high school and vocational education were introduced. These new forms of schooling were developed specifically as a sorting mechanism. The United States was receiving about a million immigrants a year, mostly from southern and eastern Europe. The newcomers were viewed as socially different, not on the same level as the Anglo-Saxon and northern European immigrants of earlier generations.

Industries in the United States were seeking laborers to work in factories. Vocational education and ability placements within comprehensive schools were both methods of channeling the lower classes into their "proper" social station.[12]

Ironically, the progressive reformers of the period did not view this tracking system as elitist, although the academic track was associated with white-collar or professional jobs, and general or vocational education classes were connected with blue-collar work. Instead they saw the provision of different types of curriculum to different social classes as democratic, because it allowed each person to fulfill his or her potential and permitted everyone to participate in the same school. Their image of democracy conveniently ignored the ways in which this channeling process automatically limited the potential of lower-class students. Equality of opportunity meant that schools would aid the lower-class student to become an assembly-line worker as effectively as they would help an upper-class student to become a bank president.

This Orwellian logic, by which elitism, in the guise of individuals finding their place in society, is defined as democracy, makes reform of the tracking system exceedingly difficult. After decades of this self-contradictory language, thinking on the subject has been completely obfuscated. The confusion is deepened by the seemingly scientific basis of the sorting process—standardized testing. Within the public-school bureaucracy, the voices that criticize this deeply ingrained practice are regarded as self-serving or naively idealistic. Tracking students according to their presumed academic merit is considered fair and democratic.

Although Catholic schools have engaged in tracking, the practice takes a very different form there than in government schools—a form that does not destroy the long-term chances of success of low-track students.[13] Instead of channeling low-achieving students into dull remedial classes or "manual arts," Catholic schools offer the same curriculum to each track, but at different levels of intensity. High-track students take more classes per day and more science or foreign language classes than low-track students. Nevertheless, a hard-working student in a low-track class in a Catholic school can gain admission to college or a find a white-collar job more easily than an equivalent student from a government school because the first student has never been sidetracked from the academic curriculum.

Minorities and School Expectations

The difference between tracking in the public schools and uniformly high expectations in private schools is most significant for low-income minority families. African-American and Hispanic children in government schools are more likely than whites to be placed in special education classes or classes with low expectations. The operative mythology in the public schools with respect to low-income minority children is the "culture of poverty" hypothesis. This thesis proposes that children from lower-class, minority backgrounds will not be able to take full advantage of education because they are "culturally deprived."

The problems of labeling, tracking, and low expectations have been discussed for at least twenty-five years, since Kenneth Clark attacked "the cult of cultural deprivation" by which public schools blame children instead of themselves. Yet nothing has changed since he wrote:

> These [ghetto] children, by and large, do not learn because they are not being taught effectively and they are not being taught because those who are charged with the responsibility of teaching them do not believe that they can learn, do not expect that they can learn, and do not act toward them in ways which help them to learn. . . . The schools in the ghetto have lost faith in the ability of their students to learn and the ghetto has lost faith in the ability of the schools to lead.[14]

Almost a decade later, the U.S. Commission on Civil Rights observed the same phenonenon of expecting less from certain students because of their ethnicity.

> Teachers praise or encourage Anglo children 36 percent more than Mexican Americans. They use or build upon the contributions of Anglo pupils fully 40 percent more frequently than those of Chicano pupils. Combining all types of approving or accepting teacher behavior, the teachers respond positively to Anglos about 40 percent more than they do to Chicano students.[15]

Since the structures of school organization have not changed, we can only assume that this process continues. Some students are labeled as intelligent or receptive and others as dull or unreceptive. The labels, which are passed from teacher to teacher, become self-fulfilling prophecies as students conform to either positive or negative expectations.

Bright students in lower-class or minority schools learn to fulfill the expectations of their teachers by becoming listless, unproductive, and disruptive because their competence is not recognized. This anticipation of limited achievement is only one aspect of the public-school culture that reinforces an image of poor and minority children as failures.

One striking piece of evidence that children from low-status backgrounds fail as a result of oppression rather than personal characteristics comes from international comparisons. Finnish students do poorly in Sweden where they are a low-status group, whereas they do well academically in Australia where their status is more favorable. The outcaste group in Japan (similar to India's untouchables) attain low scores on intelligence tests in Japan, but score higher when they move to the United States.[16] Thus, the internalization of low expectations, not a set of personal psychological characteristics, accounts for the failure of children from socially dominated groups.

Changing the Tracking System

Since the tracking system is an integral part of the public-school system, internal reform is unlikely. But a voucher system could undermine the tracking system from the outside by offering alternatives to those who have been consigned to dead-end courses of study. Returning power over education to families is a key to renewing the lives of those who have been classified as disadvantaged. The psychological and social elements of poverty—the experience of not being in control of one's own life—can be addressed only by giving to the poor the tools by which to gain control over their condition. Nowhere is this control more important than in education, and in no other aspect of life is it so conspicuously absent.

The likely effects of a voucher system on the poor can already be observed in the way inner-city nongovernment schools treat their clientele. In independent, predominantly African-American neighborhood schools that were surveyed by Joan Davis Ratteray and Mwalimu Shujaa, teachers have high expectations of all children. As one parent who responded to the survey noted: "[The teachers at an independent school] want coming to school to be a positive experience . . . [My daughter] gets up and she wants to come to school. She wants to learn. [The teachers] promote asking questions. That's a positive thing to me. She comes home with that same type of attitude."[17] Another parent had a child who had been tested and placed in a learning-disability class in a public school without the parent's being notified. She took her son out of the school and placed him in an independent school which determined that he did not have a learning disability. He had simply not been taught basic academic skills.[18] Other parents stressed the ways in which nongovernment schools, starting in preschool, pushed their children to study the kind of curriculum that would enable them to succeed in school and be prepared for college without having to take remedial classes there.

Conclusion

Government schools do not remedy the presumed disadvantages of the poor; the schools compound the sense of failure and stigma that accompanies poverty. Despite their promise to help achieve equal economic opportunity, schools perpetuate poverty in the sense of reinforcing negative expectations. They add to the sense of hopelessness of many children, and by failing to provide a decent education, they contribute to the growing number of "information poor."

Above all, schools disadvantage a child by affixing a label and then placing the child in an academic track that will maintain the effects of the label over time. This is not an accidental feature of schools that can be eliminated by judicial decree. The process of sorting is an integral part of the function of government schools.

Consequently, only by restructuring the entire educational process could we alter the ways in which schools systematically disadvantage certain students. Vouchers would not only produce smaller, community-based schools in which tracking would be unthinkable, but they would also give parents the power to leave a school if it treated their child with indignity.

6

Choice, Segregation, and Empowerment

Some critics of vouchers might affirm the positive role of community-centered schools but fear that vouchers will invite a return to racial segregation. They believe that vouchers challenge the integration ideal of public schools. Although that ideal has rarely been realized, the idea that vouchers might further erode the prospects of an integrated society would be disturbing, if true. But voluntary integration of schools, based on attraction, has been more successful in recent years than mandatory busing. A voucher system is thus likely to increase the ethnic diversity of both public and private schools.

Civil rights groups such as the National Association for the Advancement of Colored People (NAACP), however, claim that vouchers will lead to separatism, which they regard as a step backward. The president of the Milwaukee NAACP joined a lawsuit opposing the new voucher system for low-income residents of that city, because he believes that vouchers will undermine desegregation. Yet the independent schools that students can attend with vouchers are themselves integrated.

The real conflict in Milwaukee and elsewhere is not between integrationists and segregationists but between those who regard integration as an end in itself and those who treat it as a desirable objective if it improves education for blacks. A significant enlargement of the voucher system would inevitably have an impact on the city's desegregation plan, particularly if black families chose to establish new inner-city schools instead of putting their children on buses to attend schools in predominantly white neighborhoods. Tactical voluntary separatism on the basis of ethnicity will not lead to a permanent division of society, just as

separate black or women's colleges have not promoted permanent racial
or gender segregation. Nevertheless, the issue of voluntary versus
mandatory segregation will remain volatile in the years ahead.

African Americans, Integration, and Choice

The hostility of the NAACP to vouchers has some of the character of
generals fighting a previous war. Every plan for choice in education,
no matter how much it will benefit ethnic minorities, appears to some
civil rights leaders as a reenactment of the integration battles in the
South during the 1960s.

Circumventing Integration

As the federal courts attempted to eliminate segregation in the wake
of the landmark 1954 Supreme Court decision *Brown v. Board of
Education*,[1] and as the United States Office of Education sought to
implement the Civil Rights Act of 1964, whites in the South used four
methods to circumvent integration orders: (a) school closures (especially
in Virginia);[2] (b) voucher plans,[3] which the courts immediately found
unconstitutional because the vouchers were intended to circumvent
integration;[4] (c) "freedom-of-choice" plans, which theoretically allowed
blacks to attend white schools; and (d) "white flight" from cities to
suburbs, although this was used more in the North than in the South.

Of the four strategies, freedom-of-choice plans were the least effective
at preserving segregation. In Alabama, more integration occurred as
a result of freedom-of-choice plans in rural areas than took place under
court-ordered desegregation plans in big cities.[5] But even the best plans
generally produced only token integration. In the late 1960s, the federal
courts insisted that choice plans would be acceptable only if they yielded
greater integration.[6] They insisted on plans that entailed the transfer
of large numbers of both black and white students, closing some all-black
schools in the process. This offended several civil rights groups,
especially the Congress on Racial Equality (CORE), which believed that
blacks should have the option of attending black-controlled schools.[7]

As a result of the use by whites of vouchers and choice systems to
evade integration and to avoid equal educational opportunities, many
black civil rights leaders are understandably skeptical of programs to
increase the role of nongovernment schools in education. However, lumping old racist voucher plans of thirty years ago with neutral proposals
today is unfair. Overcoming de facto segregation now is a different
problem from that of defeating legal segregation in an earlier era.

Nongovernment Schools and Desegregation

The image of private schools in the South in the late 1960s as segregation academies is generally valid. In Mississippi, there were only 12 nongovernment schools in 1964; by 1971, there were 236, of which at least 163 were established to bypass desegregation.[8]

It must also be remembered, though, that Catholic schools, which still remain the predominant provider of alternative educational services to minorities, did not fit the segregation academy mold. Indeed, as Thomas Vitullo-Martin points out, sectarian schools were the last holdouts against the segregationist Black Codes in the South (laws upheld by the U.S. Supreme Court in 1917) and the first to end segregation when the law permitted them to do so.

> After the 1954 *Brown* decision struck down the school segregation statutes, private schools were the first to integrate voluntarily. In St. Louis, New Orleans, and elsewhere, Catholic schools integrated *before* the public systems. In Mobile, Birmingham, and other southern cities, whites fled to the segregated public system to avoid integration in Catholic schools. The effect of integrating Catholic schools was to break the back of resistance to voluntary desegregation in the public systems of those cities.[9]

But the positive role played by *some* nongovernment schools was ignored or forgotten by those who saw all independent schools as the enemy of the civil rights struggle.

The Nineteenth Century

The attitudes of African Americans toward vouchers have been shaped by a history that extends back further than the civil rights movement. To understand conflicting perspectives on how to achieve the best education for black children, one must go back at least 150 years to the period before the Civil War when government education was first being established in northeastern states.

From the 1840s to the 1890s, African Americans sought ways to provide an adequate education for their children despite the obstacles put in their way. As David Tyack says of this period:

> No group in the United States had a greater faith in the equalizing power of schooling or a clearer understanding of the democratic promise of public education than did black Americans. . . . Practically every black voluntary group, almost all black politicians, rated the improvement of educational opportunities near the top of priorities for their people. Yet across the nation many of the whites

who controlled systems of public education excluded, segregated, or cheated black pupils.[10]

Blocked from automatic participation in white schools, African Americans chose two different responses to segregation. In some cities, black leaders supported separate schools that they could staff them- selves, arguing that this provided jobs for black teachers and better learning conditions for their children. White teachers, they charged, were biased against their children. Either schools for blacks were established by public authorities with minimal funding, or African Americans established their own voluntary schools, relying on com- munity resources as well as philanthropy.

In other cities, African Americans fought for integration of the local public schools. In Boston in the 1840s, for example, black abolitionist David Walker denounced segregated schools for denying black children the chance to learn. He reasoned that integrated schools would be more likely to receive adequate resources. "If there were white children in the classes—in effect, as hostages—the teachers would have to teach the Negro pupils as well."[11] The integrationists believed that "separate but equal" would never be equal. They thought that if black and white children attended school together, school boards would be forced to provide them with equal education.

The debate between African Americans pursuing schools with a black identity and those who favored integration continued throughout the century without resolution. One of the political issues was the elimination of the secure professional jobs that segregated schools offered black teachers. In 1908, segregated schools in Baltimore, Philadelphia, and St. Louis employed 285, 99, and 136 black elementary school teachers, respectively.[12] By contrast, no African-American teachers worked in the integrated elementary schools of Los Angeles and Pittsburgh. Boston employed only three. Thus, whereas integration may have increased resources for black children, it practically eliminated a whole class of professional role models and sealed a major avenue of upward mobility.

The issue of choice for African Americans has always been more complex than simply becoming free of state control, because whites have often controlled both public and private sources of school support. As Joan Davis Ratteray points out, many nongovernment schools for African Americans were financed by missionary groups that had no intention of providing an academic education that would liberate blacks from manual labor.[13]

Only schools that did not depend on white sources of funding could guarantee an education that was not denigrating to African-American children. From the perspective of those who valued independence of thought, the pursuit of integration might have seemed self-defeating in terms of the loss of black teachers as role models. When black children did attend nominally integrated schools, they were (and still are) disproportionately assigned to classes for those with learning problems. This was only the most visible aspect of the systematic effort to deny equal education to African Americans—all within the public schools.

The Desegregation Strategy

In the 1960s, desegregation was pursued with the naive faith that the physical proximity of blacks and whites would improve the education of black students. Initially, this view was vindicated, for as integration began in the South, achievement levels of blacks and whites either increased or remained constant. But the early successes in schools integrated voluntarily on the part of blacks "proved hard to attain through direct policy intervention."[14] Integration increased the scores of young black children on IQ tests by a few points in some cases, but "student gains did not increase with time spent in a desegregated environment."[15]

The limitations of integration were already noted in the massive study by James Coleman and his associates in 1966 and by later reanalyses, which showed that achievement gains of blacks had derived from social class integration as much as from racial integration.[16] For the purpose of improving the level of achievement of black children, placing lower-class children with middle-class children may have been more important than racial mixing. When cities began busing children between lower-class neighborhoods for the sake of racial balance, the results were less successful than voluntary integration into middle-class schools had led everyone to expect.

The courts failed to consider the factor of social class, but that merely reflected a more general blindness. School districts were so preoccupied with the logistical problems of moving thousands of children that few paid much attention to the human dynamics in the receiving schools, an important element in schools where integration was successful. Integration policies ignored resegregation within schools, reductions in intensity of the curriculum, and changes in the culture of integrated schools. With staff inadequately prepared to deal with unfamiliar interactions between blacks and whites, the failure of massive integration to improve educational achievement is no surprise.

In terms of racial mixing alone (ignoring the academic effects) northern cities proved more difficult to integrate than the South. Blacks and whites live in greater physical proximity to each other in small southern towns than in northern industrial cities. In contrast to the

North, where resegregation in the form of white flight to suburbs often followed desegregation, many southern whites had no suburbs to which to flee when integration came. In the 1980s, southern schools were the most integrated in the nation.

The integration strategy was effectively blocked after the Supreme Court ruled in *Milliken v. Bradley* that suburbs could not be held accountable for urban segregation.[17] As a result, federal courts dropped plans to overcome regional patterns of residential segregation by requiring student transfers between predominantly white suburban districts and predominantly black urban districts. When courts failed to require interdistrict transfers to achieve racial balance, the potential for integration declined considerably. By 1983, the population of about one-half of 126 major urban areas was predominantly (more than 75 percent) black and Hispanic.[18] Black and Hispanic children in cities now have only a few whites with whom to integrate.

To achieve integration "with all deliberate speed," the courts imposed mandatory desegregation plans in the 1960s and 1970s. Initially, the results were impressive. In northern cities, however, increased racial contact in the first year of a plan was usually followed by a rapid decline, and by the fourth year, whites had abandoned the integrated schools, leaving a district less integrated than before.[19] Nevertheless, a dispersal index of integration that measured only how evenly whites were distributed among blacks often showed an improvement. That measure is, however, a misleading basis on which to claim that mandatory programs have proven superior to voluntary plans.

If one takes a more commonsensical view that sees integration in terms of the probability of a black or Hispanic student having a white classmate (which depends on both dispersal and the number of whites who stay in the district), then mandatory integration plans have been less successful than voluntary programs. In contrast to the long-term net decline in integration from mandatory programs, voluntary programs gradually increase the level of integration without leading to high levels of white abandonment of the city schools. In a study of both voluntary and mandatory integration plans in Los Angeles in 1979, the voluntary program was more than twice as effective as the mandatory program for contact between blacks and whites and equally effective for contact between Hispanics and whites. The study found similar results for cities in two states: San Francisco, San Diego, and San Bernardino, and Denver.[20]

Regardless of whether or not statistical desegregation has occurred, efforts to achieve equality by integration have been plagued in various ways by bad faith. First, desegregation by race has not involved much mixing of students of different social classes. In practice, most integration plans have brought together children of various races from low-income neighborhoods. Second, desegregation plans have forced African Americans and Hispanics to give up their schools in order to be bused to white schools, and in the process, minorities have paid the high price of losing control over their education. Third, in integrated schools, blacks and Hispanics have been disproportionately assigned to low-level classes, punished for infractions, and forced out of school at an early age. Finally, the mere fact of physical integration does not necessarily improve racial understanding or mutual respect unless the curriculum, staff development, and other aspects of a school's program create a multicultural atmosphere.[21] Integration has often meant bringing ethnic minorities into predominantly white schools and expecting the "outsiders" to assimilate the values of the majority. Even many schools that are predominantly African American or Hispanic have failed to adopt a curriculum that genuinely considers the interests of those students because whites continue to control most school boards and administrations.

Having lost sight of the ultimate purpose of desegregation suits— the creation of opportunities and choices for blacks and other minorities—several civil rights lawyers have pursued statistical measures of contact between races as their goal. This weakness of desegregation plans has been clear to at least some civil rights leaders. Derrick Bell has suggested that the Supreme Court's remedy in 1954 would have been more helpful if it had demanded equalization of resources, "required that blacks be represented on school boards and policy-making bodies in proportions equal to those of black students in each school district . . . [and five years later] imposed a freedom-of-choice plan." Since historically "black parents have sought not integrated schools, but schools in which their children could receive a good education," the remedy of the Court should have enabled black parents to choose between integrated schools and African-American schools instead of assuming that the latter were inherently inferior institutions.

> Had we civil rights lawyers been more attuned to the primary goal of black parents—the effective schooling of their children—and less committed to the attainment of our ideal—racially integrated schools—we might have recognized sooner that merely integrating schools, in a society still committed to white dominance, would not insure our clients and their children the equal opportunity for which they have sacrificed so much and waited so long.[22]

Presumably if integration had been achieved by expanding choices with vouchers instead of constraining them with rigid busing plans, this negative side effect could have been avoided.

The Continuing Controversy

The preceding brief history is intended to put into perspective the debate among African Americans who were confronted by two unenviable options: separatism without resources or integration without esteem or teacher employment. The debate was not over ends but means. Both sides wanted to achieve educational equality as a step toward economic equality. The separatists did not want segregation to be compulsory or under white domination, and the integrationists were not ready to sacrifice their cultural identity in order to assimilate into white society. Both wanted the empowerment of African Americans and an assurance that they would be treated with dignity. They merely disagreed on the wisest strategy to achieve those goals in the shortest possible time.

The controversy continues today, in part because white paternalism has prevented a transfer of genuine power to African Americans. Many of the blacks who have gained some degree of power within white institutions seek patronage and political payoffs rather than direct empowerment of all blacks. There seems to be an underlying assumption that if whites are going to control the levers of power, the best that can be done is to demand equal access to services provided by whites. That is also the standard interpretation of the Supreme Court's decision in *Brown v. Board of Education* and subsequent desegregation cases.

Patricia Lines has pointed out, however, that the usual interpretation of *Brown* is based on a misunderstanding of the fundamental issue at stake: equal control of institutions rather than equal access to resources. In *Brown*, the court rejected policies that deny blacks the right to exercise self-determination in the political process. Those policies involved official segregation in the South and various school policies that had the effect of isolating blacks in run-down schools in the North. The *Brown* decision did not mandate racial balancing. It did not mandate policies to promote equal outcomes in test scores. Instead, it deemed officially sanctioned segregation as morally repugnant, regardless of the outcomes. According to Lines, the problem with segregation was not so much separateness as the denial of political power to blacks to exercise control over their lives: "The central problem with the idea of "separate but equal" facilities for blacks was the denial of choice—the denial of the right to choose and shape education through full participation in the political process."[23]

Since *Brown*, the courts have treated segregation as a statistical issue, focusing on the number of children of different races who must be brought into physical proximity, regardless of the wishes of the black families that are supposedly benefitting. Lines suggests that the spirit of *Brown* cannot be fulfilled by providing blacks with access to predominantly white facilities. Instead, the remedy should be to empower blacks by giving them discretionary control over equal resources. This is not the same as "separate but equal." Under that doctrine, even if equal resources had been provided to black schools, decisions would still have been in the hands of white officials. That was why separate could never be equal, at least not until blacks were given direct control over the resources being spent in their names. As Lines explains, "Most courts have treated only the symptoms—the racial imbalance in schools—and have failed to treat the underlying cause of imbalance, the exclusion of blacks from participation in decisions affecting student assignment and allocation of resources to schools."[24] In effect the courts have been engaged in moving resources around in what Lines calls "a sophisticated version of musical chairs." To this day, the courts have not carried out the intent of *Brown,* because they have refused to transfer power to blacks.

What this suggests is an almost complete lack of progress since the early 1970s, when blatant school segregation was finally ended. If the problematic feature of school policy then was white control of black education, little has changed. In some instances, the situation worsened when desegregation removed what little power blacks had over their children's education.

Lines proposes that the underlying problem of unequal political power could be remedied by issuing vouchers to the victims of past discrimination. This would allow them to attend the public or private schools of their choice.[25]

Vouchers would permit those who want Afro-centric schools to establish them. At the same time, for those who prefer immediate integration, a voucher system would constitute a means of achieving that goal on the basis of attraction to a school rather than compulsion by the state. Since urban public schools have already lost most of their white students, vouchers would not threaten to resegregate urban school districts. Instead, they would increase the opportunities for more integration by improving the quality of urban education and attracting white families back to cities.

In addition, vouchers will give more blacks and Hispanics the means to attend private schools that now enroll a higher proportion of whites than do public schools. Efforts to enable minority youth to attend private schools as part of a desegregation plan were made in Los Angeles in the 1970s.[26] More recently, this aim was the basis of an integration lawsuit that was filed on behalf of the children of Kansas City District (KCD) in Missouri. Originally the court mandated the district and the state to pay the cost of voluntary transfers from the overwhelmingly black district of KCD to nearby white districts. The court was powerless, however, to require the neighboring districts to accept any of the black students from KCD, and they refused to do so. A suit was subsequently filed on behalf of a number of black students that, if successful, would require KCD to pay the cost of sending these and other students to private schools in Kansas City and nearby towns that have offered them over four thousand places.[27] Since the public schools spend approximately $6,000 per student, and the (primarily sectarian) schools that have offered to accept the students spend around $2,000 per pupil, KCD could cover this cost and actually save money. The students would receive a high-quality, integrated education. Yet the district is fighting this eminently sensible idea, while the attorneys from the earlier desegregation suit refuse to help the children, even though they privately admit the plan is good for students and for integration.[28]

The Conflict over Vouchers Today

Past conflicts among blacks about the way to deal with segregation and deprivation can be seen in the different orientations toward vouchers in the present political context. The most critical voices regard desegregation of government schools as the one and only solution to unequal treatment of African Americans and other minorities.

Others echo Professor Derrick Bell, who sums up the feelings of many civil rights leaders who have lost faith in the existing system: "Vouchers may be worth trying, things are so bad now."[29] This view was shared by 79 percent of blacks surveyed by the *Boston Globe* in March 1982. The survey was taken during a period in which the 200-member Black Parent Committee, in an ironic twist, demanded a freedom-of-choice plan to replace the court ordered integration plan.[30]

A more positive view comes from those who believe vouchers are a constructive means of allowing African Americans to build their own institutions and thereby foster a sense of self-reliance rather than dependence. Their viewpoint reflects the tradition that has considered black-owned schools an important resource for promoting black pride and enterprise.

Roy Innis, president of the Congress on Racial Equality (CORE), endorsed a tuition tax-credit plan in Oregon in 1990 that would have reimbursed families for tuition expenses at nongovernment schools. This position reflects a long-established principle of CORE that all-black schools can provide high-quality education and that African Americans should have the option of choosing between integrated schools and independent neighborhood schools controlled by blacks.

Joan Davis Ratteray, president of the Institute for Independent Education, has written extensively on the harm inflicted on the spirits and intellects of many African-American children in government schools, on the value of independent neighborhood schools for African Americans and Hispanics that are responsive to issues of ethnic identity, and on the need for vouchers to foster these types of schools.[31]

Robert Woodson, director of the National Center for Neighborhood Enterprise, supports vouchers as a method of giving parents more choice and a chance to gain greater control over the moral content of their children's education.[32] He points out that most of the trillion dollars spent to reduce poverty in the past twenty-five years has gone into the pockets of a class of professional poverty "experts," rather than to empower the poor to make decisions for themselves. Vouchers would end that pattern of dependence by providing new educational opportunities for low-income families. The neighborhood schools that vouchers would foster would create prototypes for other independent enterprises in minority communities.

In 1968, before widespread discussion of vouchers began, Kenneth Clark, the psychologist who showed how debilitating racism is to young children's self-image, wrote an article on the need for alternative forms of education. He saw that "public schools are protected public monopolies" and argued that

> alternatives—realistic, aggressive, and viable competitors—to the present public schools systems must be found. . . . Truly effective competition strengthens rather than weakens that which deserves to survive. I would argue further that public education need not be identified with the present system of organization of public schools. Public education can be more broadly and pragmatically defined in terms of that form of organization and functioning of an educational system which is in the public interest.[33]

In practical terms, he proposed a variety of parallel systems of schools, operating on a quasi-private level but in the public interest. He believed competition was the only means of overcoming the inertia of the public-school bureaucracy. Although he has never explicitly endorsed the voucher concept, his views at that time were compatible with it in many ways.

Despite the increasing number of African Americans who favor vouchers, others continue to oppose choice systems. Given the historical roots of this conflict, it probably cannot be resolved to the satisfaction of all civil rights leaders, although the ongoing failure of the public schools will increase the willingness to experiment with greater choice.

Other Ethnic Groups

Thus far, I have concentrated on conflicting views among African Americans toward vouchers. Their concerns and interests have historically been central to public debates about segregation, integration, choice, and community control of schools. The importance of rediscovering cultural roots grew out of efforts to regain a black identity in response to the dominant culture's role in effacing the history of African Americans.

In the past two decades, many of these concerns have also become more evident in other minority communities, among Hispanics, Asian Americans, Pacific Islanders, and American Indians. The result has been growing pressure within government schools for bilingual programs and a truly multicultural curriculum. There is also a growing desire among some groups to be granted the means to attend independent schools that are not dominated by the ideology of the mainstream (Anglo) culture.

A variety of ethnic groups have faced educational discrimination or exclusion at various stages in American history, and some, such as the Chinese, have established separate schools. The groups whose experience most closely parallels that of African Americans are Mexican Americans and Puerto Ricans. As a result of prejudice and oppression, these Hispanics became a caste-like minority whose children internalized the stigma imposed on their ethnicity. In urban high schools today as many as half of Hispanic students drop out before graduation.

History of Hispanic Miseducation

Before 1950, many school districts in the Southwest provided a separate school for Hispanic children if any school was provided at all. The motivation was similar to that behind Jim Crow schools for blacks: to keep a low-caste group in its place. As one Texas school superintendent explained: "Most of our Mexicans are of the lower class. They transplant onions. If a man has much sense or education, he is not going to stick to this kind of work. So you see it is up to the white population to keep the Mexican on his knees in an onion field."[34] Seldom do those in power make their reasons for oppressing others so blatant, but the motivation revealed here has been common in the provision of inadequate schools to minorities.

Like the industrial-labor schools designed to prepare blacks for menial jobs, their separate schools trained Hispanics for domestic service, garment work, or other low-status occupations. White school officials expected Hispanic children to drop out at an early age and planned accordingly. Rather than encouraging students to focus on school, counselors and teachers discouraged them from pursuing academic programs leading to college.

The legal desegregation of Mexican Americans in California and Texas ended more than six years before the famous *Brown v. Board of*

Education decision declared all officially segregated school systems unconstitutional. In 1946, the League of United Latin American Citizens (LULAC) won a case in Orange County, California, arguing that assignment to separate schools violated the Fourteenth Amendment.[35] The *Delgado* case in Texas in 1948 was even more far-reaching. It "declared unconstitutional the segregation of Mexican-Americans in separate classrooms within 'integrated' schools."[36] As in the case of African Americans, school officials continued to carry out segregation within schools by tracking Hispanic students into non-academic courses.

Yet a more important issue for many Hispanics than integration was the question of forced acculturation. Both separate and integrated schools were run by Anglos who taught Hispanic children to be ashamed of their history, their culture, and their language. "The specific acculturation measures included Anglicizing the child's first or last name, forbidding the speaking of Spanish on the school grounds, and the use of a curriculum that put Mexico and Mexican-Americans in a bad light."[37] The result for at least some children was "a sense of shame, a sense of guilt, a sense that somehow you're not good enough."[38] Out of that experience grew an interest in either special English classes or bilingual education, depending on the orientation of the parents or educators.

Hispanic Attitudes toward Education

Among Hispanics, the desire for their children to learn in a bilingual setting is almost universal. According to a 1979 telephone interview of Hispanics in New York and Los Angeles, 87 percent favored bilingual education, 10 percent opposed it, and 3 percent had no opinion.[39] Yet among those who favored it, there was disagreement about whether the primary purpose of bilingual programs should be to prevent Hispanic children from falling behind academically (36 percent) or to preserve the cultural identity of Hispanic people (34 percent).

Polls also show that a majority of Hispanics want the opportunity to attend a nongovernment school. According to a national telephone poll of 1,223 households in 1981–82, 65.2 percent of Hispanic parents responded they would be "very likely" or "somewhat likely" to switch their children from public school to private school if a full-tuition tax credit were available.[40] In a sample of Corpus Christi, Texas, residents, low-income Hispanics were the group most in favor of tuition tax deductions for parental private school expenditures.[41] A poll conducted in 1978 in California showed Hispanics favoring vouchers by a 69 to 25 margin.[42]

Assimilation or Separation

Vouchers offer Hispanics and other ethnic minorities a method by which the conflict between assimilation and separateness can be resolved. For those who want ethnically identified schools, vouchers provide the means of financing these ventures. The *option* of separate schools does not harm the cause of those who prefer integrated schools.

The presence of ethnically identified schools does not detract from the possibility of integration, *as long as the separation is by choice.* In fact, with the exception of a tiny fraction of any ethnic group, separation is not a goal per se, but a strategy to gain respect and justice. The separatist does not argue against integration, but against the concept of integration which is imposed on terms dictated by the dominant power structure.

As Jesse Jackson (who attended an all-black college after feeling "out of place" at a mainly white university) put it:

> There are schools like Harvard and Yale, predominantly white Protestant, which include some others; there are schools like Brandeis and Yeshiva, predominantly Jewish, but which accept other students; is there anything wrong with having Howard, North Carolina A&T, and Morehouse, predominantly black, but open to others?[43]

He might also have mentioned the National Hispanic University, which came into being in the 1980s in response to a need for a similar ethnically identified and culturally supportive university for Hispanics.[44]

Given the decades of resistance to integration, an increasing number of minority leaders believe that vouchers may be the only means of equalizing access to quality schools.

Conclusion

The problem of school segregation in this country has usually been defined as a legal issue of how to bring about interracial contact. The courts have focused on measurable outcomes that provide statistical evidence that integration is taking place. Thus, desegregation has drifted farther and farther from its original purpose of empowering the oppressed.

The goal of integration was never wrong per se. The question has always been how it will be accomplished and on whose terms. Thus far, integration has primarily been thought of as a way for blacks and Hispanics to fit into Anglo institutions. Genuine integration can come about only if Anglos also learn to accommodate themselves to institutions controlled by minorities. As Derrick Bell, a civil rights lawyer who participated in hundreds of desegregation cases, has observed:

> The major problem with segregation was not separation; there was nothing evil per se because a school was all black. The evil was the racism that said that white must dominate, that white schools are necessarily the best schools. You got rid of the manifestation, but racism could and does serve to undermine the potential for educating black children even in schools boasting perfect racial balance. Paradoxically, racism can best be overcome in a predominantly black school with a good component of white parents who are committed to integration and willing to work for effective schooling without being in a clearly dominant role. Regrettably, few white parents have that kind of commitment.[45]

He added that African Americans should therefore have the option of either integrating with whites or running their own schools in which they would determine personnel, curriculum, and other policies.

It is hard to see how minorities can achieve two-way integration in the absence of the economic power to control at least some schools. As long as most of the power in the political system lies in the hands of Anglos, integration will remain a largely theoretical exercise.

Rev. Leon Sullivan has summarized the situation in a brief phrase: "Integration without preparation is frustration."[46] Yet after twenty or more years of integration, most public schools are still not prepared for it. Integration remains frustration, particularly for the minorities who have been the objects of this grand social experiment.

Vouchers offer a way out of the quandary by offering opportunities for both those who want immediate integration and those who believe that creating minority-owned institutions is a prerequisite to integration. With the power to establish their own schools, African Americans and Hispanics would no longer be forced to accept whatever the Anglo majority chooses to give them.

Of course, many families will not choose schools based on ethnic identity. They will prefer schools that are based on a philosophy that cuts across class and racial lines. On the whole, vouchers are likely to increase the level of integration by fostering schools that bring diverse people together by attraction rather than compulsion. Since public schools remain heavily segregated in most cities, expanding options in independent schools could break down existing racial and ethnic barriers and achieve goals that intrusive desegregation plans have not attained.

It is important to recognize that educational separatism that is chosen by ethnic minorities rather than imposed by a white power structure may be more conducive to integration in the long run than contrived racial balancing in schools. Constructive integration can occur only among groups with mutual respect for one another's traditions, just as a healthy marriage depends on the acknowledgement by partners of each other's separate identities. Otherwise, in politics or marriage, the weaker party is forced to assimilate and lose integrity.

Radical and permanent segregation is destructive because it perpetuates misunderstanding, inequality, and subordination. But temporary, voluntary separatism can serve the larger cause of empowering those who have been oppressed. As Nathan Glazer and Daniel Moynihan showed in *Beyond the Melting Pot,* political and economic institutions promoting ethnic identity and mutual support enabled Irish, Italian, and Jewish immigrants to improve their position in American society. The success of immigrants depended as much on the solidarity of the ethnic group as on individual initiative.[47] The same process could continue to operate for oppressed minorities if they are given the opportunity to build their own institutions.

What is the proper balance between separatism and integration, independence and assimilation? No abstract formulation can answer that question. Perhaps in a multiethnic society we are destined to stumble between extremes as various groups learn to share power.

A voucher system does not push society in either direction. It is a neutral instrument that can be used for either increased separatism or more complete integration. It does, however, represent a rejection of compulsory methods of overcoming segregation and embraces instead the idea of voluntary affiliation.

7

Nongovernment Schools and Deregulated Government Schools

The pursuit of equal opportunity has been a failure because our society has sought to achieve it on a grandiose scale. In the process, we have established large-scale institutions that have undermined community and deprived people of a sense of responsibility for one another.

Government school systems have participated in that trend by becoming larger and more bureaucratic. In the school year 1937–38, there were over 119,000 school districts in the United States. In 1988–89, there were only around 15,000. Although combining small districts in rural areas may have been been beneficial in some cases, urban district consolidation has achieved only phantom gains in efficiency. In the process of increasing the size and complexity of districts, the sense of ownership of schools by the community has been eroded.

Nongovernment schools, by contrast, have remained manageable in size and have protected the sense of community that defines them.

The Advantages of Nongovernment Schools

Over the years many parents have learned from personal experience what scholars have only recently been able to demonstrate statistically: nongovernment schools are frequently better for students who are unsuccessful in government schools. This chapter will show why that is the case.

The mere fact of private ownership of an institution does not guarantee its excellence. There is no particular reason to assume that the schools of Chelsea, Massachusetts, will be better managed privately by Boston University than publicly by the former school board. The main difference is that the university will not be bound by as many restrictions on hiring and firing as the school board has been. Yet merely turning control over a monopolistic school system to a private institution is no solution. Autonomous and unregulated private schools will be as inefficient as the existing system if they are granted charters that give them monopoly control.

Nongovernment schools are effective because they are dependent on voluntary applications and tuition, and they must be responsive to changes in what families want. Without that direct accountability, nongovernment schools would easily slip back into bureaucratic routines that destroy their distinctiveness.

The purpose of examining nongovernment schools is not to privatize education. The question is how choice, community, and autonomy in combination can contribute to improvements in schools. These are the factors, not private control per se, that make nongovernment schools effective. They could be emulated by government schools, but only if some major political obstacles can be overcome.

The Importance of Organizational Characteristics

The purpose of this chapter is to consider the ways in which organizational features contribute to the quality of education. Even though some schools may attract better students than others, there are also characteristics of schools themselves that make a difference in how much their students learn. No one claims that any of these school characteristics can completely overcome differences in the family background of students. Schools are simply not capable of fully compensating for social inequality. The question is whether schools can make any difference in student achievement.

The most comprehensive study of that question is *Politics, Markets, and America's Schools* by John Chubb and Terry Moe. They compared the effects of internal organization on differences between "effective" and "ineffective" schools in both the public and private sectors. The difference between these two sectors is largely due to the obstacles to organizational effectiveness in highly bureaucratic public schools.

Effectiveness was determined by the increase or decrease in average test scores of over seven thousand high school students between the sophomore and senior years. In other words, the effect of schools was defined in terms of improvement in achievement, not absolute levels.

Effective schools were defined as those in the top 25 percent of achievement gains; ineffective schools were in the bottom 25 percent. Students in effective schools gained approximately three years of academic progress in two years whereas those in ineffective schools advanced only one year.[1]

The analysis by Chubb and Moe estimated that school organization makes a difference of about one-third to one-half of a year of academic achievement, when family background, selection bias, and numerous other factors are held constant statistically.[2] Among the organizational features that influence the effectiveness of schools, the degree of autonomy from centralized control and from union influence over hiring, firing, and seniority was by far the most significant. This is not a factor over which the principal of a government school has any control.

The key to the success of nongovernment schools is based on a variety of intertwined factors. The following sections of this chapter consider some of those factors. Finally, since the public schools will remain the primary provider of education even under a voucher system, I examine ways in which government schools could be given a chance to develop some of the characteristics of nongovernment schools in order to make themselves more effective.

Small Classes and Small Schools

Class size   The conventional wisdom argues that small class size is one of the keys to improved educational achievement. If this theory is true, then one source of the superior performance of private schools would be their small classes and the personalized attention that they offer. But Catholic schools with relatively large classes have also managed to foster high levels of achievement. Most research on class size suggests that its relationship to achievement is ambiguous. Small classes appear to be effective in improving achievement only if instructional techniques are oriented to take advantage of the small number of students.[3] Within the normal range of twenty to forty students per class, there is little variation in achievement.[4]

These findings are not equally valid for all groups. Some research indicates that class-size reduction can be important for children in early primary grades and for low-achieving students, although smaller classes alone do not guarantee improved performance.[5] Theoretically, reducing class size for those students could be accomplished in government schools, but in practice, those students are often in the most crowded schools. The political competition within public schools tends to distribute the classload of teachers according to teachers' seniority, not student needs. Public schools frequently view some children as unteachable, which makes class size irrelevant.

School size   The research on school size (and district size) is as contentious as the debate over class size. School managers presuppose that large schools are more cost effective than small ones because fixed costs can be spread over a larger base. In other words, teaching four thousand children is supposed to be cheaper per child than teaching one thousand. This penny-wise and pound-foolish mentality ignores the fact that putting children in a stockyard atmosphere is not conducive to learning. Even from a purely managerial (that is, noneducational) perspective, economies of scale are more theoretical than actual. When schools and districts grow, they increase the size of the administrative staff, the cost of transportation from outlying areas, the costs of keeping everyone aware of school policy through formal channels, the frequency of vandalism, and other hidden costs.

Educationally, the rationale for increased size calls for a minimum of only about 400 to 500 high school students. That was the conclusion of James Conant, who estimated in 1959 that that size would allow for sufficient staff specialization to offer a fully differentiated curriculum.[6] Presumably, elementary schools could be much smaller.

The most obvious advantage of small schools is their welcoming atmosphere for students and parents and collegiality for teachers. Considerable anecdotal evidence suggests that positive school climate, high student motivation, and intensity of student effort, especially for low-achieving students, are associated with small- or medium-sized schools (often imprecisely defined, but generally having between two hundred and six hundred students). In a 1964 study of schools ranging in size from an enrollment of 35 to over 2,200, students in small schools participated in more activities and were less likely to consider school an alien environment, whereas students in large schools were more likely to feel superfluous and unneeded.[7] In a 1982 survey of secondary alternative schools, in which 69 percent of the schools enrolled fewer than two hundred students, the morale of teachers and students was heightened by the commitment individuals have to the small familiar group, in contrast to the anonymity of the typical large high school.[8] Many of these small schools are especially valuable for "at-risk" students, who need a supportive atmosphere in which peer relations reinforce an ethos of discipline and hard work.

The positive social climate that is associated with small schools helps in lowering dropout rates and raising achievement levels.[9] One recent study, however, indicates that large schools are beneficial to students from educationally advantaged backgrounds and harmful to students from disadvantaged backgrounds.[10] This confirms a finding that the size of a school is unrelated to average achievement, but that larger schools have more achievement stratification: in other words, good students do better in large schools and bad students do worse.[11]

Whether small schools benefit all students or only the low-achieving students, these alternatives are especially important in inner cities, where large, factory-style schools are beset by violence, disruption, and feelings of impotence. Belief in one's ability to control one's destiny was more important than any family-background characteristic in explaining student achievement among African Americans in the 1966 Coleman report.[12] If a school can contribute to that belief by placing students in a familiar setting that instills confidence and responsibility, then it is understandable that small schools are able to improve the performance of students from low-income families.

One final piece of evidence points to the advantage of small-scale schools. On average, nongovernment schools are smaller than government schools: as of 1985, average enrollment in elementary schools was 218 for nongovernment schools and 403 for government schools, and average secondary enrollment was 541 and 721, respectively.[13] In the 1988–89 school year median enrollment in nongovernment schools (around 325) was around half as high as the median in government schools (around 650).[14] The difference between private and public schools is likely to be greater in urban areas where government schools enroll thousands. Small size would appear to be one of the factors that makes nongovernment schools attractive to families. If the reverse were true, and if bigger schools were educationally better, one would expect the private sector to discover it.

There is no administrative reason why government schools could not be scaled down in size, if only by creating "schools within schools" as District 4 in New York did as part of its choice program. Yet the mystique of economies of scale has been pushing the size of government schools upward for several generations. The most powerful political influences on school policy have no incentive to reduce school size. Administrators and teachers' union representatives have higher salaries and status when they make decisions for large numbers of people, so they have vested interests in maintaining large-scale schools and districts. Even though researchers have been documenting the socially damaging aspects of large schools for several decades, this issue has never been placed on the policy agenda. Thus, in the absence of competition from small, nongovernment schools, it seems unlikely that the managers of government schools will ever feel compelled to reduce the size of their spheres of influence.

Autonomy, Purpose, and Distinctiveness

The single greatest asset of nongovernment schools, which is sorely lacking in most government schools, is a common sense of purpose and direction. This is possible because nongovernment schools (1) have the autonomy to determine their own goals and (2) must define their specific reason for existence in a way that will appeal to a group of parents and gain their loyalty. Government schools are unable to define themselves distinctively because they are politically controlled and thus must appeal to the lowest common denominator of public opinion.

The problem that schools face is how to deal with the diversity of students who vary by interest, ability, family and cultural background, religious beliefs, level of academic motivation, and other personal factors. Government and nongovernment schools respond to this challenge in very different ways. Government schools offer diversity and choice (or the appearance of it) *inside* the school; nongovernment schools offer diversity and choice *between* schools. On the surface, this may seem like a trivial difference, but it is highly significant: the public schools offer neutral information, whereas private schools provide ideas to believe in.

Because a government school is politically controlled, it makes every attempt to remain neutral in its orientation. Few administrators exert strong leadership or give schools a clear direction. Instead of setting goals, they engage in public relations. Instead of providing leadership, they establish procedural rules and try to avoid controversy. In the absence of both goals and leadership, each teacher is permitted to teach (or fail to teach) in any manner that does not explicitly violate a rule or a strongly held belief of parents.

Without any agreement on a school's purpose (beyond some vague rhetoric about "excellence"), that school becomes a motley assortment of characters who have learned to "play it safe." The occasional teacher who breaks the mold, who teaches from conviction, and who tries to inspire students—a teacher such as Jaime Escalante, the real-life hero of the movie *Stand and Deliver*—will usually be defeated by the larger system that conspires to maintain dull mediocrity.

Even if all the teachers in a public school are individually gifted, they provide no coherent framework that shows students how their classes fit with each other and with the larger adult world of work, family, and public responsibilities. Public schools offer little help because of their moral neutrality and their choiceless choices within a school.

The teachers in a nongovernment school, by contrast, develop an orientation around a set of principles or ideas about education. In a Montessori school, the principle is discovery learning; in a fundamentalist Christian school, the principle is use of the Bible as the ultimate reference point. Ethnically identified schools have a particular cultural orientation. Alternative public schools with distinctive identities have been established for high school students who were alienated from the regular program. Unfortunately, these distinctive public schools often do not outlast their original organizers and their political base of support.

The clearly defined goals and purposes of nongovernment schools create a climate of academic and social expectations that teachers and students both agree to follow. The goals may be self-expression, scholastic excellence, community service, moral development, or any combination of them. By holding students responsible for their behavior in relation to a definite code of conduct, the school can offer a stable environment for children, even if none exists at home. James Coleman and Thomas Hoffer, in a 1987 study, found that Catholic schools outperformed prestigious private schools for children from unstable family backgrounds, regardless of family income.[15] They hypothesize that schools that evolve a network of caring relationships form a functional community that can offer the sense of connection and purpose that children need to succeed in school.

Another study of public and private high schools, *The Shopping Mall High School,* compared schools on a qualitative basis, using interviews and classroom observations.[16] The authors found that highly motivated students from educationally rich backgrounds can make use of the diversity in a government school. But the 70 percent or 80 percent of average students who are alienated, unmotivated, or indifferent are ignored or given inadequate guidance in public schools. They take classes almost at random from a menu of courses without a specific focus.

Thus, contrary to conventional wisdom, private schools are better for academically weaker students than for the scholastic elite who can function in an unstructured environment. The authors of *Shopping Mall* interviewed a mother who had placed one son in a private school and kept another son in public school:

> She knew the common stereotypes were wrong—that public schools were dangerous jungles, and that private schools were filled with students easy to teach. That kind of silly talk missed the entire point, she said. The point was the practical consumer problem of matching a particular child to a particular school. She believed that no school was better in a general sense; indeed, the public schools had worked out marvelously for her other son: "There are some kids who need more scope, who need a bigger learning environment, and there are some who absolutely need a small school." Other students "have certain needs that could be met in both public and private schools."[17]

Similarly, the admissions director at one private school pointed out that "the public schools can't be beat if the kids are really great, but when they are round about average, we can do a much better job of providing individual instruction."[18]

The issue is thus not whether private schools are better than public schools for all students, but which students will benefit from which kinds of schools. This raises the related issue of whether parents or public school officials should make the determination about which kind of school is better. There are already limited programs in the state of Washington and in California that allow certain "at-risk" students to attend nongovernment schools at the expense of a school district, but only if the district approves. In other words, school officials are sometimes willing to admit that nongovernment schools are preferable, but only when they, not parents, have control over placements.

The autonomy and distinctiveness of nongovernment schools enable them to meet the demand for patterns not available in government schools. Some independent schools in the inner city, for example, operate year-round in order to help the children retain what they learn. A long summer break upsets the rhythm of learning for all children, but it is especially detrimental for those who have no contact with reading materials in the home.

Nongovernment schools can also choose to function as single-sex schools. Recent studies indicate that boys do better academically in co-ed schools, but girls do worse. Girls seem to learn more in single-sex schools, an effect that is most pronounced in the study of mathematics and science. Furthermore, they appear to show better emotional and social adjustment, and better occupational growth in the years following school and college.[19]

This does not necessarily mean that government schools should all shift to year-round or single-sex programs, but it does suggest that parents should be allowed to decide the types of schools from which their children might benefit most.

The Value of Community

The importance of private schools is not limited to the potential achievement gains of the 70 percent to 80 percent of students who do not excel in public schools. Perhaps the most valuable function of nongovernment schools is their potential to build a sense of community in cities that are dying as a result of apathy and despair. Many schools, particularly in urban areas, drive a wedge between children and the surrounding community by denying the value of the nonacademic knowledge that children learn informally, especially from parents. Instead of binding a community together, schools undermine it and alienate children from their parents and other adults. Thus children derive their norms from fantasy images of entertainers, sports heroes, and movies, or from gangs and other peer groups.

Sara Lawrence Lightfoot has observed the problems that black children face when there is little "continuity between the profound and deeply etched learnings within their families and the social and intellectual lessons of school."[20] Her observations apply with equal force to the children of all ethnicities who are disaffected by the culture of school.

> Future strategies for designing more productive and effective schooling for poor and minority children must recognize the critical role of families as educators and the important relationships between families, communities, and schools. . . . Once school personnel begin to value the significant place of families in the educational process, they will feel more responsible to the communities they serve and to the children they teach. . . . Education may be seen more holistically, and the medium and message of school can be designed to be adaptive to the values and idiom of community life.[21]

As Lightfoot recognizes, these strategies cannot be pursued by tinkering with curriculum or staffing policies. The fundamental issues in ensuring community-oriented schools are "the balance of power between families and schools, the sense of responsibility and accountability teachers feel for the educational success of children, and the parents' sense of entitlement in demanding results from schools."[22]

Along much the same lines, Mary Anne Raywid has argued that schools are among the few institutions left that could potentially promote community among both youth and adults:

> I contend that it makes good sense today to see the schools' challenge as that of making school *itself* a strong and unified modern community. This seems desirable due to the absence of community elsewhere and the fact that communal needs are apparently not being met in any other way. . . . There seems no reason why schools cannot be designed to represent coherent persuasions that ultimately might enable them to function as chosen reference groups for the adults as well as the youngsters affiliated with each school. A school that began with the initial advantage that its constituents had selected it could, by virtue of that, possess the capacity and the groundwork for community. . . . In this way, schools might conceivably come to be chosen communities for the parents affiliated with them, as well as for their students.[23]

Unfortunately, Raywid, like many others steeped in the supposedly liberal tradition of the common school, cannot embrace the kind of policy that would enable school-centered communities to form. She warns us that "certainly not all communities are good," then proceeds to explain that she would have "extensive misgivings" about communities formed around fundamentalist schools, presumably because they indoctrinate their children with ideas she regards as false.[24] Thus, she favors "communities," but only those that are approved by the public-school establishment.

While white liberals debate the merits of community as an academic exercise, the breakdown of community for ethnic minorities is literally a matter of life and death for their children. In the absence of other forms of community, teenagers may be drawn into self-destructive youth gangs. Community-based schools that are oriented toward children and youth who are hostile or indifferent to public schools would not instantly remove the causes of gang activity. Yet these schools could help teenagers develop peer relationships and become contributing members of society.

For example, community-based schools could institute cross-age tutoring, which has been shown to be effective in raising the achievement level of both tutor and tutee. A number of cross-age tutoring programs in inner-city schools in the 1960s proved successful not only in raising the test scores of tutors with below-grade reading levels but also in improving their self-confidence.[25] Even more significant, one of the programs, in Newark, hired tutor supervisors from the community, most of whom had not finished high school themselves. The loyalty and sense of responsibility built up among the fourteen- and fifteen-year-old tutors is perhaps best measured by the fact that 98 percent of them showed up during and after the riot of July 1967, although half of the tutees failed to come back afterward.[26]

In theory, this sort of community-building process could occur in public schools, as Mary Anne Raywid proposes. However, community is practically impossible to achieve in government schools because (1) parents and other nonprofessionals have so little power, (2) community-building practices upset the bureaucratic routines of schools, and (3) the restraints imposed by collective bargaining reduce the flexibility in hiring or in using the school's budget to pay students as tutors. The political compromises necessary to run a public school prevent the conditions for community except in unusual cases.

Implications for Government Schools

Nongovernment schools have positive characteristics that are lacking in government schools. One reasonable inference to be drawn is that vouchers would enable at least some families to gain a better education by transferring their children to nongovernment schools. But what about those students who remain in the government schools? Will the educational opportunities in those schools expand as external competition forces them to copy the practices of the private sector, or will such opportunities decline as the schools lose resources? This question lies at the heart of the voucher debate, and it cannot be answered with any certainty because there are very few cases of a public quasi monopoly being forced to compete for customers with privately owned service providers.

If a district loses students who transfer to nongovernment schools, its officials are not likely to respond creatively to this outside competition. They are oriented to following specific bureaucratic routines. From their perspective, the effect of students leaving school will be the same as declining enrollment due to any other reason. School administrators tend to be managers, not innovators. They have been rewarded for avoiding change and controversy. Instead of initiating plans, they will seek political support to maintain existing programs.

A voucher system will not change the behavior of administrators unless laws are modified to give them a chance to compete on an equal basis with nongovernment schools. States must provide public schools with the autonomy and the capacity to respond flexibly to changing demands. Reforms that allow government schools to function with greater autonomy are largely useless, however, if they are not combined with a policy that enables parents and children to choose among alternative schools. Parental choice without school autonomy is empty; autonomy without choice is tyranny. Vouchers include both autonomy and choice and thus run neither risk. But reform within the public sector must account for both sides of the equation if it is to succeed.

Independent Public Schools

One approach that partially resolves the problem of inflexibility in the public sector is the creation of independent public schools. This is the method proposed by John Coons and Stephen Sugarman in their draft legislation in California. The concept is that any government body (city, county, state) could establish schools of its own. School boards could charter schools that would be independent of the state education code and of board control. Because the latter schools would be independent, they could not rely on support if they did not attract students. But they would remain public schools insofar as they could not have any religious orientation.

The purpose would be to create public schools that could compete successfully with private schools. This mechanism for establishing new schools would enable the school board to respond quickly to changing demands, without waiting for legislative changes to make public schools more flexible. Yet since the new schools would be as independent as nongovernment schools, the unions would probably encourage the school board to delay in providing the schools with space or legal charters or other prerequisites for getting started. Any voucher system will be under attack in the courts for some years after its adoption, and the board may use that as an excuse to avoid acting.

Charter Schools

The Minnesota legislature has enacted a process for chartering independent government schools, which are called "outcome-based schools," although initially it is limiting the number of such schools statewide to eight.[27] These schools will be freed of most of the requirements of the state education code. They will be evaluated entirely on the basis of outcomes, as outlined in a contract of up to three years with the school board that charters them. The schools are to be established by state-certified teachers who want to operate an independent school as a nonprofit corporation or a cooperative with minimal supervision by the school board. A school may establish selection criteria based on interest but not ability; selection among applicants who meet the criteria will be by lottery. The school must match the racial and ethnic diversity of the area in which it is located. The teachers are permitted to form a collective bargaining unit, but since the governing board of the school will be primarily composed of teachers, that possibility seems remote.

The charter-schools approach enables selected schools to operate freely in developing curriculum, staffing policies, administration, and mission. The schools can focus on particular sectors of the school population if the founding teachers so desire: students who are behind in school, those who are unable to function in a regular program, those with a special interest in drama, or any other group. This is an example of how a school with autonomy can be selective and distinctive without being elitist.

Opting Out

An alternative method of providing autonomy to schools, known as "opting out," has been developed in England. Denis Doyle, Bruce Cooper, and Roberta Trachtman describe how the system works:

> In 1988, as part of the Education Reform Act, the nation created a whole new category of "grant maintained" schools, supported by direct grant from the central government, setting them free from

Charter Schools: Alternative to Vouchers?

The aim of a voucher plan is to increase autonomy, diversity, and community in education. Yet vouchers may not be the only method of reaching the desired goal.

Minnesota has initiated a program in which licensed teachers will be allowed to operate their own independent schools under contract with a local school board. Each "charter" school must meet certain basic requirements. It is not allowed to screen students, inculcate a religious doctrine, charge tuition, or discriminate in admissions. The school must also specify its intended instructional outcomes in a contract with the school district that charters it. In operations and personnel, however, the school will be self-managed and free of the state and local bureaucracy.

If the law works as intended, new schools could be established that would serve as alternatives to the regular public schools. Families would thus acquire a range of options. Most choice programs in the past have had limited success because they provided no mechanism for expanding the supply of new schools. The charter-school policy solves that problem.

One surprising feature of the program in Minnesota is the interest that the St. Paul branch of the National Association for the Advancement of Colored People (NAACP) has shown in creating a charter school that would provide both education and social services. (This is significant because the NAACP has consistently opposed vouchers that could enable them to start similar joint service institutions.)

Albert Shanker, president of the American Federation of Teachers, has also endorsed the concept, despite his opposition to vouchers. (The Minnesota law allows only certified teachers to work in charter schools, which means this policy poses less of a threat to teacher unions than vouchers do.)

A number of other states are considering similar legislation. The chief drawback of the entire policy from the perspective of voucher supporters is the failure to include sectarian schools. But the debate about charter schools will at least reveal the ambiguity of the concept of public schools. If independent charter schools are perceived as public, then an important psychological barrier to vouchers will have been broken.

political and bureaucratic constraints of local authorities. Under this program, any state-run school may, with a majority vote of its parents and trustees, apply to the national government to "opt out" of its local education authority and become an independent school, with the same level of funding by the central government.[28]

The most immediate effect is that because funds go directly to the schools, with no local administrative costs extracted, the schools have 15 to 20 percent more money to spend on education. They have the discretion to buy as many or as few services from the central bureaucracy (or from other sources) as they wish. Instead of waiting for the district bureaucracy to reform itself, the parents and teachers at a school site can simply bypass the district office altogether.[29]

Local bureaucrats have testified to the effectiveness of the plan by reacting hysterically.

In one case, the school board tried to sell the school and its grounds, rather than have the school opt out. Parents were threatened, and black parents were told that the new school would discriminate against them. One local school authority even took out newspaper ads urging parents not to vote to become grant maintained. Another ruled that the sports teams at the opt out school could no longer compete against teams from the district. Petty bureaucrats can be petty, indeed.[30]

These responses are an indication that genuine reform has taken place. The single best measure of whether a plan creates genuine autonomy is the volume of the voices raised against it. In contrast to school-based management, a policy in some American school districts that gives the appearance of autonomy to each school without relinquishing real power over budgets and personnel, opting out actually transfers power.

In order to accomplish the opting-out procedure, a state would have to provide a mechanism by which an individual school could develop its own board of trustees. Once the school opted out, presumably the district school board would have to transfer title to the property to the new trustees. One feature of this approach which does not apply in England, however, is that the school would still be required to participate in a district-wide desegregation plan. This requirement might be lifted once a voucher system began to increase the range of choices open to black and Hispanic children.

An approach that creates less school autonomy and that represents less of a departure from existing law would be a system of allowing a high school and the "feeder" junior high and elementary schools to opt out of the district and form their own district. Newly created school districts would be allowed to "secede" from large school districts if a majority of the voters in the smaller district approved the measure. Although this would not generate the level of autonomy found in nongovernment schools or in British grant-maintained schools, it would allow citizens in inner cities the same degree of control over their local schools that suburbanites have.

Either of these approaches would diminish the power of the teachers' unions. The unions would be less able to dominate school-board elections in small districts (or the trustees in individual schools) than they can control urban school boards where there is no effective political opposition to the unions. Teachers would be better off, however, because the unions would be forced to compete for membership in each school or school district. With less union and administrative control over their classroom activities, teachers could enjoy a new level of professionalism.

In the absence of a system of choice that included nongovernment schools, opting out would also involve increased segregation in urban areas. The courts might declare unconstitutional any legislation that provided for the creation of autonomous districts without ensuring that existing racial balance be maintained. If the new districts were created as part of a system that included vouchers and interdistrict choice, however, there is no reason why the policy should be declared unconstitutional.

Revision of State Laws

The Coons-Sugarman proposal for independent public schools and the Minnesota plan for charter schools have one major advantage over opting out and the creation of smaller districts. They authorize the independent schools to be free of the provisions of the education code. Since states, not school boards, are increasingly the primary governing bodies of schools, achieving independence from local boards would provide little genuine autonomy. The fundamental problem with school governance in this country is the accumulation of decades worth of state laws regarding curriculum, textbooks, personnel policies, and every other conceivable aspect of school life.

Another approach, more radical than either independently chartered public schools or opting out, would be revision or elimination of large sections of a state's education code. The most important features of state law that limit the flexibility of government schools are the provisions that specify personnnel issues. State laws restrict the flexibility of districts and schools by requiring that (1) all teachers have a state credential; (2) a credentialed teacher be present for all instruction, even for programs that could be handled by teacher aides; and (3) all hiring, firing, transfers, and other personnel decisions be carried out according to the rules set by collective bargaining. Laws and collective bargaining also restrict the hiring and firing of noninstructional personnel. Thus districts and schools are seldom free to determine the size of the budget for custodians, maintenance workers, food service personnel, and specialized staff who work outside classrooms.

Any school that cannot determine its own staffing patterns lacks control over the basic elements of the education process. The key to granting financial autonomy to schools involves allowing them to determine the balance between equipment and personnel and between instructional and noninstructional personnel. Given the option, students might agree to accept certain janitorial duties if the money saved were to be spent on something they especially valued. In a small autonomous school, that kind of choice can be negotiated internally. An autonomous school could also decide how to balance its needs for teachers and aides (including older students), how to divide tasks between them, how much to pay them, what kinds of work to assign them, the credentials they require, and the content of what they will teach. This can only be accomplished by removing the state laws that either specify these policies or give teachers' unions effective control over them through collective bargaining.

Ironically, granting autonomy to schools would empower teachers even as it reduced the power of the teachers' unions. Autonomous government schools would be in the same position as nongovernment schools are today: they offer good working conditions as an inducement for teachers to join them.

Conclusion

Nongovernment schools are generally superior to government schools because the former are required to be responsive to clients. If an independent school were given effective monopolistic control of most students in an area, the quality of its service would presumably deteriorate over time.

The characteristics of nongovernment schools are important, however, because they must satisfy participants. Nongovernment schools are smaller and less bureaucratic than government schools. With their autonomy they can establish distinctive programs with clear purposes. They are thus able to target their programs to the mediocre and unmotivated students who are neglected in government schools. A school with internal agreement about its purposes also has the advantage of constituting a community. This increases the satisfaction of teachers and the performance of students.

Vouchers will provide all students with the means to attend a nongovernment school if they and their parents choose that option. But competition from nongovernment schools may not be sufficient to make government schools responsive to family needs. Thus, when vouchers are enacted, government schools should simultaneously be freed of the regulations that make them ineffective. They should be granted autonomy, including the freedom to determine their own mix of personnel and working conditions. In other words, all schools should be given the chance to function as nongovernment schools now do.

PART III

EMPIRICAL EVIDENCE IN SUPPORT OF VOUCHERS

How will vouchers actually affect education? Will difficult students be left behind in the race for the best schools, as opponents claim? Or will entrepreneurs, former teachers, and neighborhood activists open a range of schools with varying constituencies so that every child will have an opportunity to participate in a true community of learning? Will the government schools respond to the challenge of parental choice by overcoming their organizational inertia, or will they become more insulated and defensive?

There are dozens of questions about the actual operation of a voucher system that can be answered definitively only with experience. At present we must rely on indirect experience from existing nongovernment schools and choice programs that are somewhat similar to an education voucher system. I have already suggested that the evidence from most public-school choice plans offers misleading images of a voucher system: if the supply of schools is determined by administrative fiat rather than the changing interests of families, choice is a meaningless exercise.

A full-fledged voucher system has not yet been tested. (Experiences in Milwaukee and Vermont are partial exceptions, applying only to a limited number of students. They are considered in Chapter 10.) In the absence of full, statewide projects, empirical evidence from other sources provides significant clues about how a voucher system would affect students from low-income families.

The most important evidence comes from the experience of poor children in nongovernment schools. In Chapter 7, this issue was considered in general terms. Chapter 8 is concerned with the more detailed effects of nongovernment schools and with some examples of inner-city private schools that work. It also deals with the probable effect if churches and other community organizations were enabled to establish schools with the help of vouchers.

The next most significant information comes from the GI Bill and other scholarships that have provided college choices to low-income students. These are voucher programs because they provide funding to individuals rather than institutions. Their effectiveness is discussed in Chapter 9.

The effect of aid to nongovernment schools in other countries and of voucher-type systems in the United States also provides information about the likely consequences of vouchers. That is the subject of Chapter 10.

8

The Experience in Nongovernment Schools

W hen most people think of private schools, they have a mental image of boarding schools for the wealthy or exclusive day schools in idyllic settings. Of course, there are such schools, and they do indeed charge high tuition that hinders most low-income families from enrolling.

Yet there are also hundreds of sectarian schools and other schools in urban areas that serve a very different population. These are also private schools. Presumably more of these schools would come into existence under a voucher system. In the case of Catholic schools, vouchers would reverse the financial pressures that are currently leading to the closure of heavily subsidized schools in low-income areas. The purpose of this chapter is to examine the effects of these urban schools on low-income families in order to provide evidence of the potential of vouchers.

Low-Income Students in Nongovernment Schools

Even without any state subsidies, a total of almost four hundred thousand children from families with incomes below $15,000 were attending private schools in October 1987.[1] This represents about 4 percent of the families in that income range, almost half the rate of middle- and upper-income families with considerably more disposable

125

income. The interest of the poor in private education is revealed in the opinions they express about how they would react to subsidized choices.

A 1988 poll showed the urban poor favoring vouchers by a 62 percent to 17 percent margin.[2] In another national survey, over half of the households with incomes below $15,000 said they would switch schools if offered a tax credit that covered full tuition expenses. These figures are indicative of the number of frustrated inner-city low-income families that would choose an alternative to their assigned public schools if provided with a voucher. By contrast, only one-third of families with incomes above $50,000 said they would use the credit.[3] Presumably the public schools in wealthy neighborhoods are already moderately effective, and the rich who prefer private schools have already enrolled their children in them. The fact that the poor would use the credits to switch more often than the rich (and that 59 percent of urban families would use them compared with only 38 percent of suburban families) is not surprising.[4] The desire of the urban poor to escape from the schools provided by the state reflects the poor quality of those schools.

Anecdotal evidence suggests that students from minority and low-income families who are able to gain access to low-cost sectarian or independent schools as a result of vouchers will attain higher achievement levels than they would otherwise. In one study of inner-city private schools in which 70 percent of families had incomes below $15,000 and 35 percent of the families had a single parent, most of the schools that tested transfers from public schools accepted large numbers of below-grade-level students.[5] The schools were able to raise test scores in math and reading approximately to grade level. In a study of urban Catholic high schools, students from families of all income levels (very poor, moderately poor, and nonpoor) raised their achievement in vocabulary, reading, and math from below national norms to above-average levels.[6]

The tremendous achievement gains in the public-school choice model implemented in East Harlem (from the bottom to the middle level in New York City in just over a decade) also reveal the value of providing options. The kinds of schools that were started in District 4 are similar to the kinds of programs that would likely emerge under a voucher system in both the public and private sectors. Since this district contained a higher proportion of poor families than any other district in the United States, the achievement gains are not attributable to the income or social status of the residents.[7]

Moreover, according to national data analyzed by Coleman and Hoffer, Catholic-school students consistently outperformed public-school students of the same socioeconomic status. Students enrolled in the Catholic schools improved three grade levels in reading between the tenth and twelfth grades, whereas public-school students with similar family backgrounds raised their scores by only two grade levels. The same improvement differential was found in vocabulary, math, and writing. There was almost no difference in science and civics.[8] Although the use of standardized grade-level estimates may have exaggerated discrepancies, there seem to be real differences for the average student. Of greater importance, however, is the small variation within Catholic schools between the achievement levels of rich and poor students, whereas in the public schools the gap is wide. Thus, the superior results of Catholic schools are not a function of a small number of star performers. The schools' achievements are due more to the consistency of their curriculum for all students.

One of the most surprising results of the Coleman and Hoffer study is that expensive private schools are not consistently better institutions than public schools. To some extent the high scores in the elite schools merely reflect the caliber of the student population, not the schools' teaching effectiveness. In reading, vocabulary, and writing, private-school students led equivalent public-school students by 1.5, 1.0, and 0.6 grade levels respectively. But in math and science, students from the same socioeconomic backgrounds scored 0.3 grade levels higher in public than in private schools.

Another significant set of findings of the Coleman and Hoffer study deals with the different dropout rates at the three types of schools: public, Catholic, and private. When the authors looked at differences in dropout rates (controlling for family income), they discovered that private schools in which individualism is emphasized and community downplayed have the highest dropout rates while Catholic schools have the lowest. They also provide evidence of the ability of Catholic schools to provide a supportive and nurturing environment for children from single-parent households or from homes where the parents are neglectful and do not talk much to their children. In Catholic schools, children with these "structural and functional deficiencies" are no more likely to drop out than their friends from supportive families. In public and secular private schools, the differences are staggering. In public schools, children from neglectful families are more than twice as likely as children from supportive families (21 percent to 9 percent) to drop out; in secular private schools the figures are 28 percent and 4 percent; in Catholic schools, where the community works together, the figures are 3.4 percent and 2.5 percent.

Perhaps the most surprising finding by Coleman and Hoffer was that the feature that accounts for the greatest variation in school success is not family income but the integrity or lack of integrity of the family.[9] Surprisingly, when socioeconomic status is statistically controlled, the dropout rate in elite private schools is higher than in public schools. Private schools with an individualistic orientation do little to prevent dropping out.

Some scholars have questioned the validity of the results demonstrating the superiority of Catholic schools. Yet even if the difference in achievement is somewhat exaggerated, there must still be a reason why inner-city parents make such intense efforts to enroll their children in Catholic schools. The main issue is what factors account for the difference in achievement. Coleman and Hoffer believe it is due to the functional community surrounding Catholic schools. Their data also indicate that part of the difference lies in the less rigid tracking in Catholic schools. A higher percentage of students of all backgrounds are encouraged to take academic classes in Catholic schools than in public schools, which in itself reveals the workings of a community— one that does not divide its members into winner and losers.

Aggregate test scores do not tell the whole story. Low-income parents choose independent or sectarian schools because they desire schools that teach values, that are relatively free of violence, that are not cynical about their children's chances of success, and that are concerned about the total welfare of their children. All of these concerns and interests can be summarized in a single word: trust.

For many parents in ghetto neighborhoods, the public schools cannot be trusted to perform their basic duties: they have neglected their responsibilities. Similarly, the school staff does not trust the parents and does not want their active involvement in school affairs, despite all of the rhetoric about parental participation. In small towns, a mutually trusting relationship may still exist between parents and public school staff. In cities, the relationship between staff and families is impersonal, regardless of how sincere the concern of teachers may be for the welfare of the children assigned to them. The school in the neighborhood is often not of the neighborhood, particularly if all of the staff are outsiders.

In contrast to the social distance found in government schools, the essential ingredient in the relation established between parents and private school staff is trust. The closest approximation is the relationship between the members of a religious congregation and the clergy. This relationship might be filled with tensions and conflicts, but no church or synagogue could survive long if the congregation and clergy related to each other on an impersonal, rule-governed basis.

Case Studies

Schools are not statistical abstractions. Their success or failure depends in large part upon the personality of their leadership, but only if the rules of the system allow those leaders to exercise authority.

In general, boards of government schools control district super-intendents and principals far more thoroughly than the boards of nongovernment schools bind their principals. That is not invariably the case. From time to time, a dynamic superintendent or principal emerges in the government schools. He or she gains attention, often during a controversy over a new program or personal leadership style. Eventually, however, the system removes or restricts this person with imagination and energy. Some government schools have managed temporarily to resist inertia and to establish a more productive environment for learning. Since change in the public sector usually involves "buying off" the interest groups that keep the system locked in place, effective leaders are generally ones who can bring in extra revenue.

In the case studies that follow, I have included both government and nongovernment schools. Some alternative government schools have worked out creative programs for youth who are having difficulties in standard schools. Since part of the aim of a voucher system is to encour-age innovation in government schools, it is as important to highlight their programs as those in nongovernment schools.

The point of these case studies is to demonstrate that idealistic citizens or institutions can establish community-based programs that are aimed at low-income and school-resistant students. The fact that schools of that sort have been in existence for decades without any subsidy undercuts the claim that only schools for the elite will emerge under a voucher system. Presumably if there have been people who cared enough to start schools for the oppressed despite having to scramble for funds, more would consider doing so if they could receive an operating subsidy.

The focus in these case studies will be on schools that serve lower-class children on terms acceptable to their parents. In the 1960s and 1970s, a number of free schools were established with good intentions by white, upper-middle-class "radicals" who saw themselves as helping the poor. Often these schools were structureless institutions in which the students determined what and how they would learn. Although vouchers might encourage a new generation of white idealists to start similar schools, they will fail if the methods are not appropriate for inner-city children. Black parents rejected the type of education being offered to their children in many of the free schools because it was as defective in its own way as the indifference of the government schools. As Jonathan Kozol explains in *Free Schools*, middle-class whites made the mistake of assuming that ghetto children would teach themselves the academic skills necessary to succeed in the marketplace.

> It is, far too often, the rich white kids who speak three languages with native fluency, at the price of sixteen years of high-cost,

rigorous, and sequential education, who are the most determined
that poor kids should make clay vases, weave Indian headbands,
play with Polaroid cameras, climb over geodesic domes.[10]

Presumably, this naivete has largely disappeared in the ensuing
decades, although it might surface in different forms. Significantly, the
experience of the early 1970s reveals that parents, particularly black
parents, were able to distinguish between quality and faddishness in
education. Schools survived only if they offered programs that helped
children succeed.

Some academically successful schools, however, were not able to
sustain themselves because of financial problems. Many of them served
families that could not afford to pay more than a minimal amount of
tuition. Teachers could not long endure on idealism and $200 a month.
Consequently, most of the schools that have survived either charge an
amount for tuition that has excluded the poorest families, or they have
received support from a church to compensate for low tuition.

Westside Preparatory Academy

Perhaps the most famous independent, black-run school in the United
States is the one initiated by Marva Collins in Chicago.[11] Started in her
home in 1975 with fewer than thirty children, aged four to thirteen,
the school grew to an enrollment of around three hundred students in
1988. Ms. Collins's method involves pushing students from a young age
to achieve at a high level. She requires each student to read a difficult
book every two weeks and to write a composition daily. Students also
study math, social studies, and Spanish. To maintain this level of
intensity, she cuts out art, music, gym, and even recess. She demands
that students speak standard English because she believes that allowing
black students to speak a street dialect at school denies them a chance
to compete in the outside world of work.

By the time children are nine or ten, they are reading Chaucer,
Shakespeare, Emerson, Dante, and Booker T. Washington. The children
not only learn to read; they enjoy reading these difficult works. Such
accomplishments do not depend on attracting high-level students. The
neighborhood in which she opened her school was one of the poorest in
Chicago. Some of the students in the school had been classified as
mentally retarded in government schools, yet under the tutelage of
Marva Collins they advanced several grade levels in a year. Most
important, the students become convinced that they have the intellectual
power to set their own limits rather than allowing themselves to be
confined by the expectations of others.

St. Leo

In 1970, St. Leo in Milwaukee closed as a Catholic school.[12] In 1977, it reopened as a community school with 280 students, 98 percent of them African American. Unlike some community schools that have avoided the use of standardized tests, St. Leo has administered them to its students. The results have been dramatic. On entering St. Leo in 1977, the fifth graders were months or years below the national norm in every tested area; when they graduated from eighth grade in 1981, they were well ahead of the grade-level norms in all but one skill.

Skill	Months below grade level in 1977	Months above grade level in 1981
Vocabulary	24	7
Reading comprehension	24	5 below
Spelling	9	24
Capitalization	13	24
Punctuation	14	21
Word usage	20	8
Math concepts	12	7
Problem solving	19	8

These gains were achieved in a school in which 85 percent of the students qualified for government-funded meals. The poverty and the scores of incoming students indicate that this school, not family background, was responsible for the rapid learning that occurred.

Monroe Saunders School

In 1965, Bishop Saunders started a church in Baltimore, and in 1977 he opened an elementary school intended "to allow children to grow up without feeling that there is a necessary separation of God and life."[13] Nevertheless, the school was not a "Bible school" in a narrow sense. Rather, the religious atmosphere set the tone for the school by promoting discipline and principles that bound faculty, parents, and children together.

The student body of two hundred was entirely black, but some of the teachers were white. This was an intentional policy to teach children to deal with all races, witnessing the teachers both in positions of authority and as subordinates to the school principal. Parent volunteers made an important contribution to the school.

Class size varied from fifteen to twenty students. Tuition was set at $2,800 in 1991, but the actual cost per pupil was around $4,000. Part of the cost involved bringing half the students to school by bus. The church subsidized the difference between tuition and costs. The cost per pupil in the Baltimore public schools that year was around $4,500.

The school was not very selective: it admitted 94 percent of applicants. Yet since it was located in a middle-income area and since it charged a significant amount of tuition, it did not enroll many students from low-income families. It avoided status competition among students by requiring children to wear uniforms.

Sheenway School and Culture Center

Begun by Dr. Herbert Sheen in 1971 after he had opened a medical clinic in Watts, the school was intended to serve as a community center of learning.[14] The school today enrolls students from preschool through high school. It is affiliated with a martial arts academy and a theater arts academy.

The tuition is $2,600 per year, far below the $6,000 cost of educating equivalent students in Los Angeles public schools. Moreover, the Sheenway program runs year-round, with only two weeks of vacation a year. Since inner-city children lose much of their cognitive gains over summer vacation in other schools, this is a very important feature of the school's success.

Some students attend on partial scholarship, in return for which their parents must volunteer more hours than parents who pay full tuition. Some volunteers teach once or twice a week in special classes such as dance, Chinese, architecture, and computers. Others are involved as aides or in maintenance.

Dolores Sheen Blunt, the current director, operates the school in an open style without rigid class times or grade levels. The aim of the school is to help children learn to apply knowledge from school to concrete situations, not simply to memorize facts. One aspect of this experiential approach is a camping program in which troubled children are given opportunities to learn and to regenerate inner balance by direct contact with nature.

Sheenway has not sought any government assistance, but Ms. Blunt supports the idea of a system that would provide opportunities for parents to choose between government and nongovernment schools.

St. Thomas Community School

In 1968, the Catholic Archdiocese of New York began a process of turning over a parish school in Harlem to a community organization that would run the school as an independent institution. In 1971, a parent body accepted full responsibility as trustees of the St. Thomas Community School, originally an elementary school but now a high school as well.[15] Twelve board members are parents and three are community members. Tuition was $1,500 in 1988.

Children in nearby government schools at the time were reading and computing two grades below the average level. The approximately one hundred students at St. Thomas, however, have consistently scored at or above grade level. That success is not due to selective admissions: the trustees decided from the start that admission was to be on a first-come, first-served basis. The main purpose of maintaining the school when the church was ready to close it was to provide children in the neighborhood a chance to attend a high-quality school that made serious academic demands on them. The school atmosphere and parental involvement have enabled minority children to achieve far more than they would have in their assigned schools.

One key element of the school is helping parents understand their role as co-teachers of their children. By participating in the school, parents learn that they can help their children by reinforcing academic lessons in the home. Increasing numbers of jobs within the school are filled by parents.

As a truly community endeavor, the school originally sought to serve as a distributor of household products and cosmetics. The intent was to provide income simultaneously to the school and to parents, thereby helping some families to remove themselves from welfare rolls. This proposed business venture was not allowed in New York, however, because it was classified as pyramiding. Nevertheless, other fundraising activities were conducted in ways that enabled parents to benefit directly (in the form of reduced tuition). This is an indication that the school has always been conceived of as a community enterprise, a place of economic significance for parents as well as an academic institution. This feature is especially important in urban ghettos with high unemployment. A school that can serve as a center of neighborhood enterprise will gain credibility by proving its immediate value.

Humboldt Community Christian School and New Concept Development Center

Humboldt Community Christian School, with about two hundred mostly Hispanic elementary students, and New Concept Development Center, which enrolls about one hundred black elementary school students, are two other examples of schools that finance themselves partially with business ventures.[16] Both are in Chicago. Parents and former students at Humboldt raise money by operating a thrift shop. About one-third of the operating costs of the New Concept school are covered by a publishing company and bookstore on the premises.

Highland Park Free School

Founded in 1968, the Highland Park Free School was intended to offer an alternative to the Boston city schools in which African-American children were being systematically miseducated.[17] An essential element of Highland Park was the insistence that every classroom contain both a certified teacher and a community teacher and that they would work closely with parents and community groups. Initially the school had difficulty finding enough certified teachers who could appreciate from personal experience the problems and issues facing the inner-city children enrolled in the school. Community teachers received training to enable them to become certified teachers under a new form of school certification. This is an important innovation that would allow independent schools in inner cities to develop their own teachers after a transition period of relying on teachers from outside their communities. At Highland Park, the dual-teacher policy created some tension between the certified teachers, who were predominantly white, and the community teachers, who were black. Because of their concepts of "professionalism," the certified teachers often had difficulty accepting the community teachers as equals.[18]

Allen Christian School

Rev. Floyd Flake, the founder of the Allen Christian School in Jamaica, New York, had made an important observation in his roles as dean of Lincoln University (an African-American school) and Boston University (integrated). At the former, when black students performed poorly, professors and administrators could put pressure on them.

> They did not feel that it was a White system that was degrading what they thought were their intellectual capabilities and skills. If a student failed and was sent home for a semester, that student usually came back a much better student. In the White school, Black students felt that because they had gotten to the institution, no one could tell them they had deficiencies, whether it was reading, writing, math, or other skills. When we developed programs to try to address those skills, they would not participate.[19]

This brief account explains not only why Rev. Floyd Flake believed in the importance of establishing a school in 1982 in conjunction with his African Methodist Episcopal church, but also why compensatory programs are so often destined to fail. Unless a school program overcomes the resistance of students, it cannot succeed.

The focus of the school is on discipline, principles of Christian thought, African-American culture, and high educational expectations in math, reading, writing, and a foreign language. Parents are told not to send their children to school if they will not allow their children to be disciplined (which means reprimands, not spankings and beatings). The school consciously differentiates itself from government schools where discipline is frequently harsh or ineffective or both.

Islamic School of Seattle

Not all of the independent schools in the United States are either Christian or nonsectarian. There are a few schools representing non-Christian religions. Many of them, and others that focus on ethnicity, are supplementary schools, functioning on weekends. A few operate a full educational program. (Perhaps more of the ethnic weekend programs would attempt to operate full-time day schools if vouchers were available.)

The Islamic School of Seattle is a full-time day school that combines secular instruction with study of the Koran and the Arabic language.[20] The time devoted to the latter subjects varies from half an hour to an hour and a half per day, depending on grade level and other factors.

Not all the teachers are Muslim, but only those sympathetic to Islam are acceptable as teachers. There have been some differences of opinion about the relative weighting of Arabic studies and studies conducted in English. Regardless of how that particular balance is worked out, a significant feature of the school is the way in which Islamic thought permeates all subjects: science, art, music, and social studies. In fact, the school has considered developing and publishing social studies texts for other Islamic schools because the faculty considers the treatment of Islamic countries to be negatively biased in existing social studies texts.

Another important feature of the school from the perspective of the Islamic community in Seattle is the fact that it has created employment for a small number of Islamic women who are thereby relieved of the conflicts involved in working in a non-Islamic environment. This element of employment within a community instead of relying exclusively on outsiders is a characteristic of many community-based schools, but not all of them highlight it in their descriptions of themselves.

An Anonymous School

In his book *Free Schools,* Jonathan Kozol described an unnamed school in Roxbury (south Boston) with eighty students and six teachers. (Presumably the anonymity was intended to protect the school from outsiders coming to study it.) Rather than providing a list of statistics about the school, he chose to reveal the quality of caring that made the school special. I quote from Kozol's description of this particular school because it symbolizes the characteristics of numerous other inner-city community schools, past and present, Christian and nonsectarian, that have struggled to survive against desperate odds.

> There is . . . a strong, emphatic and disarming atmosphere of trust, of shared endeavor and of conspiratorial exhilaration between children and adults—a sense of trust which builds at all times on the recognition of the unjust and intolerable conditions that surround their school . . . There is . . . a real sense of stability and of sustained commitment in regard both to the present lives and to the future aspirations of the children in the school. . . . [That commitment] involves them in the most painstaking labor of medical referrals, legal battles, food-stamp hassles, landlord-tenant confrontations, difficult introductions and complex affiliations with more traditional independent schools and with rich people's colleges, job prospects and the like, all of which are the visible evidence and the daily confirmation of the fact that it is the survival of their children and not the slogans of the moment they believe in.[21]

The independence of the school does not guarantee the dedication that Kozol describes. It merely guarantees that the dead hand of bureaucracy will not crush dedication that arises spontaneously.

Options for Youth

The Options for Youth program in Los Angeles is significant because it is a nongovernment school that is operating with public funds.[22] The school receives the average daily attendance (ADA) funds that the Los Angeles Unified School District receives from the state. (The district continues to receive the categorical funds for these students, even though the district provides them with no direct services, only administration. This is the type of deal that entrepreneurial schools have to make with districts in order to survive.) Yet Options for Youth is privately managed. It contacts students who have dropped out of school and offers independent study and tutorial services until the student returns to a regular school or accumulates enough credits to graduate.

Under California law, nongovernment schools can receive government funds as long as the school is under the control of a school board. In this case, the control amounts to little more than a requirement that teachers have a state-approved credential. The way in which the school is run is largely up to its director.

One of the innovative features of the program is aimed at students who are so alienated from school that they will not come to the site where the program is conducted. Instead, tutors are dispatched to the homes of the students to pick up independent study assignments and to go over them with the students.

Although this approach might not be as successful as a program that creates a sense of community among students, it is better than the existing government schools for many students. According to John Hall, director of Options for Youth, some parents have called him to ask how to enroll their children who have not yet dropped out of school but who are learning little.

Test results also indicate the success of the program. Students in Options for Youth generally gain one year of skills for each year of participation. In other words, they are not catching up with students reading and doing math at grade level, but they are learning faster than comparable students in the Los Angeles public schools. Since the budget of Options for Youth is less than half of what is spent per pupil in the public schools, the success is due to the motivation of the teachers and the students in a program that gives them freedom.

Oakland Street Academy

Another unusual combination of public funds and private enterprise is the Oakland Street Academy.[23] This school of around 180 students receives ADA funds from the state on the same basis as Options for Youth. It was originally funded by the U.S. Department of Education's experimental schools program. Currently, the Oakland district pays the Urban League of Oakland to run the school. The Urban League hires the teachers, some of whom are state-certified while others operate under a district waiver of certification rules. Each teacher takes personal responsibility for 15 to 20 students, serving as a counselor and making home visits.

The Oakland Street Academy accepts primarily students who have either dropped out of school or who are not functioning well in regular high schools. The program involves all students in reading literary classics, learning algebra, and writing research papers. As one former teacher put it, there are no remedial classes "full of second grade spelling worksheets which some [students] say predominated in other urban high schools."[24]

Another attractive feature of the school for African-American students (the overwhelming majority in Oakland) is the inclusion of black authors in the curriculum. Without neglecting such authors as Shakespeare and Dickens, the school also exposes students to Maya Angelou, Malcolm X, Alice Walker, and Piri Thomas. As one student said, "This is the first place that I found out that the black man had done anything important." A statement by John, a former student, describes well the anonymity of public schools that he escaped by choosing the Street Academy: "I was invisible. I sat in those other schools for two years, and I did nothing. I spoke to no one and no one spoke to me. Finally, I said, Man, I'm invisible here.' So I got up and walked out the door and I never went back."[25] John later graduated from the Oakland Street Academy reading above grade level.

Schools in Prince George's County, Maryland

In the public sector, school districts are the units that operate with some degree of legal autonomy. Occasionally, the principal of a particular school will gain enough community support to carry out an independent policy. In general, however, districts and superintendents have more power than principals to establish distinctive programs. That is precisely why giving more power over hiring, firing, budget, and curriculum to individual schools (and less to central offices and unions) is the key to the reform of government schools. Until then, one should primarily consider school districts, not schools, when looking for examples of high-quality education in the public sector.

The schools in Prince George's County, on the eastern border of Washington, D.C., had long been in a state of decline when the school board hired John Murphy as the superintendent in 1984.[26] The district was divided over busing, tax support for schools had been cut, and enrollment had declined by 28 percent in ten years.

Perhaps Murphy's most important characteristic is that he does not allow schools to blame children for failure. Instead he fires or transfers ineffective principals and demands that schools set high expectations for students. In Suitland High School, for example, where an accreditation report noted that "thirty percent of [the] faculty have lost interest in the teaching act," Murphy put a new principal, Joseph Hairston, in charge. Hairston issued transfer notices to seventeen teachers. Some of them had been sleeping in class. The teachers' union filed a grievance, but all except two of the teachers were transferred. (One wonders, of course, where these teachers were placed.) Average SAT scores have risen by over 125 points in the five years since then.

In another school, the failure rate on the ninth-grade Maryland writing test went from 50 percent to 4 percent in five years. Overall, student achievement scores rose during Murphy's tenure in office from twenty-first to tenth out of twenty-four Maryland districts.

The emphasis on measurement of achievement through tests took its toll, with less measurable elements of the curriculum put on hold in order to show gains. Nevertheless, the magnet program in Prince George's County enabled the schools to make significant gains. It is important to note, however, that unlike managers of nongovernment schools, who have succeeded on shoestring budgets, Murphy almost doubled the size of the budget during his time in office. In addition, ongoing conflicts over his methods eventually led him to leave the district (for Charlotte, North Carolina) in 1991. How much of the improvement in student achievement will outlast him remains to be seen, but it seems likely that the district will return to the normal level of bureaucratic inertia soon enough.

Conclusion

The advantages of nongovernment schools have been shown both statistically and anecdotally. Both sources of evidence point to the value of schools that utilize the strengths of a community rather than treating students as isolated individuals.

Contrary to the prevalent image of nongovernment schools as elitist, the evidence cited in this chapter indicates that some have been established for students failing in regular government schools. Alternative programs help students achieve their potential, provide an atmosphere conducive to academic effort, and, in some cases, offer a curriculum that promotes self-esteem by emphasizing the historical achievements of ethnic minorities. The overriding purpose of each of these schools is to help children and youth from poor backgrounds to have a chance to participate fully in American society. All of them reject the "culture of poverty" concept by which schools blame students for failing. They seek to restore the confidence that regular government schools have undermined.

A series of examples is inconclusive. Perhaps the number of people who establish community-based schools for low-income families is so limited that vouchers will not induce similar schools to come into being. Vouchers do not guarantee improvement; they only make it possible. Nevertheless, one can reasonably suppose that if entrepreneurs have opened these schools and operated them in part with funds from bazaars, car washes, and rummage sales, more will follow in their footsteps when funding is not such an overwhelming obstacle.

Parents whose children are not learning in their current schools want alternatives. They have flocked to the kinds of schools described in this chapter. Vouchers could enable far more of these schools to thrive and far more parents to be satisfied.

Perspectives on Schools and Community

Horace Mann Debates over the control of education date back to the middle of the nineteenth century. Most histories of education credit Horace Mann and his colleagues with the creation of the public schools. These accounts generally ignore the fact that public schools primarily replaced existing "voluntary" schools instead of adding new schools. The purpose of the compulsory government-run schools was to inculcate a common ideology. The primary models for this "liberal" school system were two militaristic states: ancient Sparta and nineteenth-century Prussia. (*Print from the Library of Congress. LC-US262-60506.*)

Polly Williams Through the persistence, dynamism, and eloquence of Wisconsin state representative Annette "Polly" Williams, Milwaukee became the first city in the United States with an education voucher system. Ms. Williams argues that all families should have the right to choose where their children attend school, not just the rich. After repeated efforts to reform the Milwaukee public schools, she gained bipartisan support for a voucher system to allow 1,000 children from low-income families to attend nonsectarian private schools. Both she and the voucher plan remain the center of controversy. (*Photo courtesy of Annette Polly Williams.*)

Will integration suffer under a voucher system? Genuine interracial understanding comes about when children enjoy learning together, not when they meet statistical standards of courts or school boards. Within the public schools, voluntary integration programs have been more effective than mandatory plans. A voucher plan could have the same positive effect. Predominantly white private schools in the suburbs of Kansas City, Missouri, for example, have offered 4,000 places to black children under a proposed integration plan that would make use of vouchers. (*Photo from UPI/Bettmann.*)

Sheenway School Although there are a few African-American schools that date back to the nineteenth century, most of the hundreds now operating have been started in the past twenty years. There is no typical model; each school has its own orientation and philosophy. The Sheenway School in Los Angeles is one example. It began as the vision of Dr. Herbert Sheen, who used his own money in the 1960s to start the Sheenway School and Culture Center. Now run by his daughter, Dolores Sheen Blunt, the school enrolls eighty students and provides year-round instruction. It remains a source of initiative in a community dominated by dependency. (*Photo courtesy of Sheenway School and Culture Center.*)

Ex-servicemen as college students, 1946 The GI Bill has served as a prototype voucher system since 1944. It allowed millions of veterans to choose the type of training or college education they would receive after completing military service. Its overwhelming success encouraged Congress to use the voucher model again in the Pell Grant program, which gives scholarship money to low-income postsecondary students. Vouchers have also been provided for the funding of daycare for poor families. If vouchers work for the very young and for adults, why not for schoolchildren? Despite its claims that vouchers will destroy public education, the National Education Association did not fight the GI Bill or Pell Grants—because those programs did not threaten NEA interests. (*Photo from UPI/Bettmann.*)

Klan marchers in Ashland, Oregon, 1920s   Although critics of vouchers sometimes present the specter of schools with extremist orientations, historically groups such as the Ku Klux Klan have strenuously opposed any schools (especially Catholic schools) not run by the government. In 1922, the KKK in Oregon was instrumental in the passage of legislation forbidding the operation of private schools in that state. In 1925, the U.S. Supreme Court overturned the legislation as an unconstitutional infringement on parental rights. (*Photo from Oregon Historical Society. No. OrHi 49676.*)

Berlin school children and their teachers, 1933 One of the standard features of totalitarian societies is their unwillingness to endure institutions that are not controlled by the state. Fascist and Communist governments have both eliminated nongovernment schools as threats to their social order. The Nazis, for example, considered private schools superfluous, particularly religious schools that served as an alternative object of loyalty. After World War II, when the occupation government tried to impose neutral, state-run schools modeled on the American system, Germans resisted. An education system controlled by the state reminded them of the Nazis' German Community Schools. Thus Germany, like most industrialized countries, provides state support for independent or sectarian schools. (*Photo from UPI/Bettmann.*)

Are private schools elitist? Playing on the distorted image that non-government schools are bastions of elitism, some critics charge that a voucher system will lead to skimming or "creaming" the best students from the public schools. They also complain that it will lead to "white flight" to the suburbs. But in inner cities, the children in nongovernment schools are from poor families who want their children to learn. These are the families that will flee the deteriorating public schools that have treated them with such contempt. Those with money have already deserted the ship. The beneficiaries of vouchers are those who have not had a chance to choose. (*Photo from UPI/Bettmann.*)

A student and her mother accept a tuition award from the CHOICE Trust As in other cities around the country, poor children in Indianapolis have had to endure a lack of educational opportunities. In the belief that an educated workforce is in the long-term interests of the nation and of business, the Golden Rule Insurance Company offered to pay half of the private-school tuition for Indianapolis children from low-income families. This private voucher program, administered through the Educational CHOICE Charitable Trust, is almost as large as the Milwaukee plan funded by the state of Wisconsin. The project provided funding for 700 students in its first year. Other corporations that observe this example may be encouraged to follow the lead of Golden Rule by establishing pilot programs in their cities. (*Photo from the Educational CHOICE Charitable Trust. Photographer, Ron Neal. Used by permission.*)

9

The GI Bill and Other Federal "Vouchers"

The single largest source of information about how vouchers will work is the evidence that can be derived from the GI Bill, Pell Grants, and other federal programs of direct student aid. These programs have functioned as voucher systems for postsecondary education, both public and private. In addition, federal programs such as food stamps and housing vouchers provide limited evidence about administrative issues related to education vouchers. In particular, experience with those programs can help to dispel potential concerns about corruption.

The Original GI Bill

The GI Bill (the Servicemen's Readjustment Act), enacted in 1944, provided a tuition subsidy to any of the sixteen million armed forces personnel to continue their education or training as they returned to civilian life. The original purpose, however, had little to do with education. The aim of the GI Bill, in addition to offering one more benefit of military service, was to reduce the immediate impact on the economy of a massive number of people looking for jobs. Nevertheless, with over a million veterans enrolling in the fall of 1946, it had a tremendous effect on education, almost doubling the number of students in college in two years. In its seven years of operation, the program assisted a total of

7.8 million veterans, most of whom attended trade or technical schools rather than academic institutions. An estimated half-million veterans attended college and could not have done so without the subsidy. Schools were forced to expand almost overnight, but they managed to absorb the onslaught of students.[1]

Opposition to the GI Bill was minimal. James Conant, president of Harvard, and Robert Hutchins, chancellor of the University of Chicago, attacked the plan for elitist reasons. They feared that unsuitable veterans would force a watering down of the curriculum and convert colleges and universities into "educational hobo jungles." Congress ignored these protests, however, and Conant later endorsed the results of the GI Bill enthusiastically.

Retrospectively, the almost total lack of opposition seems remarkable. Where was the National Education Association that today regards vouchers as a dangerous threat to public education? Where were the educational professors who now decry choice as contrary to the American common school tradition? Where was the American Civil Liberties Union, which consistently attacks vouchers that would pay tuition in sectarian schools, when funds from the GI Bill were used for that purpose in higher education? Indeed, where was the Supreme Court that until 1983 consistently struck down aid to sectarian elementary or secondary education as violating the separation of church and state, yet allowed federal funds to pay tuition at church-established colleges and universities?

The basis of these inconsistencies has little to do with principle and much to do with politics. Specifically, in 1944 no group had a vested interest to protect by blocking vouchers for veterans. By contrast, unions representing elementary and secondary teachers fear that if vouchers enable students to attend private schools, the public schools will lose funds and teachers (that is, union members). In addition, the anti-Catholic bias that has pervaded attitudes toward aid to elementary and secondary sectarian schools since the middle of the nineteenth century had no parallel in higher education. Most private colleges and universities were founded by mainline Protestant denominations. Therefore, neither the education establishment nor the Protestant establishment had much reason to fight the GI Bill.

The only opposition, based on the fear by elite university presidents of lowered standards, now appears ironic. In the current debate over vouchers, the argument has been made that the disadvantaged will not make use of vouchers. In the 1944 debate, Conant and Hutchins believed that intellectually unqualified veterans would make excessive use of the vouchers and overwhelm their universities. The original fears turned out to be largely unfounded. The GI Bill was regarded as an overwhelming success, despite some problems that will be discussed below.

Other Programs to Increase Access and Choice

As a result of that success, the concept of providing vouchers to students for attendance at postsecondary schools became widely accepted. In addition to renewing the GI Bill after each war, Congress has added several income-based scholarship programs. The largest grant program available for low-income students at present is the Pell Grant program, formerly called the Basic Education Opportunity Grants.

Unlike the GI Bill, which provided benefits in return for military service, the later entitlement programs were aimed at widening educational opportunities. They were intended to increase both access and choice for students who would otherwise be denied options in postsecondary education. As a result of the increased availability of grant funds, blacks and Hispanics began in the 1970s to catch up with whites in enrollment in higher education.[2] Between 1970 and 1976, the percentage of black eighteen- to twenty-four-year-olds in higher education rose from 16 percent to 23 percent. Hispanic enrollment increased from 13 percent to 20 percent from 1972 to 1976. White enrollment remained constant at 27 percent.

From 1976 to 1985, however, scholarship aid diminished. By 1985, the proportion of eighteen- to twenty-four-year-old blacks and Hispanics participating in higher education had declined to 20 percent and 17 percent respectively. The proportion of whites remained constant. Although a variety of changes had taken place during the intervening decade, this decline among blacks and Hispanics can be partially attributed to the reduction in real expenditures for federal grants to students from 1976 to 1985. The decline in grants was somewhat offset by loans, but this did not sufficiently compensate students from low-income families. During the period from 1976 to 1982 the number of students enrolled in four-year colleges or universities increased by 7 percent, while enrollment in proprietary (for-profit) schools, which generally offer short-term programs, almost doubled.[3] Presumably a large portion of that increase in proprietary enrollment was constituted by black and Hispanic students who were discouraged from attending four-year schools by the decline in grants.

Since scholarships designated for the poor improved their educational opportunities for a short period, there is reason to believe that vouchers for elementary and secondary education would also improve choice and access to quality schools. Voucher systems can be limited to low-income families in the manner of the Pell Grant program. But a voucher plan for elementary and secondary school would probably include families of all ethnicities and income groups. The more comparable program would be the GI Bill, which was not income-based.

As David O'Neill and Sue Ross noted in their study of the effectiveness of the GI Bill for veterans with low preservice educational attainments:

> The use of vouchers is often advocated on grounds that the trainee's freedom to choose his course of study ensures that providers will be responsive to the interests of trainees and, at the same time, will seek to be efficient in the provision of services. Opponents of vouchers often object that those with limited prior education, who are most in need of training, are also those least able to make wise choices among training types and institutions.[4]

One purpose of the O'Neill and Ross study was to determine which is the best way to deliver education training services: directly in the form of government-run programs or indirectly by providing vouchers. They discovered that those receiving vocational training supported by the GI Bill earned around 10 percent more per year after training than a control group that received no training. They estimate that this earnings differential is about twice as great as that effected by the government-run Manpower Development Training Administration programs.

Who Used GI Bill Benefits?

O'Neill and Ross determined that training under a voucher system was particularly effective for blacks. This contradicts the widespread belief that this group underutilized the potential benefits of the GI Bill and that those who did take advantage of it were not provided with useful training.

> Prior to training, the earnings of blacks were in the neighborhood of 15% lower than the earnings of similar non-blacks. After training, there was no significant racial earnings differential. Clearly, blacks gained much more from training than similar non-blacks . . . provid[ing] positive evidence that a voucher type system can be relied on to help blacks participate in the labor market on an equal footing with other segments of society. . . . [In addition,] training reduces the percentage difference between groups with less than a high school education and those with more education.[5]

Nor are these remarkable findings due to low participation rates among blacks. For both high school graduates and nongraduates, blacks utilized the GI Bill more than nonblacks. In addition, within every range of scores on the Armed Forces Qualification Test, blacks used the GI Bill more than nonblacks.

O'Neill and Ross also found that veterans with higher levels of prior education were more likely to make use of the GI Bill benefits than those without high school degrees or with no college education. This gap is not surprising, since veterans with more prior education had more options for future education or training: from correspondence courses to college and graduate school. Most of the difference in participation rates was between high school dropouts and high school graduates, which is a difference that would not exist in a voucher plan for elementary and secondary students. Moreover, as O'Neill and Ross point out, this gap narrowed in the years prior to their analysis, as the military services made more of an effort to provide remedial training prior to discharge and to notify veterans from low-education backgrounds of the opportunities available to them. Throughout the period from 1972 to 1976, as benefit levels increased, growth in participation rates among educationally disadvantaged veterans was far higher than for their better educated counterparts. This suggests that part of the reason for lower participation rates among the educationally disadvantaged may have been the failure of benefit levels to keep up with the rising cost of education. If those with low education levels are generally poorer than those with more schooling, total benefit levels would influence participation rates.

Opportunities for Education—
and for Corruption

The experience of the GI Bill and other entitlement programs reveals that a voucher system unleashes pent-up demands for education options. The question is whether there will be a compensating increase in the supply of education services. As we have already seen, the supply of available education services rose swiftly and dramatically in the first two years of the GI Bill. Colleges and universities managed to make room for twice as many students in that short time, and the number of proprietary schools multiplied rapidly. Some form of education was supplied to all who wanted it and on short order. If the government had been directly responsible for creating enough new schools to meet the new demand, far fewer veterans would have benefitted from the program.

Nevertheless, critics of the GI Bill have argued that the Veterans Administration did not adequately regulate the types of schools or training institutes that would be eligible to receive federal funds. They complain that "fly-by-night" companies opened schools and bilked both ingenuous veterans and taxpayers. The extent to which this was true bears on future voucher plans for children. Voucher critics maintain that naive, low-income families will invest in education programs of limited value for their children based on deceptive advertising and aggressive sales techniques.

There were in fact charges in 1945 and again in 1951 and 1952 that the GI Bill had spawned a number of institutions that had bilked the government by inflating their charges or, in the case of dummy corporations, by charging for nonexistent services. Many of the institutions involved in this scandal were proprietary schools, although nonprofit schools were also apparently engaged in creative accounting. The problem actually arose from the fact that the *initial* GI Bill was not precisely based on voucher principles. The portion of the payment for tuition went directly to the school rather than to the veteran. The amount of the payment varied with the school's tuition. Thus, each school had an incentive to raise tuition to the maximum allowed by the government stipend. The government had created conditions that were almost inevitably corrupting.

To correct that problem, when Congress renewed the GI Bill in 1952 for Korean War veterans, payments were made directly to the veterans, who could then stretch their funds by attending public universities rather than private ones.[6] Some private colleges and universities resisted this innovation because it hurt their chances of attracting students. University administrators revealed themselves as managers of subsidized corporations who protect their own interests just as other corporate leaders do. In the battles over the exact formulas by which federal scholarship aid would be distributed, public institutions favored flat-rate grants that increased the advantages of enrollment at low-cost state-run universities. Private colleges and universities lobbied for a provision that limited grant aid to one-half of tuition. Grants based on a percentage of tuition helped high-cost private schools. Each type of college fought for aid based on its institutional position, not idealistic concern for the best interests of students.

Congress decided to provide flat-rate individual, rather than institutional, aid. By 1958, 62 percent of the new GI Bill's beneficiaries attended public postsecondary schools. This may have reduced the federal funds for private schools, but it also eliminated the basis for deception and corruption in the original GI Bill by setting a precedent for funding individuals, not institutions. This became the principle upon which later scholarship plans and modern voucher proposals were founded. When the grant amount was provided directly to veterans, the grantees had an incentive to seek low-cost institutions, whereas before they had had no reason to be cost conscious. From that point on, the complaints received by the Veterans Administration have been primarily (85 percent) related to late payment of benefits, not to inflated charges from institutions.[7] Subsequent abuses did not involve institutions so much as individuals who enrolled in courses but did not attend. This procedure allowed them to collect the subsistence allowance as part of the GI Bill package. Obviously, this particular sort of cheating would not exist under a voucher plan that did not include a subsistence allowance. Moreover, the Veterans Administration estimates that in 1974 its overpayments due to this sort of deception amounted to only 1½ percent of total disbursements.[8] The tiny amount of abuse under the revised (1952) law suggests that a school voucher program would also be subject to only limited corruption.

Congress had closed the loophole by which schools had been able to charge excessive tuition under the original GI Bill. Still the question remained in the minds of many as to whether proprietary schools were valid educational institutions.[9] The leaders of American education have perpetuated an aristocratic bias against proprietary vocational institutions, regarding schools that are established by entrepreneurs as having only base material motives. From the lofty vantage point of a respectable university that receives millions in grants from the government, profit seeking and education are regarded as incompatible. As a result of this hypocritical snobbery among opinion leaders, proprietary schools have always had difficulty receiving a fair hearing in public. The fact that millions of people have learned in these proprietary schools skills that led to better employment opportunities has little bearing on the animosity toward such schools.

Proprietary Schools and the GI Bill

The appropriate measure of the value of proprietary schools has nothing to do with whether they generate a profit for their owners. Instead the question is whether they provide high-quality education and training at a cost equal to or below that of nonprofit schools.

Obviously, schools that engage in fraud or overcharge for inadequate classes would not meet this test. Newspapers have periodically reported cases of schools that have indeed engaged in deceptive advertising and enrollment of unqualified students in order to profit from federal student aid. There is no evidence, however, indicating how widespread these practices are or have been. With over one million students enrolled in more than 5,500 proprietary schools in 1982, misrepresentation by some schools is not surprising.[10]

A handful of unscrupulous operators can tarnish the image of an entire industry and create a scandal, especially if the evidence is based on anecdotal accounts. Yet no evidence has ever been presented of a consistent relationship between low quality of education and the profit-seeking orientation of institutions that provide educational services. O'Neill and Ross point out that one criticism found in newspaper stories about proprietary schools has been that they spend too much (over 40 percent of their budget in some cases) on advertising and recruitment.

> Although a large expenditure for advertising is always taken to be a bad thing, the precise argument is never spelled out. In another context—that of delivering manpower services to the disadvantaged—these activities are respectable and are called "outreach." It is also noteworthy that there is no evidence that any large volume of complaints is received by VA regional offices from abused veterans. Officials . . . were queried by the authors on this issue. . . . Both [officials] said the number of complaints received each year was minute relative to the number of students being served.[11]

In fact, during the recent era of declining college enrollments, public and nonprofit schools have been emulating the aggressive marketing practices of proprietary schools, the same methods for which the latter have been faulted in the past.

Stories that confirm the prejudice of elite educators against proprietary schools are reported in the press, but neither the overall efficiency nor the particular success stories of those schools are made available to the public. Despite the fact that proprietary schools are cheaper to run than public schools, this advantage is frequently concealed by cost comparisons based on tuition. These figures are misleading since government-owned schools are tax consumers but proprietary schools are tax providers. In addition, proprietary postsecondary school programs are more efficient because of their shorter duration. If the time cost (lost income) of attending classes is considered, the net cost to students of proprietary school programs is a fraction of the cost in public sector programs: 51 percent as much in computer programming, 30 percent as much in auto mechanics, 60 percent in electronics, and 27 percent in secretarial programs.[12] In other words, even from the students' perspective, proprietary schools are cheaper because they allow students to complete programs quickly and begin earning money.

A second way in which proprietary schools are superior is in their effectiveness in training students for the job market, largely because their reputations depend on their ability to provide skills in demand by business. Proprietary schools led the way in the field of training computer programmers in the 1960s, years ahead of public schools.[13] In contrast to the public sector, where new course and program offerings require years of advance planning, committee evaluation, and bureaucratic review, a private entrepreneur can initiate a new course of study or training in a matter of months, although always at the risk of failing to attract students or to place them in jobs. Risk, efficiency, and flexibility are closely related to one another. By eliminating risk (and the potential for rewards), the public sector also stifles innovation.

A third measure of the advantage of proprietary schools is their completion rates. According to one study, 46 percent of students in public vocational programs completed their courses, whereas 63 percent finished private vocational programs.[14] Since Wellford Wilms found that graduates of public and private programs have approximately similar rates for job placement, the probability of employment for an entering student is about 50 percent higher in a private than in a public program.

This extended discussion of proprietary schools is not intended as an endorsement. The purpose is merely to dispel the notion that millions of people were bilked under the GI Bill by choosing to attend proprietary schools. Although job-oriented schools such as these are likely to be started under a voucher system, in the long run they will probably be less popular than comprehensive academic programs.

Comparative Corruption

Experience with federal scholarship programs should dispel fears about possible corruption in voucher programs. Other federal programs that allow the poor to make choices provide similar evidence.

The seriousness of corruption is largely a matter of perception. High level graft is usually much more complex and harder to understand than the petty graft involved when someone sells food stamps or uses them for liquor. There is widespread outrage when a family cheats the government out of a few thousand dollars in Aid to Families with Dependent Children (AFDC) benefits. By contrast, few comprehend the ways in which institutional corruption costs taxpayers billions of dollars. In large organizations, responsibility is diffuse, and the public is uncertain who is to blame when scandals occur.

In dollar terms, the direct provision of services is likely to produce far more corruption than a voucher program. In the case of food aid, for example, surplus commodity programs are much more open to corruption than food stamps. Fraud by users of food stamps is generally for hundreds of dollars. By contrast, a dishonest manager in a surplus commodity program could make tens of thousands of dollars by misappropriating commodities. Yet if one evaluated these programs according to column-inches of text exposing abuse in local newspapers, then the petty scams of some poor individuals would make food stamps (or similar voucher plans) seem far worse.

Corruption in federal health care programs is also conducted primarily by well-respected institutions and doctors, not by indigent patients. Estimated fraud in Medicaid, which is around 25 percent, is perpetrated almost entirely by nursing home operators, physicians, and pharmacists.[15] Reducing fraud by providers in health care is especially difficult because there is no obvious way to enable consumers of health services to hold providers accountable.

The incentive for corruption is greater in programs to construct public housing than in housing voucher programs. This was made abundantly clear in 1990 when Congress held hearings on overpayment and influence peddling in the Department of Housing and Urban Development (HUD). Rudolph Penner of the Urban Institute explained that corruption arose because the HUD rehabilitation programs were complex and allowed administrators discretion in awarding contracts, a condition that created incentives for graft. By contrast, housing vouchers (under Section 8 of the Housing and Community Development Act of 1974) provide small amounts of money to many people. Those vouchers are less prone to kickbacks and influence selling. As Penner noted in response to a question about the difference between housing vouchers and construction subsidies: "I'm not saying there isn't theft and some fraud in those [voucher] programs, but I think it's very minor compared to what we see in the others."[16] The total cost of HUD's corruption was estimated at four to eight billion dollars. A million cases of petty fraud would have to occur to equal that figure.

The same principle applies to education vouchers. The potential magnitude of fraud is minimal when individuals receive benefits directly. By contrast, corruption in school districts can cost taxpayers millions of dollars. Fiscal mismanagement of school districts often borders on fraud and sometimes crosses the line. The Oakland and Richmond school districts in California went bankrupt because of financial mismanagement and amid rumors of embezzlement and widespread fraud. Although spending a district into bankruptcy without even minimal financial auditing (as Richmond did) may not be illegal, its repercussions for students are perhaps worse than embezzlement. Yet according to California State Controller Gray Davis, many other districts besides Richmond follow slipshod financial procedures of the kind that caused Richmond to self-destruct.[17]

Nevertheless, the public scrutiny of individuals' behavior under a voucher system will be intense. If a school superintendent hires a nephew as an education consultant or orders unnecessary new carpets for the central office, the expenses will be buried in the district budget so deeply that only a few insiders will be aware of these types of professionalized corruption. But if one individual were caught in a kickback scheme with a private school under a voucher plan, the case would create a furor. The same newspapers that have failed to unmask corruption in giant education bureaucracies would be full of stories of how parents may be cheating their children out of an education. Individual corruption makes a good human-interest story; collective corruption is too complex to receive extensive treatment.

Conclusion

Experience with individual entitlement programs for postsecondary education provides some evidence that sheds light on proposed voucher plans for elementary and secondary education.

On the demand side, the availability of scholarship aid has increased the number of students attending postsecondary institutions. The GI Bill and later entitlement programs such as the Pell Grant program allowed millions of low-income students, particularly minorities, to participate in higher education.

On the supply side, the voucher-like programs encouraged a rapid increase in the size and number of postsecondary institutions that students could attend. By funding students rather than institutions, the federal government created an incentive to expand school enrollment. College attendance doubled, and hundreds of proprietary schools came into being, with mostly positive results.

The difference in the potential for misuse of institutional aid and misuse of vouchers is evident in an analysis of corruption in other federal programs. Isolated cases of graft or kickbacks in voucher-type programs receive media attention, but little attention is paid to the pervasive corruption in almost any program involving direct service provision.

The battle over elementary and secondary school vouchers is in many ways a repetition of the federal conflicts between support for individuals and support for institutions. In the case of vouchers, employees of public schools prefer direct institutional support because they are already the beneficiaries of the policy. Thus the arguments of public-school respresentatives are as self-serving as those of the private-college presidents who fought to preserve GI Bill payments made directly to their schools in 1952. Congress chose to ignore institutional interests at that time. A voucher system would override similar entrenched interests today.

10

Voucher-like Education Systems: Europe, Commonwealth, United States

S ystems of choice in education in other countries provide some insight into the way a voucher system would operate in the United States. In addition, three states (Vermont, Minnesota, and Wisconsin) now operate small-scale programs that involve subsidies of parental choice. Finally, several states, including California and the state of Washington, allow school districts to contract with private companies to provide educational services for special-needs groups. There is considerable evidence from these limited programs that vouchers can indeed work in education, for rich and poor alike.

Educational Choice in Europe

Any discussion of tax-supported nongovernment schools in Europe or elsewhere must begin with a recognition that no country uses a true voucher system as the basis of education financing. The financial arrangements involve direct financing of nongovernment schools rather than providing scholarships to families and allowing them to choose a school or join other families in starting one. In most cases the government provides funds to the schools on the basis of their actual costs, which gives the schools less incentive to economize than would a per-pupil subsidy. But, a few countries, particularly Denmark, tie aid directly to enrollment levels and also allow parents to start new schools, thus closely approximating a voucher system. In most countries the alternative schools must conform to state guidelines that make them less distinct from government schools than would be the case under a true voucher system.

Even direct funding of nongovernment schools allows parents to exercise some choice, particularly between schools that represent different religious options. After centuries of religious wars, European countries have learned the importance of pluralism rather than mere toleration. As a result, the nations of Europe not only fund schools that represent the official state religion, they also provide support for other sectarian schools. In countries with Protestant or secular orientations, this primarily involves support for Catholic schools.

France

In France, the conflicts in education policy stem from the French Revolution. The Republican hatred of the Catholic church as one of the pillars of the ancien regime persists in the twentieth-century conflict over government subsidies to Catholic schools. Since the state provides the teachers in all schools, there is a threat to the religious character of the Catholic schools. Since 1977, however, Catholic-school principals have been entitled to reject any prospective teachers who do not share the school's convictions, thus giving the schools a chance to maintain a distinctive focus.[1]

The experience in France provides some interesting insights into the controversy over whether a system of subsidized parental choice will lead to elitism in the private sector. The French are also debating the adoption of a true voucher system, but the present system gives some indication of how choices affect different groups within society. Sociologist Robert Ballion points out that the middle class is better able to make use of the existing choice mechanisms because the present system lacks "a formalized and generally understood mechanism for the exercise of parental choice."[2] Yet when they know of options, working-class parents make school choices that are fairly similar to those of middle-class parents. Despite information obstacles, in the school year 1976–77, students from working-class homes made up 21 percent of private-school enrollments (as compared with 38 percent of public-school enrollments).

Just as in the United States, many of the most prestigious secondary schools are run by the government. The same skills that enable the French middle class to make disproportionate use of private options also make them "more aware of the possibility of manipulating the public system to the benefit of their children" than working-class families. By contrast, "a whole sector of non-Catholic private schools specialize in giving a second chance to students who have experienced academic failure in public schools."[3] Thus, whereas the public system is elitist in the sense that only the upper echelons of society can make effective use of its best schools, at least some nonelitist choices are available among nongovernment schools.

The moral of the French experience would seem to be that a system of choice that is convoluted and hard to understand is likely to be inequitable. In America this applies to the existing system of "choice" in public schools that permits upper-middle-class families to manipulate the system to their advantage, while most families are consigned to schools in which they have little voice or control over what happens to their children.

Germany

Germany has had a long history of "confessional schools" that were based on the Catholic or Protestant orientation of the majority of citizens in a district. During the Nazi period, confessional schools were supplanted by uniform state schools, specifically so that the state could impose its ideology on children. The implicit challenge of confessional schools to the power of the state under the Nazis is Germany's most important lesson to other democracies. The fact that the Nazis felt compelled to dismantle these schools is indicative of the perceived threat they posed to totalitarian government. Certainly, neither the Catholic nor the Protestant schools were radical politically, perhaps less so than the government schools to which socialists presumably sent their children. Yet government schools were more easily coopted by the Nazis.

After the war, when the occupation government sought to impose uniform, nonconfessional schools on all children, there was strong resistance: "The American model of a common school, dependent exclusively on State and local government and ignoring confessional differences, seemed to some Germans uncomfortably close to the Nazi's German Community School."[4] Thus, at public insistence, all German states provide for some form of public financing of traditional confessional programs, either within the public schools or as separate schools. Since a decision in 1987 by the Federal Constitutional Court, states must support nongovernment schools on a neutral, nondiscretionary basis. Significantly, the court ruled that failure by the government to provide support for private schools forces those schools to rely on family resources and makes them exclusive schools for the upper class. In other words,

the court found that the *absence* of financial aid to private schools led
to economic segregation, whereas public support could make them
equally accessible to all elements of the population without regard to
family income.

> Only when [private schooling] is fundamentally available to all
> citizens without regard to their personal financial situations can the
> [constitutionally] protected educational freedom actually be realized
> and claimed on an equal basis by all parents and students. . . . This
> constitutional norm must thus be considered as a mandate to
> lawmakers to protect and promote private schools.[5]

If this mandate were thoroughly implemented, Germany would protect
the ability of dissenting groups to control their own education more than
any other country in Europe.

The protection of the right to educational opportunity of Turkish
guest-workers or other minorities in Germany has not been a strong
tradition. Perhaps because these minorities have had a tenuous legal
status as temporary residents, they have not made efforts to develop
a strong school system for their children. The primary "minority" group
that has established alternative schools has been made up of parents
who respect the philosophy of Rudolf Steiner, the founder of Waldorf
schools. Approximately 53,000 students, less than 1 percent of the school
population, are in Waldorf schools.[6]

Preserving freedom of thought depends on protecting the institutions
in which unorthodoxy can flourish. The Nazi experience suggests that
politically controlled state institutions are more vulnerable than
independent institutions to the influence of an extremist group that
seizes power. Although this may seem outside the experience of the
United States, the suppression of minority voices has long been part
of the American tradition: from deportation of so-called radicals in the
1920s, to internment of Japanese Americans during World War II, to
the infiltration and destruction of various African-American, Hispanic,
and Native-American rights groups in the 1960s and 1970s. The capacity
to form independent schools cannot alone protect minorities. But the
absence of institutions in which minorities can keep alive their traditions
is a major obstacle to preserving their identity.

Denmark

In Denmark, as in Germany, most of the private schools that are publicly
funded are distinguished from state schools on the basis of religious

affiliation.[7] In Denmark, any group of parents representing more than twenty-eight students can found a school at state expense on the basis of a shared philosophy of education.

The average size of alternative schools in Denmark is 172 students; the average for government-run *folkeskoler* is 360. (The comparable figures for the United States are around 325 and 650. Thus the non-government schools in the United States are only half as large as the government schools, but both are almost twice as large as the equivalent schools in Denmark.) The average class size in both types of Danish schools is fewer than nineteen students.

State subsidies of alternative schools have amounted to an average of 78 percent of their operating expenses per pupil. The rest of the operating costs plus capital expenses are covered by parents and by donations. Despite the limitations on state subsidies and the additional costs to parents, the alternative schools are accessible to all income levels.

The schools are not expected to carry the burden of social integration. Social classes live in different parts of cities and thus attend different schools, which Danes view as normal. At any rate, there is little extreme poverty. In these circumstances, state support of alternative schools is not socially divisive. As an Organization for Economic Cooperation and Development (OECD) report explains:

> It is evident that the private schools are not perceived in Denmark as elite schools for the rich, conferring social and educational advantages on a minority. . . . [S]ome private schools serve as the public school in areas where the municipalities see no point in incurring the cost of setting up a new school.[8]

Some private schools in rural areas are resented because they are more selective than government schools, but as Peter Mason notes, "There is no evidence that going to a private school gives any special social advantages in career or life generally."[9] Thus, even though schools are, to some extent, differentiated by social class just as are neighborhoods, this is not perceived in Denmark as a source of economic inequity.

The purpose of the state subsidies to alternative schools in Denmark has not been primarily to equalize opportunities. Rather, they aim to protect diversity. Schools have been founded by a variety of groups such as Montessori and Waldorf educators, humanists, Jews, Muslims, socialists, and Germans (members of the German minority in Schleswig). More than any other country in the world, Denmark has had a long commitment to pluralism and choice in education. State schools represent the perspective of the state church, the Danish Evangelical

Lutheran church. But instead of trying to force everyone to conform to the state religion, the Danes have preserved freedom of religion by offering freedom of choice among schools.

The Netherlands

The Dutch have been equally insistent on protecting religious freedom and diversity within the nation's schools. In fact, more than two-thirds of the students in the Netherlands attend nongovernment schools at state expense. Approximately 85 percent of those independent schools are confessional. Most of the remainder are so-called Free Schools. All schools are required to meet state curriculum guidelines. Thus the main differences between schools are in the quality of the teaching staff and, to some extent, in the religious values espoused. The confessional schools, as a result of their history of a central religious hierarchy, sometimes adhere to their professed values in a purely formal manner. The Free Schools, by contrast, have retained more independence, more distinctiveness, and a stronger sense of purpose.

The 1920 Law on Education enables parents to start a new school by joining with others in a formal organization to request state financing. In small municipalities, the law requires only 50 families; in larger cities, 125 are required. The important feature of this arrangement is that parents are not bound to accept the options offered by the state or by religious bodies.[10]

The fundamental social issue in the Netherlands is the conflict between those who want everyone to attend schools with a neutral character (common schools) and those who want schools that have distinctive orientations.[11] The latter have prevailed for almost a century in the Netherlands. The longstanding acceptance of alternatives, however, is being called into question in a "new school struggle" over whether schools should be pluralistic within schools (the common-school approach) or pluralistic between schools (the distinctive-schools approach).

Although this conflict has been ignited in the past by arguments over whether financing a uniform state system of education is better or worse than funding confessional schools, the issue has been raised anew by the recent establishment of Muslim and Hindu schools. For several years, while local authorities delayed, those groups had demanded schools that represent their perspectives. They have been able to receive state funding only since 1988.

The fact that religious and ethnic minorities have chosen separate schools is threatening to those who imagine that the multicultural instruction in supposedly neutral public schools is sufficient. The parallel with the situation in the United States is striking. Just as many blacks,

Hispanics, American Indians, and other minorities in the United States are unsatisfied by the tokenism inherent in the way cultural diversity is treated in public schools, the Hindus and Muslims in the Netherlands are unhappy with public schools that trivialize their religions or study them as objects rather than as living faiths. As one leading Hindu pointed out, "You don't bring a Hindu child up as a Hindu by organizing a Hindu festival or an exotic day. Our philosophy of life does not find a place in the public school. . . . We don't want the superficial alone, and that's why we want a Hindu school."[12] Or, as a Muslim argued, "If someone doesn't know his own culture well, he can't understand other cultures. No one can stand on the air!"[13]

The issue for both Hindus and Muslims is the same as it is for minorities who want vouchers in the United State: who will have the power to govern the schools they attend? If minorities do not control the schools their children are in, they will be forced to accept the marginal position to which the dominant culture assigns them. In the public schools, they will always have second-class status.

The Dutch struggle between paternalism and empowerment of minorities serves as a mirror for the conflicts within American schools. The Dutch leaders who prefer a public-school monopoly attack those who want their own schools by arguing that this contributes to segregation and polarization. The Muslim quoted above, however, notes that the concern about isolation and separatism is hypocritical, since Muslims and Hindus are largely isolated already in the public-school system. The effect of this hypocrisy has been to maintain a pattern of oppression in the guise of being concerned and helpful. As in the United States, the ideal of unity has traditionally been achieved by denying minorities the right to teach their children differently. By providing minorities with funds for their own schools, the Dutch have overcome this inequity. Americans have yet to learn from this example.

Canada, Australia, New Zealand

Three British Commonwealth countries are similar in many ways to the United States. All have federal systems of government. None has an official church, and each has a provision in its federal constitution preventing establishment of an official church. Yet none of them has interpreted this as a wall of separation between church and state that prevents their governments from supporting the education of children in church-run schools. In all three countries, as in the United States, aid to schools is a joint federal-state issue. Thus education policies are a complex mixture of funding sources, rules, and politics.

With the exception of a couple of Canadian provinces, none of the systems of support for nongovernment education come close to a voucher system. Rather, they all suffer from the same problem as France: by receiving direct subsidies from the government and accepting the state curriculum, sectarian schools run the risk of becoming fully secularized and indistinct. The law in each country guarantees that the "special character" of the independent schools will be respected, but the dependence on state support has a corrosive effect.

This problem arises because funding is provided in the form of direct aid to schools rather than following each child. In theory, the government could restrict its power to control the nongovernment schools, while still protecting consumers from fraudulent advertising or breach of contract. Under any program of direct state grants, however, schools are liable to be subjected to excessive state regulation and a loss of distinctiveness.

Direct funding also limits the power of the state to provide special help to the most disadvantaged students. In Australia, for example, funds are allocated to nongovernment schools on the basis of a complex formula known as the Educational Resource Index. Since 1985, government policy has been aimed in theory at increasing support for the "neediest" schools. Because of the nature of the school funding formula, however, a school's "need" is defined not by the income or status of the population served but by the school's income and expenses.[14] An obvious inequity arises when a school serving a low-income population receives less aid than one with higher expenses that serves middle-class families. Fairness is almost impossible when government directs aid to institutions rather than to individuals.

Despite such drawbacks, families in the three Commonwealth countries are still much freer than those in the United States to choose among a variety of schools at a reduced cost to themselves. In Australia, about 26 percent of the population attended nongovernment schools in 1985, over four-fifths of them in either Catholic or Anglican schools. In New Zealand in the same year, only about 3 percent attended nongovernment schools. That figure was down from 9 percent in 1981 as a result of the "integration" of most nongovernment schools into the government sector. Even sectarian schools, including the 250 Catholic schools, are regarded as government schools in New Zealand. At the same time, the remaining independent schools continue to receive modest subsidies from the government. The official figure for nongovernment school attendance in Canada is low (around 5 percent) for the same reason: students in Catholic schools under provincial jurisdiction are classified as public school students.[15]

The history of state aid to nongovernment schools in British Columbia, Canada, is distinctive. Since British Columbia became a

Canadian province only in 1871, it did not have a provision requiring separate schools within the public sector for the minority Catholic population (a requirement under the earlier British North America Act that applies to other provinces). Thus, when it approved the Independent Schools Support Act of 1977, providing funds to nongovernment schools according to enrollment, this amounted to a departure from its past denial of aid to those schools. The grant amounts were quite small, ranging from 9 percent to 30 percent of public-school costs, depending on the degree of regulation accepted by the school. A combination of direct funding of schools and low subsidy levels had the effect of raising revenues marginally in existing private schools without creating much incentive to start new schools. According to Prof. Donald Erickson, who has studied the British Columbia system extensively, the schools became less responsive to parents and the sense of community was undermined when schools became partially dependent on direct government grants.[16] A voucher system, by funding families rather than schools, could have avoided that loss of cohesion. Schools would still depend on the voluntary commitment of families.

Direct provision of aid to truly independent schools in Australia and New Zealand is similarly limited to a small portion (less than 25 percent) of the total cost of a nongovernment school. The effect of this financing limitation is to force schools to make a trade-off between egalitarianism and independence. Those schools that wish to maintain a distinctive program must charge relatively high tuition fees to cover costs. Thus, even with a partial state subsidy, they must remain at least somewhat elitist in order to survive. If they wish to receive a sufficient subsidy to be able to accept low-income students, they must give up their independence (like the majority of private schools in most Canadian provinces and in New Zealand) and become part of the state system. Thus, the poor are still unable to gain access to distinctive educational programs.

United States

Most states in the United States have not allowed public funding of nongovernment education since the period of the Civil War. Before that time, public support of private schools, both Protestant and Catholic, took place in a number of states. The form of support varied from city to city and state to state. In some cases, the city or state provided funds for general support of nongovernment schools or for the education of the poor in them. The distinctions between public and private or between sectarian and nonsectarian education were extremely fluid in this period.

Where the government provided no schools, charitable societies often established them.

Daniel Moynihan describes how the state of New York initially funded church schools and how that policy was reversed as a result of political battles between 1805 and 1825.[17] This pattern was repeated throughout the country from around 1850 onward. The anti-Catholic, anti-foreign Know-Nothing party was sufficiently powerful to prohibit the use of government funds in nongovernment schools. Of the more than four hundred members of the Massachusetts state legislature, which set the tone for the rest of the country in educational policy, all but three were members of the Know-Nothing party in 1854.[18]

An interesting example of how nongovernment schools came to be excluded from public support can be seen in condensed form in California. California was admitted to the United States in 1850, when the national turmoil over the control of education was becoming intense.[19] From 1850 to 1855 (except for one school year, 1852–53), all schools in the state, sectarian and government-operated, received a pro rata share of tax money. In 1855, at the behest of a number of vehement anti-Catholics, the state legislature required all schools to merge into a single nonsectarian system. The law wiped out virtually all of the independent Protestant schools, which became secular public schools; but the Catholic schools struggled to survive. In 1861, when legislation was introduced to reinstate the pro rata system of dividing school taxes, the nineteenth-century equivalent of a voucher system, the bill was again attacked as a Catholic ploy despite the open support for it among a number of Protestant clergy.

This xenophobic and anti-Catholic spirit persisted for many decades (and has never entirely disappeared from American life). In the 1870s, many state legislatures enacted Blaine amendments to their constitutions (named after James G. Blaine, a candidate for president in 1876 and later a secretary of state), prohibiting public funding of parochial schools. That action indicates that no one at the time believed the U.S. Constitution sufficient to effect a separation of church and state with respect to school finance. That doctrine of separation has been applied only since the Supreme Court misread the intent of the Establishment Clause of the First Amendment in *Everson v. Board of Education* (1947).[20] The language of the First Amendment was intended only to prevent the establishment of a *national* religion and the preferential treatment of one religion over others. In *Mueller v. Allen* (1983), the Supreme Court held that state aid to sectarian schools does not violate the Establishment Clause if the aid is neutral between religious and nonreligious institutions.[21]

The main point of this sketchy history is that the policy of excluding nongovernment schools from public funding is rooted in religious intolerance rather than educational idealism. Whereas Europeans resolved the same religious tensions by providing government funds to sectarian schools, Americans generally followed the opposite course until recently.

Vermont

A few states have not followed the general pattern, however. Since 1869, Vermont has operated a quasi-voucher system in high school education at local discretion.[22] (Around thirty towns in Maine follow a similar pattern, but little published information is available on Maine's policies.) With the approval of the local school board, parents may elect to send their children to a government school in another district or to an independent school, in or out of state. The school board then contributes a sum equal at least to the average cost of tuition at a Vermont unified high school, while parents assume all extra costs. The governing boards of 95 out of 246 towns follow this procedure instead of building their own high schools or joining a unified high school district.

The policy is not a true voucher system because it restricts choices to schools approved by the local school board, and the board has the right to reject a parent's request to send a child to an alternative school. In some cases, a town requires all of the students in its jurisdiction to attend a nearby nongovernment school. In other cases, the town allows parents to choose. About one-fourth of the ninety-five towns have vouchers that apply to elementary school as well as high school.

Despite a Vermont Supreme Court ruling that prevents payments to sectarian schools, some payments continue to be made to Episcopal schools that have clergy on their boards and that hold chapel services.[23] Either the definition of sectarian is unclear, or the law is not being enforced. In practice, Catholic and fundamentalist Protestant schools are excluded, but public funding of students at old, established Protestant schools is permitted. This is in keeping with the century-old practice of considering mainstream Protestantism "nonsectarian."

The state's eight requirements for nongovernment schools are (1) specific courses; (2) attendance records; (3) progress assessments; (4) statement of school objectives; (5) a faculty with adequate training, but not necessarily credentials; (6) formal support of the U.S. Constitution and laws by the faculty; (7) student immunization; and (8) periodic approval by the state.

The Vermont program has worked well for over a hundred years without controversy or any of the catastrophic consequences predicted by opponents of public funds for private schools in other states. In fact, some families moving into the state have deliberately located in townships that have a voucher system. Although superintendents do not like the competition from nongovernment schools, they welcome the opportunity to attract students from nearby towns.

Vermont's experience shows that choice is compatible with high-quality education. Despite the state's poverty (it is thirty-ninth in per-capita income), Vermont students in 1982 ranked third on the Scholastic Aptitude Test (SAT) out of twenty-two states that use it extensively. This performance cannot be attributed primarily to choice. It is more likely due to the strength of community in Vermont's small towns.

Not being urbanized, Vermont is not as socially or ethnically heterogeneous as many other states. Still, there are considerable differences in family income and social status. At least one private-school headmaster has noted the positive effect of publicly funded students in an otherwise homogeneous school: "We especially like having kids from Kirby on the voucher plan because it broadens our student body mix. Otherwise, we would have only children of parents who could afford the tuition on top of the property taxes they pay to support the public schools."[24] Thus, at least in some cases, permitting choice leads to social integration rather than the further segregation by social class that voucher critics fear.

Minnesota

Outside of New England, Minnesota is the only state that has had a longstanding policy to assist parents who choose to send their children to nongovernment schools.[25] Since 1955, parents have been allowed to deduct school expenses from their state income tax. The law impartially allows deductions for spending on both government and nongovernment schools, which was a major factor in the Supreme Court's decision to hold it constitutional in 1983.[26] Moreover, the law explicitly includes sectarian schools, unlike laws in Vermont and Wisconsin.

This policy is a far cry from a voucher system, however, since it benefits only those who can already afford tuition at nongovernment schools. It permits deductions of $650 for an elementary student and $1,000 for a secondary student. One should keep in mind, however, that this is a deduction from taxable income, not a tax credit. For a family with a marginal state tax rate of 10 percent, those figures amount to a reduction of only $65 or $100 in the amount of tax owed. That is not sufficient to increase appreciably either the demand for or the supply of alternative schools.

Thus far, efforts to establish a voucher system in Minnesota have failed. Instead, Minnesota has established a policy that permits inter-district transfers among government schools. In addition, the state has adopted a postsecondary options program whereby high school juniors and seniors can attend state or private colleges at state expense. This is a unique sort of voucher system, but it is limited to a small number of students (2 to 3 percent) who have chosen to leave high school early. On the whole, students with negative school experiences have already given up hope by the junior year, especially if they are years behind in reading and math. Nevertheless, a few dropouts who might have left school permanently have taken advantage of this program.

Since 1987 the High School Graduation Incentives Program has also operated, giving secondary students (twelve years old and over) who are falling behind in school, pregnant, or addicted to drugs a chance to attend a "nonprofit, nonpublic, nonsectarian school that has contracted with the school district of residence to provide educational services."[27] Although the program has been in effect only a short time, around six hundred students each year have already taken advantage of it.[28] From 1990, elementary school students became eligible for the program as well; and in the fall of 1991, sectarian schools became eligible to sign contracts with districts. If a school signs a contract, it is required to accept any student who seeks admission through this process, subject to space available.

Milwaukee

In contrast to Minnesota and Vermont, where tax deductions and vouchers have been around long enough to be taken for granted, the experimental voucher system in the city of Milwaukee was the center of controversy even before it began in 1990. The conflict originated when Rep. Annette "Polly" Williams sought passage of a bill in the Wisconsin legislature to authorize vouchers. Republicans and conservative Democrats favored the proposal, while liberal Democrats fought it. Throughout the first year of the system's implementation, the conflict persisted as the result of a lawsuit brought by the teachers' union, the Milwaukee schools superintendent, and the head of the Milwaukee NAACP. Aiming to overturn the legislation by any legal means, they attacked it in court on technical grounds (the use of a budget bill as the vehicle for passing the legislation).

As a result of the difficulty experienced by those trying to get the legislation passed, the voucher plan in Milwaukee was watered down by compromises. In its first year, funding was provided for only one thousand students. The voucher amount (around $2,500) was based on average daily attendance (ADA) funds that the state would have provided to children in the district anyway. Local property taxes were not added to the voucher amount. Schools accepting voucher students could not charge extra tuition; few of the families benefitting from vouchers could have paid much on their own. Students were not allowed to redeem their vouchers at sectarian schools or at any of the nongovernment schools in the suburbs of Milwaukee. The choice of possible inner-city nongovernment schools was extremely limited. Finally, the uncertainty surrounding the future of the plan may have made some parents reluctant to take advantage of the offer.

A unique feature of the Milwaukee plan is that it is limited to children from low-income families. This includes children of several races. The plan sets aside half of the funds to pay for students from poor families already enrolled in nongovernment schools. The other half of the money is intended to help students transferring from government schools. Despite the fact that the funds are targeted to the poor, the program has been attacked as inequitable. This suggests that opponents completely ignore differences in types of voucher systems.

Given the legal turmoil and uncertainty over the future of the program, it is not surprising that schools and parents have been dubious about participating. Even in the absence of uncertainty, those who want to take advantage of the program would face another difficulty: inner-city private schools have a limited capacity for new enrollment. Only a long-term, stable policy that stimulates the creation of new schools will enable the voucher plan in Milwaukee to fulfill its goal of expanding opportunities for the poor.

Conclusion

No political jurisdiction has a pure, unfettered voucher system in which parents are provided by the government with school fees and allowed to determine how they will be spent. But a number of countries (including many that I have not mentioned in this chapter, such as Japan, England, Spain, Italy, and Sweden) provide some funding to nongovernment schools. In these countries, any distinctions between schools are based not so much on the source of funding as on the religious or ideological orientation of the curriculum. With the exception of the remaining Communist nations, the United States is one of the few countries in the world that draws such a sharp line between government and nongovernment education.

Experiences in Europe and elsewhere emphasize the importance of guaranteeing the freedom of nongovernment schools from government control. Many Americans who favor independent schools are fearful that a voucher system will bring increased regulation of sectarian education in its wake. The history of state support of Catholic schools in France suggests that the threat is real if the proponents of truly independent schools are not strong enough to win a clear victory over those who insist on government regulation and control. Where the political will exists, however, the problem can be solved by amending state constitutions to limit the power of state legislatures to regulate nongovernment schools.

Examples such as the experiences in British Columbia, Australia, and Minnesota indicate that very limited state subsidies of nongovernment schools are not beneficial to those who cannot afford the tuition. If the poor are to gain access to independent schools on a large scale, the amount of the voucher should be close to the level of existing per-pupil spending. In Denmark, where the system most closely resembles a voucher system, there is no perceived social stratification between government and nongovernment schools.

The Nazi insistence on wiping out schools that provided a center of loyalty independent from state and party is a reminder that centralized political control of education can easily become antidemocratic. The protection of minorities and of dissenting viewpoints depends on the strength of institutions other than those controlled by the state.

Although there are a few states in the United States that have permitted government funds to be used in nongovernment schools, the barrier of sectarianism remains an obstacle to the generalization of this policy. The nation's first voucher system for low-income families, in Milwaukee, was hobbled from the start by the political necessity of eliminating parochial schools from eligibility. It has been said that anti-Catholicism is the anti-Semitism of American liberals, and evidence of this attitude is most plainly seen in the history of education.

In the aftermath of Vatican II, mainline Protestants have increasingly found common ground with Catholics. Europe has shown how sectarian differences in education can be resolved. In each case, the support of separate schools has led to greater rather than less loyalty to the nation. When parents are allowed to determine the method of transmitting culture to their children, they have a stake in the system that enables them to do so. European democracy has been strengthened by separate schools. Americans could learn from the example.

PART IV

ANSWERING CRITICISM OF VOUCHERS

A lthough many of the criticisms of education vouchers are nothing more than shrill invectives against those who would "destroy the public schools," there are also some reasoned arguments against vouchers that should not be dismissed lightly.

Chapter 11 considers three different ways in which critics have charged that vouchers will contribute to inequality: differences in information, disparities in capital investment, and separate socialization experiences. (Significantly, the critics do not explain why vouchers would be worse than the present system. They simply show how inequalities would develop under a voucher system.) My response in each case is that there are likely to be differences in the ways people of different social classes make use of vouchers, but differences are not necessarily inequalities. Unless we assume that middle-class behavior patterns are the norm for everyone, there is no reason to be alarmed by the mere existence of variations in the way people learn about and operate programs or learn in school.

Chapter 12 addresses the complex problem of selectivity. In simple terms, critics of unregulated vouchers have made the assumption that if schools are allowed to choose who attends them, "hard to teach" children will be left out of good schools. Specifically, they charge that the poor and minorities will be relegated to public schools as dumping grounds. Again, this charge is not made in a comparative framework. Public schools already have subtle ways of ridding themselves of troublesome children or of confining them to dead-end classes and programs. By contrast, there is considerable evidence that outside of a small number of elite private schools, admissions criteria are used more often to create for students a sense of a school's importance than to exclude those who are different.

In Chapter 13, I respond to those who fear that vouchers portend a fragmentation of the country into feuding factions, each with its own school. The issue is whether schools should serve diverse communities or a single national community. The increasing uniformity of government schools suggests that they are based on some form of assimilationist ideology. By contrast, vouchers could potentially establish a number of diverse communities. Paradoxically, the freedom to establish a school reflecting one's own philosophy is likely to bind people into a community more effectively than students' forced attendance at an institution with which families have a negative connection or no connection at all. There is a growing need for closeknit communities in which youth can participate and gain a sense of belonging. A large and abstract national community cannot fulfill that purpose.

The problem of establishing accountability is the topic of Chapter 14. Some people imagine that political and professional control are necessary to maintain accountability. They argue that a voucher system would remove the constraints that ensure quality in education. They ignore the fact that accountability to parents has proved to be an effective quality-control mechanism over the years in existing nongovernment schools, while accountability to objective standards or to professional authority has not guaranteed high-quality education in government schools. The job market remains an external method of evaluating the results of the educational process. Public schools are unresponsive to changes in the job market because they are not accountable for their failure to prepare students for work. Vouchers can increase students' future ability to satisfy employers, but there must be a reciprocal exchange. Employers could motivate students by clarifying the skills they will need to gain employment. Finally, however, to avoid leaving behind those who cannot keep up with the current pace of technological change, our society must consider a fundamental restructuring of the economy in ways that preserve community rather than destroying it.

Chapter 15 brings Part 4 to a close and sums up the issues raised in the book as a whole. In concluding this volume I review prospects for broadening our choices and examine some of the political motivations that underlie the ongoing conflict over vouchers.

11

Problems of Information, Investment, and Socialization

Having considered the foregoing chapters, a skeptic might admit the values of nongovernment schools—their capacity to build community, their ability to specialize, their small size, and their purpose and distinctiveness. This skeptic might also agree that government schools could be improved by providing them with autonomy, particularly in the area of personnel. Yet, the question might still remain as to whether the benefits of autonomous schools will be available to the child whose parents are poor or illiterate.

The issue is not whether vouchers would improve the education of all children in ghettos or in dysfunctional families. No policy will end human misery. The appropriate question is whether the lives of a significant portion of children will be better or worse as a result of vouchers. In other words, the effectiveness of vouchers should be discussed in a comparative framework. Most of the critics of vouchers offer no new alternatives; they assert that vouchers will not work, but their proposed alternative is to recycle the failed solutions of the past. They ignore the debilitating climate of despair that permeates the present school system.

Critics seldom explain why they believe that lower-class families will be unable to make use of vouchers. In fact, some of the arguments to this effect are based purely on middle-class arrogance: the assumption that people without money are not bright enough to know what is in their own best interests. However, critics have raised three significant institutional issues concerning the effects of vouchers on the poor:

(1) disparities in the information available to people of different social classes, (2) disparities in capital investment in neighborhoods of different classes, and (3) the divisiveness of sorting children according to parental preferences that reflect the biases of their social class.

Information Differences

Critics cite the potential failure of information to reach parents as an obstacle to the effective functioning of a voucher system in a poor neighborhood. If this were a problem, it would be an even greater obstacle for recent immigrants with limited English ability. This is an important issue because the principle of choice depends on knowledge by families. If parents have no way of finding out about educational options, the whole purpose of the voucher system will be defeated.

In Chapter 3, I discussed briefly the experiment in the Alum Rock school district in the early 1970s, in which parents were allowed to choose among alternative programs in the public schools. Researchers found that differences between the designated schools or classes were relatively insignificant, thus limiting the range of true choices. At the same time, information about the choices was limited to that provided by the school district. In the absence of any nongovernment schools in the program, there were no alternative sources of information such as advertising or radio announcements. Nevertheless, a study of the information system in the Alum Rock experiment does provide some insights about the ways in which families make choices.

The Alum Rock study discovered the unsurprising fact that wealthy, educated parents had more awareness of the program and had access to more modes of information than poorer, less-educated families. Sixty-seven percent of the poorest families knew of the existence of the program, but 74 percent of the nonpoor knew about it. That difference does not point to a socially significant disparity. Moreover, initial differences in knowledge about the program disappeared over several years.[1]

The Alum Rock study does not address the issue of how the spread of information under a true voucher system would affect the poor. Michael Olivas has discussed more extensively than any other analyst the potential inequity in voucher plans stemming from lack of information.[2] He concludes that vouchers are unworkable for the disadvantaged as a result of this "fatal flaw." I challenge that idea in the remainder of this section.

Some of the problems to which Olivas alludes are transitional issues, such as the confusion likely to ensue in the initial stages of a voucher system concerning eligibility for federal funds for categorical programs targeted to low-income students. This type of problem, which can be alleviated over time with admininstrative experience, should not be lumped together with more fundamental information barriers.

Olivas argues that developing the information necessary for "diagnosis of language minority children for bilingual education classes" would pose serious administrative problems. Yet parents are fully capable of determining whether or not their children need bilingual education without complex diagnostic procedures.

Certainly diagnostic information is important. Diagnostic tests help pinpoint latent learning disabilities at an early age, so that children do not need to fail in school before being helped. But government schools are not currently evaluating students on a routine basis, and a better diagnostic system should probably be instituted whether a voucher system is adopted or not. Yet, given the history of falsely classifying minority students as learning disabled, the diagnostic system might need to be managed independently of the schools. If diagnostic tests are carried out, parents should have the power to determine what sort of schooling is most appropriate to deal with any problems that are identified. Otherwise, diagnosis becomes one more tool of control by school officials.

Olivas also claims that it would be difficult to provide information to the children of migrant farmworkers about all of the schools along their migration route. Yet migrant children would probably be best served by using vouchers to hire traveling tutors to work with several families. The failure of the current system to provide this sort of simple solution is just one more indictment of an organizational structure that is more concerned about jurisdiction than education.

As evidence of the failure of the poor to learn about services available to them, Olivas points to the underparticipation of very poor families in social service programs (food stamps, housing subsidies, family assistance, elderly benefits, and others) as a result of poorly designed information networks. In most of those social programs, a person must undergo a bureaucratic ordeal to demonstrate eligibility. In some cases, the information system for social programs has been deliberately designed to be obscure so that even eligible people will be deterred from signing up for the benefits. After several discouraging encounters with state and federal bureaucracies, the poor often stop seeking information unless they can see some tangible reward from it. Those who see themselves as powerless do not generally value information because it seldom helps them gain control over impinging events.[3] Universally available education vouchers would function differently. The poor would gain a sense of power as they exercised choices, even if they were not optimal choices from the perspective of a middle-class professional. If eligibility were guaranteed and easy to establish, the poor could expend their energy on real choices instead of administrative rules.

In addition to these misguided concerns, Olivas also raises a legitimate concern that official-looking printed information materials would be a barrier to families with limited literacy. Even Olivas recognizes, however, that the poor are not impervious to information; they simply prefer oral communication: "Yet the poor do develop sources of information, particularly in minority communities, where the ethnic press, bilingual advertising, minority radio programming, church-related channels, and folk-grapevines are employed to disseminate information."[4] He cites one case of a program for nursing mothers where "95 percent of the women had heard of the program by word of mouth," despite an extensive effort to contact potential clients with printed media.[5] Olivas inexplicably concludes from this reliance of the poor on oral sources that dissemination of information about voucher programs will be "difficult, if not impossible." A more logical conclusion is that presenting information through alternative media should be mandated for a voucher system.

The more fundamental problem, according to Olivas, is the complexity of information that would have to be transmitted about each school in order to permit school choice to function.

> The voucher proposal would require, at minimum, information on costs (over and above the voucher amount), transportation, racial composition, teacher quality, curriculum, school history (e.g., college-bound graduate rates), entrance requirements, adequacy of facilities, location, school environment (e.g., open classrooms or traditional arrangements), and many more qualitative and quantitative criteria.[6]

From this set of requirements, Olivas determines that the data system about alternative schools would be so complex as to baffle poor families. He foresees the processing of forms as complicated as the Financial Aid Form of the College Scholarship Service, which is far more difficult to understand than federal tax forms.

Olivas is correct in his perception of the dangers of allowing a bureaucracy to destroy the voucher system by overloading it with information requirements. If a family came to see a counselor in a low-income neighborhood to find out about options, however, the information could be presented in terms that responded to the family's concerns. Neighborhood workers who could make home visits could be trained as counselors, thus making the process less alien and ensuring the availability of counselors with appropriate non-English-language skills. Nor would counselors have to work full time. They could function like notaries or tax preparers who only work part time upon request by a client.

Realistically, what would be the questions that a family might want to know about alternative schools? In many neighborhoods, the first concern in the minds of parents is whether the children will be safe, a question entirely overlooked by Olivas. Are there many fights at the school? Is there on-site supervision before and after school? What does the administration do to stop drugdealing at the school? Beyond trying to ensure the physical survival of their children, the parents will have a variety of other concerns. Will they teach my child to read and calculate? Do teachers demand hard work? Will there be enough order in the class to make learning possible? Do the teachers primarily rely on books or do they teach the children to learn from experience too? Does the curriculum conform with or at least not violate the values of our family?

Finding the names of schools that fit these criteria would not be extremely difficult. Any nearby school that offered safety, discipline, and a reasonably adequate academic program would quickly gain a good reputation. The names of well-known local institutions, such as churches or community groups, that chose to start schools would be easily accessible by oral transmission. Those institutions might also serve as information clearinghouses and counseling centers to help parents make wise decisions. If a YMCA can put on a program to help children raise SAT scores, it could just as easily provide a program to help parents choose a good school. There is no reason to assume that family decision making would have to occur in isolation.

Moreover, given the general preference of parents for neighborhood schools, the range of realistic choices for most families would be among three or four schools, a number that would not tax the ability of an oral culture to make fine distinctions in matters of quality. For high school students, those choices would be more dispersed and distinctive than for elementary schools (thus requiring more information), but by that age, students themselves have a better idea of what they want from school, assuming they have been provided with enough positive experiences in earlier years to want schooling at all.

A small number of parents in low-income neighborhoods would still choose to send their children on long busrides to more affluent areas even after safe, orderly, and effective schools were established in their neighborhoods. For those parents, the criteria described by Olivas would become more critical. Perhaps there would need to be regional counselors as well as local ones in order to make wider options available, especially for high school education.

Olivas also ignores the fact that orally transmitted information is in some ways better than the typical announcements of bureaucratic organizations. In particular, information provided by personal reference would have the advantage of containing a judgment about the quality of schools that would be more useful than lists of objective data. Parents of all social classes are interested in subjective evaluations of schools by people they trust, although middle-class parents may be more swayed by numerical measures (test scores or college placement rates) than lower-class parents. The latter are likely to be skeptical of statistical averages, not because of greater mathematical sophistication, but because of a tendency to trust concrete, personal relations more than abstract, impersonal ones.

One of the most disquieting aspects of Olivas's analysis is its disregard of the inequities in the transmission of information in public schools as they are presently constituted. In elementary schools, minority and low-income children are channeled into low-achieving tracks without the approval of parents. The counseling system in the typical high school offers so little curriculum information that students in the bottom track complain that they are often not even told what classes they need to meet graduation requirements. Under current conditions, schools make choices for students and keep parents in the dark. Even an imperfect but open information process under a voucher system would be better for parents than a closed paternalistic system that categorizes students with little or no parental participation.

Capital and Emotional Investment in the Inner City

The second characteristic of low-income areas that has generated skepticism about the benefits of vouchers for minorities and the poor is the lack of capital investment in their neighborhoods. In recent years, inner-city areas that are heavily populated by ethnic minorities have been subject to negative investment, or a reduction in the number of manufacturers, wholesalers, and retailers.

This experience gives rise to fears that relying on vouchers will leave poor neighborhoods devoid not only of shopping centers but of decent schools as well. Henry Levin, an educational economist, argues that

> there would probably be far fewer sellers of educational services to the children of the poor [than to the children of the rich]. . . . The schools that now serve the poor could not hope to obtain the better teachers since such personnel would probably prefer to teach for more money in a middle-class school rather than for less money in a ghetto school.[7]

Vouchers, Information, and the Poor:
Experimental Evidence

The poor can make intelligent use of information when confronted with choices under a voucher system. That competence has been clearly demonstrated in experiments with vouchers for housing and daycare.

In the Experimental Housing Allowance Program (EHAP) in the 1970s, low-income families in a dozen American cities were supplied with housing vouchers.* The vouchers produced less segregation by race and class, and at less cost, than direct provision of housing. The experiment revealed that the level of formal, preparatory counseling services made little difference in clients' ability to rent housing that met federal standards. But "responsive services"—assisting people when they asked for help—made a significant difference.†

The poor have also shown they can make effective use of daycare vouchers. Projects in Hudson County, New Jersey, and Hennepin County, Minnesota, enabled low-income parents to use vacancies in privately run daycare programs.‡ Each participant received information about alternative programs. Contrary to a demeaning image of the poor, parents made concerted efforts to find good daycare. They engaged in comparison shopping before enrolling their children in particular programs, and they paid extra for quality care once they received a subsidy.

In these voucher programs the poor made efficient use of information from responsive assistance to find housing or from direct advisory services to choose day care. Perhaps an education voucher system should experiment with information systems of both kinds to determine which better meets the needs of families.

---

* Joseph Friedman and Daniel H. Weinberg, eds., *The Great Housing Experiment* (Beverly Hills: Sage Publications, 1983).
† William L. Holhouser, Jr., "The Role of Supportive Services," in Friedman and Weinberg, p. 120.
‡ Barbara Catterall and Carol Williams, *Voucher Subsidized Child Care: The Hudson County Project* (Trenton: New Jersey Department of Human Services, 1985). Barbara Scoll and Roger Engstrom, *Hennepin County Grant Purchase of Child Day Care through a Voucher System: An Evaluation and Use of Technology* (Minneapolis, Minn.: Hennepin County Community Services Department, 1985).

Although the general disinvestment in low-income areas gives this argument a certain plausibility, several invalid assumptions are being made. Specifically, educational results are not simply a function of investment. Schools are not established nor do they become successful on the same logic as businesses.

First, churches and other groups have founded inner-city schools and subsidized them for decades. With money from vouchers, those schools could expand, defunct schools could be reopened, and new schools could be established.

Second, money is important in running a school, but educational quality does not directly correlate with school expenditures. Average spending per student in constant (inflation-adjusted) dollars increased by almost 60 percent in the 1960s and by almost 30 percent in each of the following decades.[8] If money could buy excellence in education, students in 1990 would be two and a half times better educated than students in 1960. Yet there has been stagnation or decline instead of improvement.

Third, Levin suggests that all the good teachers will choose the suburbs if vouchers enable more independent schools to open in those areas as well as in the inner city. This prediction would carry weight if the experience in government schools formed a sufficient basis for its assumption. It is true that the public schools offer no incentive for a caring teacher to remain in a school in the ghetto. The teacher not only has to have the energy to deal with the students; he or she must also do battle with an administration and a union that are concerned primarily with money and power. Under those circumstances, government teachers are understandably eager to teach in schools with little threat of violence and with highly motivated students who share the middle-class values of the teachers. Presumably, urban public schools are frequently forced to accept teachers who are less competent or more burned out than the ones suburban schools are willing to hire.

By contrast, however, many excellent teachers are likely to choose to work in nongovernment or autonomous government schools in low-income areas if the schools are well-managed and safe. Although money is a factor that influences teachers, it is far from decisive. Some are already willing to work for a salary 20 or 30 percent below the public school salary schedule in order to participate in institutions with a sense of purpose and accomplishment. Even if suburban private schools pay high salaries, some dedicated and inspired teachers will choose to work in ghetto schools where parents and community leaders strive to achieve a vision for their children. The fact that independent schools would be permitted to hire teachers without credentials would also increase the supply of eligible educators.

Fourth, the danger of losing good teachers to the suburbs, even if true, would not be decisive. In autonomous schools, individual teaching skills are not so critical to success as school organization and management. Effectiveness in independent schools depends on visionary leadership, consistency of curriculum, a collegial relationship among teachers, and a positive school environment that enhances overall student performance. In short, in the private sector and in a few public schools, good schools create good teachers more than the other way around. By contrast, successful practice in the disjointed atmosphere of a public school demands a virtuoso performance from teachers. In the absence of consistency of purpose, there is no structure of support for high-quality teaching. A government school builds its reputation on the basis of the social class of its students or a few outstanding teachers. Only rarely is the success of a government school attributed to excellence of management or the ability of the faculty to work well with each other or with parents.

Fifth, the analogy that Levin makes with other businesses is largely misleading. Manufacturing has declined in cities due to changes in the world economy. Knowledge-based companies have moved to the suburbs to locate near highly skilled workers. (That is another reason why improving the qality of urban education is crucial.) Wholesale and retail businesses have left low-income areas because the level of effective demand (that is, the money consumers are able to pay) is less than in rich suburbs. The relevant comparison would be to ask whether retail stores would open in low-income neighborhoods if the government offered families a voucher to buy consumer goods. A retail or wholesale business requires a large initial investment in the form of inventory. By contrast, a school necessitates little up-front capital because most of the expenses are for wages. The primary requirements for opening a school are strong leadership and a reliable stream of clients who can pay tuition consistently. Vouchers would provide the funds, and there is no evidence that visionary leaders are lacking in low-income areas.

Given the low costs of starting a school, vouchers would provide residents with the opportunity to create their own institutions in conjunction with community organizations or as extensions of daycare centers. They would not have to wait for outside investors to deem the market sufficiently profitable. Such activity takes place on a small scale already in the absence of any subsidy. The schools described in Chapter 8 are but a few of the hundreds of community-based schools that have been established despite financial obstacles in low-income or minority neighborhoods.

In summary, the claims that poor children and youth will be harmed by the failure of an education "market" to invest in the low-income areas of a city are greatly exaggerated. The possibility of finding talent in poor communities and using local available skills, rather than disregarding them, is only likely to occur under a voucher system. Human resources, which our current bureaucratic sytem of education allows to atrophy, could be profitably invested rather than squandered.

Vouchers and Class Socialization

The third argument made by critics of vouchers regarding their presumed negative effect on the poor is the danger that they will widen the social gap between the middle class and the poor. Henry Levin recognizes that existing schools already sort students according to social class by means of residential patterns and within-school tracking. Yet he believes that vouchers would exacerbate that tendency by matching schools and students even more precisely. "Under the existing system there are at least some poor children in middle-class schools and some middle-class children in working-class schools. But to what degree would this be true under a system of educational vouchers?"[9] Levin proposes that integration by social class would diminish as a result of choices made by parents because of the differences in values of middle-class and lower-class families.

> It is reasonable to believe that lower-class parents will select highly structured schools for their children that emphasize a high degree of discipline, concentration on basic skills, and following orders. In contrast, . . . [middle class parents] are more likely to stress a great deal of freedom in the school environments of their children with a heavy emphasis on student choice, flexible scheduling, few significant rules, and light enforcement of those that exist. . . . If parents choose those school environments that they believe will maximize the probability of success as defined within the context of their experience, the working-class child will be provided with schooling that will reinforce working-class orientations while children from higher classes will attend schools that will orient them toward the upper echelon of the occupational hierarchy.[10]

In other words, Levin is charging that vouchers would reinforce the process by which values are transmitted from parents to children. Schools would thereby strengthen class inequalities rather than challenging social-class boundaries as the liberal theory of education envisages.

As with other critical perspectives on vouchers, there is a grain of truth in this argument. Its validity, however, is based on categories that treat social classes as homogeneous units. Levin implies that all middle-class families prefer unstructured, open-ended education while all lower-class families prefer more rigid and authoritarian patterns of instruction. Yet there is considerable variation among families of each social class in the type of educational environment they want for their children. In one study of choices that parents made about sending their children to inner-city Catholic high schools, both lower-class and middle-class parents emphasized academic reputation as their primary reason for choosing a school, although academic excellence was the first choice for the lower-class parents less often than for middle-class parents.[11] The main difference was that the poorest families chose discipline more often than the middle-class families did. One might attribute this to some inherent class difference, but it is also due perhaps to hard-won experience about the importance of a school with a more structured environment than street life offers.

Contrary to Levin's expectations, limited evidence indicates there would be less segregation by social class in a system of school choice than in a system of assigned attendance. In a unique study, Ellen Anderson Brantlinger interviewed parents from lower-class areas in a midwestern school district.[12] Most of the respondents were white, although there were a small number of black families represented. Thus, her study revealed how the poor feel about integration by social class in the absence of any racial considerations. Her findings showed that lower-class families prefer schools with a mixture of social-class backgrounds. They did not like the social-class segregation that assigned their children to schools in which almost everyone was poor. Therefore, under a choice program, presumably at least some would select a school that was partially composed of richer families. It is interesting to note, however, that 80 percent of her respondents insisted that they did not want to send their children to the predominantly high-income schools on the other side of town, either. Lower-class parents knew of too many cases in which rich children had tormented poorer students, and they did not want their children to suffer that indignity. They wanted social integration, but only if it occurred on terms that helped their children rather than hurting them.

Indeed, much of the discussion by middle-class critics about social-class segregation by vouchers displays the very prejudice that most upset the respondents in Brantlinger's study. There is a strong assumption in these criticisms that there is something inferior about the moral values of the lower class. The poor endure these snubs in the public arena quite often, but especially so in the context of school politics where subcultures clash most openly.

Children from minority and low-income communities need the assurance that success does not require them to reject their families and culture. Yet that is the message they receive in school. As long as schools are perceived as institutions that are run by and for the middle class, operating in the ghetto like embassies of a foreign power, loyalty to the rules of the school will appear to be treason. Alternative ways of organizing formal education could make school a less antagonistic environment for these children.

Levin's criticism is especially ironic because his arguments about school vouchers are directly contrary to his arguments on behalf of vouchers for adult education and training and his support of community control of education. In his criticism of vouchers for children, Levin argues that even if nongovernment schools fulfill private or individual- istic aims better than government schools, they do not fulfill the public or social goals of schooling.[13] He claims that vouchers will lead to social and economic divisiveness and that they will fail to guarantee adequate political socialization. Yet in 1979, Levin proposed that everyone over the age of sixteen be provided with an entitlement (that is, a voucher) for occupational training or academic education.[14] He considered this approach equitable and not socially divisive, and he gives no explanation as to why children younger than sixteen should be treated in a quali- tatively different manner. Also, in 1971, Levin favored community- controlled schools despite arguments that they would be socially divisive. In his article on community-controlled schools, he observes that a central feature of democratic education is the mixture of children of all backgrounds, but that schools based on geographic communities would be racially separatist.

> In this respect the community school appears to be both socially divisive and antidemocratic. But blacks are frequently among the first to point out that the concept of the "melting pot" has been a historical myth as far as black Americans are concerned. The fact is that blacks presently live in a separate society, and neither legal remedies nor the putative good will of the white community have been able to give them housing, education, and other social activities in an integrated setting. . . .
>
> If we assume that a healthy America requires the full economic, political, and social integration of blacks and whites, the real question is how to achieve such a goal. Paradoxically, black cohesive- ness appears to be a more effective strategy than any other existing alternative. The reason for its promise is a simple one. This society responds much more quickly to demands from powerful constituen- cies than it does to requests from weak ones, and black community is the basis for black political potency.[15]

Having so eloquently made the case for tactical separatism to achieve integration on the basis of equality, not submission, Levin makes it hard to understand why he is so resistant to vouchers.

Conclusion

The issues raised by critics and discussed in this chapter all conceive of schools as modern, impersonal organizations narrowly focused on cognitive skills. If we imagine, however, that schools can emerge from communities based on personal loyalty, many of these issues lose their relevance.

The problem of providing information to poor families is minimized if schools form communities and knowledge spreads by word of mouth. Most of the details required by parents to judge schools are best conveyed among people on the basis of trust. Lower-class families may seek different kinds of information from middle-class families, but the former are capable of discovering exactly what they want to know.

The general lack of capital investment in low-income areas does not signify that investment in education in those areas under a voucher system will be inadequate. Visionary leadership may be the most important form of investment needed in starting a new school. Community groups and neighborhood organizations will be able to supply much of the social capital that is needed. Little other up-front capital is required as long as a funding source such as vouchers exists.

Concerns about the potential separation of social classes and the reinforcement of rigid patterns of behavior are greatly exaggerated and misguided. Lower- and middle-class families will overlap in their school choices, although complete integration by social class is unlikely under any circumstances. If given the opportunity to choose, lower-class families will not choose schools where they are patronized and treated as less than full members of the community. The fact that values may be different, on average, in middle- and lower-class families is no reason to continue supporting a school system that alienates the children of the poor. The best way to improve the morale of lower-class children in school is to give them the chance to attend schools where they can feel they are participants in determining their own future, not passive objects whose lives are decided by others.

12

Selective Admissions and the Question of Elitism

A dvocates of the public schools criticize nongovernment schools for being elitist. Yet, as pointed out in Chapter 8, a surprising number of low-income families send their children to nongovernment schools. In the 1987–88 school year, approximately 5 percent of the children in nongovernment schools came from families with incomes below $10,000 per year.[1] Considering that the upper-income limit of that group was only about $833 per month, the prospect of paying even minimal tuition on top of rent, food, and other basic expenses must be daunting indeed. In fact, it is a sign of the desperation of poor families to leave the public schools that *any* family below the poverty line would choose to forgo free schooling and send a child instead to a school where tuition must be paid. This is a heroic act entirely overlooked by those who criticize nongovernment schools as elitist.

Critics refer to the fact that nongovernment schools enroll disproportionately large numbers of white, upper-middle-class children. This charge contains just enough truth to be misleading. Nongovernment schools are slightly elitist in the sense that high-income families use them more than low-income families, but that is only because most of the latter cannot afford tuition without government help. The fact that the poor do not make more extensive use of private schools is hardly surprising. Indeed, one of the main rationales for vouchers is that they would enable low-income families to overcome the financial barrier to admission to most nongovernment schools.

Only a very small proportion of private schools charge tuition higher than the amount spent per pupil in public schools (that is, the approximate amount that would be provided under a voucher system). As of the school year 1985–86, median tuition at private schools nationwide was $1,100 per year.[2] Breaking this estimate down, the median was $825 for Catholic schools, $1,200 for other sectarian schools, and $3,000 for nonsectarian schools. Approximately 6 percent of private schools charge no tuition. The high-tuition schools accounted for only about 12 percent of the total number of nongovernment schools (2,702 out of 21,625). In other words, the image of private schools as expensive and elitist is not borne out by the facts.

In fact, the public-school system has been more elitist than the private sector. In states lacking tax-equalization plans, rich suburban districts often spend several times as much per child as the poorest districts. Even when spending is equalized between districts, as in California, elitism remains by virtue of residential segregation that corrals the poor into some schools and the rich into others. Although private schools often provide need-based scholarships, suburbs are not in the habit of offering rent subsidies to enable the children of poor families to attend their elitist public schools.

Ironically, federal tax laws have historically reinforced this suburban subsidy by allowing a tax deduction for property taxes. When tax rates were progressive and the marginal tax rate for a wealthy family was 50 percent or even 70 percent, then the equivalent percentages of the property taxes they paid were effectively reimbursed by the federal government. This made it relatively painless for rich suburbs to increase spending for schools from property taxes: the nonrich were subsidizing them. By contrast, the tuition paid by a lower-income family at a low-cost nongovernment school is not deductible.[3] Thus the federal government has promoted public elitism but not private egalitarianism.

Entrance Requirements and Elitism

The issue of entrance requirements is more complex. The point that voucher opponents make repeatedly is that public schools are required to accept everyone, whereas private schools are able to pick the least troublesome and most motivated students. This argument that nongovernment schools cream the best and leave the rest for the government schools goes back to the original debates over the common school. Horace Mann attacked independent schools for drawing away the "best scholars" from the schools under his command.[4] Yet, then as now, this assertion was not backed with evidence.

Informal Selectivity in Government Schools

It is not quite true that government schools are required to accept every student. A government school is required to accept only those who can afford a house in the district. If a student is expelled from a school district, he or she cannot automatically gain admission in another district. The receiving district has some discretion. Even if a student is admitted to a school, the authorities can, if they wish, find cause to remove or transfer a "difficult" student. Although some schools apply this power inappropriately, it is clear that they should have the right to expel students who endanger the lives of other students and that acceptance at another school should be voluntary. I want merely to emphasize that government schools are not truly all-inclusive and that there are children under the age of sixteen who are not in school because they have been excluded from school.

Government-school officials are not honest about the surreptitious methods of controlling who enters and who leaves. They are also dishonest about the fact that once inside the school, students are not guaranteed an education. Schools still operate tracking systems, and high-track classes have admissions criteria as tough as those in private schools, but those criteria are seldom public or formal.

According to Sally Kilgore, public schools with a number of college-bound students set "minimum grade point averages and standardized test scores for college track or honors programs."[5] These public schools operate as if they had elite private schools within them. A disproportionate number of those who are excluded by these elitist practices in both the public and private sectors are economically poor.

Selectivity in Nongovernment Schools

Ironically, the selection process in nongovernment schools probably involves less creaming than in the public sector. The assumption that selectivity in nongovernment schools is elitist ignores (1) the small fraction of total private-school enrollment formed by expensive, exclusive schools; (2) admissions criteria in nonelitist schools that merely ensure a match between the interests of the school and the interests of students and parents; and (3) the value of rituals of selectivity to strengthen the pride students have in themselves and their schools.

Inner-city and parish-based Catholic schools, for example, are unselective in their admissions with respect to income or academic ability, but they are selective in requiring a sincere interest in academic work. Many of them do not exclude students on the basis of the initial screening. They merely use it as a device to ensure that parents and students will take the school and its academic program seriously.

In other programs, such as Montessori or Waldorf schools, selectivity is associated with specialization more than with elitism. The admissions process is designed to ensure a fit between the principles of the school and the goals of parents. Some schools have a clear policy of refusing to admit students whose parents see nongovernment schools primarily as a refuge from integration.

John Coons and Stephen Sugarman, the authors of *Education by Choice* and of several efforts to place a voucher initiative before California voters, believe the state should regulate admissions criteria of private schools that accept vouchers. In an effort to protect the rights of unwanted students, they propose a variety of possible "open enrollment" policies that would require nongovernment schools above a certain size to admit some of their students nonselectively. They fear that the use of ability tests to select among applicants will lead to a practice of screening out the children of low-income families and of minorities.[6]

The concern of Coons and Sugarman is out of proportion to the dimensions of the problem, however. I will divide their misgivings into two parts. First, they are worried about the existence of elitist schools that will evoke resentment among those who are not admitted to them. Second, they suggest that some students will not gain entrance to any school if schools have control over admissions.

On the first issue, Coons and Sugarman ignore the distinction between the role of schools as educational institutions and as prestige systems. The mere fact that some schools set high entrance standards to guarantee a name for themselves does not prove that they provide high-quality instruction. The empirical evidence suggests that relatively nonelite Catholic schools teach students at least as effectively as selective private schools. Denying children access to elite schools does not mean denying them a decent education, as long as entrepreneurs and community groups continue to establish schools for underserved children as they have in the past.

The evidence from limited- or controlled-choice plans, which make no provision for new schools, indicates that merely reserving positions in elite schools for disadvantaged kids is not especially helpful. Schools geared toward middle-class students with high motivation to succeed may be worse than useless for inner-city kids who may need more structure and external motivation. As Abigail Thernstrom suggests in her study of choice programs in Massachusetts:

> In terms of SAT scores and the like, the Andover public school system beats the Lawrence system by a mile. But if the Andover school system were to take over the Lawrence schools, or if teachers and

administrators in the two communities were to trade places, the result would not be a rapid improvement in the educational performance of Lawrence students. At least, such improvement is very unlikely. The affluent suburban school systems around Boston to which Metco students are bused have not done as well as expected with that inner-city population. Those systems do not dispense educational magic; they have no educational secrets known only to them. Arguably, they are *less* equipped to deal with the students who bring a host of social ills to the schools and are already woefully behind in reading by the early grades. T.C. Williams High School (in Alexandria, Virgina), described by Patrick Welsh in *Tales Out of School,* was extremely successful with its students from the middle class, but it did miserably with low-income children.[7]

This might seem to be a case of blaming the victim once again, but that is not the case. Elsewhere Thernstrom cites a study showing that focus schools—ones that have clearly defined goals, such as Catholic and some magnet schools—have been effective with inner-city children.[8] These schools establish firm rules and demand both academic excellence and personal responsibility. They also provide personalized attention. If we are truly concerned about the poor (and not merely engaged in symbolic concern), the distinction we should be paying attention to is not between elite and ordinary schools, but between focused schools and ones with no distinctive character.

Interestingly, Coons and Sugarman themselves recognize and accept the range of admissions requirements for postsecondary schools. Since a college degree or a trade school certificate has become a prerequisite for an increasing number of jobs, one might reasonably conclude that any problems of elitism should be addressed initially at the postsecondary level. Yet few Americans object to the existence of schools such as Harvard or Stanford as long as other schools can provide a decent education. In fact, given the emphasis on research at many famous universities, undergraduates often receive better instruction at smaller, less well known schools. According to research conducted by Ernest Pascarella and Patrick Terenzini, there is

> no evidence that selective admissions policies, expansive libraries, big endowments and scholar-filled faculties have any real influence on the amount of knowledge or skills students acquire on campus. . . . More important than selectivity or prestige is the quality of teaching, amount of faculty-student interaction, what courses are required, and what kind of programs are offered.[9]

The authors do note, however, that higher future earnings are related to the prestige of the university attended. School prestige is probably related to the ability to select highly motivated students, however, not to the effectiveness of a college.

What is lacking in the elementary and secondary school market is the equivalent of the many small liberal arts colleges that provide a solid education without tremendous prestige. That is precisely the niche that could be filled by the introduction of vouchers.

The existence of prestige schools with competitive admissions (and no exceptions for low-achieving students) may even give ambitious students a goal for which to strive. As long as admissions criteria are not used as a subterfuge for exclusivity on the basis of race or social class, they can act as a spur to hard work, just as they do in Japan. The problem at present is that most private schools, whether or not they have competitive admissions, are financially out of the reach of most low-income families. There will be an incentive to strive for the highest levels of academic achievement only when selectivity is combined with adequate financial aid.

In their criticism of elitism, Coons and Sugarman also argue that entrance tests are likely to be an unreliable measure of ability and that their use would unfairly discriminate against the poor. If, however, tests do not accurately distinguish between the talented and untalented, then relying on them should have a democratizing influence. If tests are unreliable measures of ability, then ability levels will be evenly distributed between schools that use tests as the basis of admissions and those that do not. That will not prevent some schools from having more prestige than others, but few have suggested that public policy should attempt to equalize that ineffable quality.

The second issue that Coons and Sugarman consider is far more serious. On the basis of pure speculation, they raise the specter of children being left out of decent schools altogether if the state does not intervene to protect them:

> If no private providers appeared who catered to otherwise unwanted children, this could lead to enormous family frustration. Even if such providers did appear, this could lead to the establishment of special dumping-ground public and private schools, which would be sorry places indeed.[10]

This is a peculiar concern coming from advocates of a measure that would enable a variety of new schools to come into existence. Their statement implicitly reflects a zero-sum view of education: the notion that if one child receives a quality education, it is thereby denied to other children. Since the actual educational process is largely a function of creating conducive relationships and motives, however, the benefits received by one child do not detract from the benefits received by other children.

The concern expressed by Coons and Sugarman about last-choice schools serving as a dumping ground is valid for limited-choice programs. In the public sector, in order to create magnet schools, other students *must* attend zoned schools to make the magnet schools attractive. In that case, the system is structured to make zoned schools into dumping grounds. This would not be the case, however, if families were able to choose among nongovernment schools, including new ones established in response to demand. The only significant question would be how quickly new schools could come into existence.

The theory of a dumping ground is also flawed because it presupposes a multitude of children that no school would admit except under duress. Who are these mythical children who cannot gain admission to schools that are no more selective than a daycare center? (The issue is not whether children are able to gain admittance to a first-choice school, but whether they can select a school with which they are moderately happy. The fact that popular schools with waiting lists are likely to be replicated will make this easier.) The children that the typical teacher complains about are ones who are disruptive, not those who are slow learners. For a teacher who wants to feel successful the latter may be less enjoyable to teach than bright children, but they are not likely to be ostracized from schools.

A more plausible case could be made that disruptive or defiant students would be left out of schools, but, upon examination, even this argument is weak. In a worst-case scenario, all of the troublemakers might be put in the same school. That is already the case to some extent with detention schools and in continuation high schools. That pattern would probably be mitigated instead of enhanced by vouchers, however. Some kids cause trouble because the schools they are forced to attend seem like prisons to them. Few kids start school resistant. They learn to hate school, because it is dull, because of the regimentation, and because they have little or no say over their assigned school or class. If they had options that fit their interests and motives, they would be likely to behave in ways that would increase their chances of admission. Children's negative behavior is not a fixed quantity; it varies in response to the way they are treated.

There are in fact some people who enjoy the challenge of working with kids who are bright but defiant or who are angry and humiliated because the school has not helped them learn to read. Ideally, improving elementary schools by increasing access to schools of choice will reduce the number of high school students with attitude problems. Even if no such change occurs, however, there will always be some people who like

to work with teenagers in trouble. Many of those people do not have
teaching certificates, so they have not had a chance to work in schools.
Vouchers can be used by nontraditional teachers who want to bring
education to kids where they live rather than forcing the kids into an
alien environment.

Requiring schools to admit specific types of students does not
alleviate the hypothetical problem of dumping grounds. Compulsory
desegregation led to dual systems within the walls of supposedly
integrated schools. If schools are forced to accept students who do not
conform to their selection criteria (for example, a child who needs
structure in a school that emphasizes self-direction), they might react
by establishing dual systems with special programs for the exceptions.
Unless the courts want to micromanage schools on a day-to-day basis,
they cannot prevent this kind of response.

Positive Aspects of Selective Admissions

The positive features of selectivity are often ignored in the desire to
achieve the elusive goal of fairness. Allowing schools to be selective
achieves two goals: it heightens morale by creating a distinctive identity
and focus of loyalty, and it enables schools to specialize.

Heightening Morale and a Sense of School Identity

A school that lacks control of admissions can easily be demoralized by
a small fraction of students who do not agree with the purpose of the
school or who are simply not ready for it. A school with open admissions
(that is, without even an admissions interview to determine the com-
patibility of school and family in terms of desire to learn) may be unable
to enforce any standards. If a teacher assigns homework and 15 percent
of the students consistently ignore it, the teacher may eventually assign
less homework. The least motivated and most alienated students can
effectively determine many of the crucial academic policies of the school.

The main purpose of selectivity is not to weed out applicants. A
number of Catholic schools that require some form of admissions
screening take virtually all of their applicants. Rather, the admissions
process is a way for some schools to say, "This is what we are about.
We are serious about education. If you want a place to play, go elsewhere.
If you think learning is important, we welcome you." Presumably, the
school that explains its purpose from the start also has a right to remove
students who refuse to live by its rules. Otherwise, the initial agreement
or contract that the school implicitly makes with the students and their
families cannot be maintained. Nevertheless, anecdotal evidence

indicates that schools that function as a community are very reluctant to expel students. Most of these schools bend over backwards to work with students in order to retain them rather than simply giving up on the hard cases.

Failing to create and maintain some clear purposes and standards is a disservice to students, particularly to those who are likely to face discrimination in the job market. The real world of employment and of street-life is harsh. If children believe they are entitled to attend a school, no matter how badly they behave, they will feel contempt for the rules. School, particularly high school, then becomes a place to "hang out" or, for the enterprising, a place to sell drugs or carry out gang vendettas.

By contrast, selectivity is a way to instill pride in a school. As Sally Kilgore discovered in her research, many nongovernment schools create "an aura of selectivity . . . as a mechanism to encourage certain positive beliefs about the applicant, his or her potential peers, and about the school itself. . . . In these instances admission procedures are ritualistic events, not screening devices."[11] Whether a school or program uses academic standards or some purely ritual form of the admissions process, selectivity is vital to the success of any school that wishes to develop a distinctive character and create a sense of belonging for its students. The single most important entrance requirement in many nongovernment schools today is an indication of a willingness to abide by the rules and to work. Without common consent to that norm, a school will dissipate its energies as government schools do and fail to motivate students to live up to their capacities.

If selectivity is positive in nongovernment schools, it should also be permitted in government schools, once they have become autonomous and vouchers have given families alternatives from which to choose. As James Coleman argues:

> There is no reason why public school principals should have less freedom to expel students than does a private school headmaster: the child has a right to attend school at public expense, but not a particular school. With a voluntary clientele, a public school can establish rules and require that students live up to them, just as can a private school.[12]

The idea is not to exclude a student from school altogether but to make it clear to all parents and students that schools are educational institutions, not baby-sitting services.

The students who have the most to gain from selectivity are low-achieving or average students in bad schools who are ignored under current policies. The lack of selectivity in schools harms the typical student from a lower-class background who is in a school permeated by violence or low standards of behavior.

Under a voucher system, presumably a student would have several schools from which to choose: from one to three government schools plus several nongovernment schools. If a student were not accepted at any of them, and if he or she were truly interested in obtaining an education, the parents could join with similar parents to hire a tutor for a few hours of lessons a day.

Specialization

Even without this tutoring option, there is reason to believe that selectivity will be positive rather than negative under a voucher system. Above all, new community-centered schools will define niches and meet an unsatisfied demand.

Some schools will specialize in students who are unwanted elsewhere: the apathetic or unmotivated students who have no strong interests or academic abilities. Many of the students who cause trouble in the impersonal environment of a standard public school would be welcomed in a school that channels students' energies constructively. That was the experience in New York City's District 4, where one of the first schools established under the choice program, the B.E.T.A. (Better Education Through Alternatives) school, was designed for disruptive students. As Sy Fliegel, the architect of the choice program, has said:

> B.E.T.A. is the kind of alternative school that is always supported by everyone, even those people who do not support alternative education. Basically it says, "Give us your troubled youngsters, and we will take them off your hands." . . . The B.E.T.A. School was a success from the first day it opened. We were able to provide these "acting-out" youngsters with a learning environment that accepted them as individuals who had difficulties adjusting to the regular school program. Three years after opening, it was cited as a model program.[13]

Another specialization that is of interest to some ethnic minorities is education that emphasizes the history and cultural heritage of their ancestors. Some schools might thereby appeal almost exclusively to a single ethnic group. A strong case can be made that this type of school would be constitutionally acceptable as long as it were one of several choices available to families, in contrast to the segregated schools to which minorities have been involuntarily assigned in the past.

A third form of specialization involves limiting a school to boys or to girls. One sociologist has proposed that the main factor in the superior performance of Catholic students in the study by Coleman and Hoffer may be the large proportion of single-sex Catholic schools. Students in those schools consistently outperform those in mixed-sex Catholic schools as well as students in public schools.[14] This analysis suggests that the adolescent subculture, which shifts the focus of school from academics to social interaction, may be partly responsible for low levels of academic achievement. If that is the case, then any school that attempts to minimize that subculture (instead of catering to it, as the public schools do) may be able to raise academic performance. Undoubtedly this form of specialization will not appeal to many families, but subsidizing school options could make it available to a larger number of students.

Conclusion

In summary, nongovernment schools are selective, but rarely elitist or exclusive. Instead, they use selectivity to develop distinctive charac- teristics and school spirit. The process of interviewing prospective families is used to create a sense among students that they are important and that the school will demand a lot from them. Financial aid to low- income families will reduce the disparity of access to private schools, but it will not reduce their selectivity. Selectivity merely implies specialization as well as the potential for creating a community on the basis of common values and interests.

Public schools have traditionally had selective entrance require- ments, based on the ability of families to buy or rent in the attendance area of a school. Furthermore, government schools have long had selec- tive programs based on academic ability, but these criteria tend to be relatively invisible because they are internal and seldom made explicit.

Selectivity allows schools to specialize in terms of ideology, academic content, or type of student. Without it, every school will tend toward generic uniformity. In order for a school to maintain its identity, it must have some means of ensuring that only those parents who agree with its principles send their children to it. The public-policy issue is thus not whether schools should be selective and specialized but what criteria are legitimate for those purposes. Increasing specialization of both government and nongovernment schools could help the millions of students who are now ill-served in one-size-fits-all schools. Rather than harming the poor and minorities, selectivity could enable them to receive a far better education than they do at present.

13

Community or Communities

E ducation vouchers would enable groups that share a commitment
to common goals to create and strengthen institutions based on
those shared ideals and personal loyalties. In other words, vouchers
would promote the revival of distinctive communities.

Opponents of vouchers believe that loyalty to limited communities
will detract from commitment to the larger pluralistic community. They
worry that schools based on ethnic identity will not teach children to
participate in an integrated society and that restrictive ideologies will
undermine the capacity of children to think for themselves. Those critics
fear parochialism. They promote uniform schooling based (in theory at
least) on liberal principles of critical inquiry and intellectual tolerance.
Finally, the proponents of a national identity stress the value of
promoting assimilation by mixing children from all walks of life in the
school setting.

At the extreme, those concerned about the need for a unifying school
system or curriculum point to Ulster (Northern Ireland), Quebec, Sri
Lanka, Lebanon, and Yugoslavia as examples of what can happen if the
binding forces that hold a nation together are loosened by tribalism or
separate identities. But these examples have no bearing on the issue
of education vouchers. Almost every society has tensions among ethnic
groups within it. The willingness of diverse groups to work together
depends on whether their rights are considered and whether the
dominant group treats minorities fairly. Violent conflict arises when
one group is economically and politically suppressed for long periods

by another group in power, not because groups are allowed control over their own institutions.

The proponents of distinctive communities believe that strengthening the family, the neighborhood, the church, or any other particular source of identity does not interfere with a healthy degree of loyalty to the society or nation as a whole. Developing a love of one's nation (rather than blind obedience to its leaders) depends on fostering concrete experiences of commitment to an immediate community. Those experiences can then be generalized into a devotion to the common good. Thus religion-based schools that inculcate in students a sense of social responsibility are more likely to produce citizens who operate out of civic duty than are public schools that promote individualism and indifference to moral issues.

Mandatory school attendance does not instill commitment to a nation's values, particularly if it alienates families by suppressing particular group affiliations in the name of national solidarity. As Europeans learned after centuries of religious wars, tolerating diverse communities (and giving state aid to their schools) promotes social harmony far more effectively than imposing a single institution on everyone.

A voucher system would foster national loyalty by honoring differences instead of denying them. Schools that emphasize traditions and ideas that are neglected in government schools and that represent unorthodox values would come into being. The state or nation that made those options possible would obtain the respect and appreciation of families that now feel their views are excluded. As John Coons observes with regard to vouchers:

> The effective way to create social trust is for society itself to display that trust [in parental choices]. . . . Our institutions will finally begin to generate allegiance to core values when they have come to deserve it by respecting the dignity of ordinary citizens.[1]

Promoting participation in distinctive communities can strengthen rather than weaken loyalty to a larger, inclusive nation. Catholic schools have produced citizens at least as loyal and patriotic as government schools. In a nation of communities, national unity can thrive in the midst of multiple loyalties. Particular traditions need not be displaced to establish an encompassing national identity.

Mixture and Separation

By creating greater opportunities for families to choose schools with particular traditions, voucher proposals raise the question of how people of diverse backgrounds can live together as one nation.

At one end of the spectrum of opinions are those who regard the United States as a "melting pot," a nation in which gender, religious, ideological, regional, and ethnic differences are and ought to be dissolved into a unified American character. From this *assimilationist* perspective, education should inculcate this character in all children in order to bring about their complete assimilation into the national culture. Historically, the national culture was defined in terms of white, Anglo-Saxon, Protestant values. Those who did not conform to those values were taught to feel ashamed of their differences.

Most liberals have embraced *multiculturalism,* which proposes that the school curriculum should include all the cultures that have contributed to American society.[2] The precise nature of that inclusion is ambiguous, however. Some multicultural curricula treat non-Western culture as ornaments on a tree, as if various traditions provide anecdotes that are interesting, but peripheral to the central Euro-American culture. Philosophical, medical, agricultural, and legal systems of other cultures are consequently viewed as "backward" unless they contributed to modern Western modes of thought. This approach to multiculturalism is as ethnocentric as the pure assimilationist view. A second concept of multiculturalism regards no tradition as the standard or norm by which to judge others. In other words, it regards America as an eclectic society that encompasses many subcultures. A curriculum developed from this perspective would therefore seek to avoid presenting any cultural values as normative except purely univeral ones. Yet this raises the contentious question of whether any universal values exist. Given the tendency to regard one's own values as universal, this view can easily revert, in practice, to the assimilation of minorities into the majority value system.

A third perspective on diversity in American society is *cultural pluralism.* This view emphasizes and values the continuing distinctiveness and autonomy of subcultures, particularly those based on ethnicity. Unlike multiculturalism and assimilationism, which regard American history as many streams flowing into a single river, this model might describe subcultures as streams that flow in separate channels. Although some of the proponents of this view favor complete economic and social separatism, the majority prefer what John Higham and Nathan Glazer have called *pluralistic integration.* This involves separate "ethnic nuclei," which are to be "respected as enduring centers of social action," but also maintains "a common culture, to which all individuals have access."[3] As Glazer points out, this approach has the virtue of reflecting what ethnic groups want (the availability of groups with distinct identities) without "the dismantling of what is after all a great, integrating, culture. . . . "[4] Michael Novak pithily summarizes the pluralistic personality as one that is "deep in its own traditions and yet open to those of others."[5]

According to cultural pluralism, true multiculturalism is possible only if members of subcultures nurture their distinctive traditions. The dominant culture tends to ignore or feel threatened by the histories of subcultural groups except when those histories reinforce and contribute to the myths of the dominant culture. For the assimilationist and most multiculturalists, there is no place for autonomous traditions. Pluralism, by contrast, stresses the tactical value of limited separatism, a choice that many families make in order to retain a historical tradition and a personal identity within it.

The assimilationist vision of a single national community is the implicit rationale for compulsory attendance in common schools and for busing to achieve integration. But policies that mechanistically combine diverse groups have failed to bring about social harmony. By bringing together children of different races and classes without initiating programs to overcome mutual suspicions, government officials have made a travesty of their goals of assimilation. By papering over differences and conflicts, public schools have exacerbated the problems of separatism and produced none of the hoped-for benefits.

Competing Views of Democracy

The debate about the nature of the national community and constituent communities relates to competing views about the nature of democracy. If democracy meant primarily acceptance of the will of the majority, then a network of state schools representing the interests of the dominant culture and social class would be democratic. But democracy is not based on conformity to the will of an all-encompassing national community. Instead, democracy means protection of the dissenting views of diverse communities. The common school, which seeks to break down particular loyalties in order to strengthen devotion to the nation, is a potentially dangerous instrument of authoritarian government. The fact that Horace Mann drew his inspiration from ancient Sparta and contemporary Prussia, rather than from states that valued dissent, should give us pause in celebrating the institution he founded as "democratic." The simplistic connection between public schools and democracy is also brought into question by the fact that the Nazis, the Ku Klux Klan, and Communists all shut down alternative (particularly sectarian) schools that were not controlled by the state.[6] As Hitler's secretary, Martin Bormann, explained the Nazi position on educational diversity:

> The creation of an ideologically objective school system is one of the
> most important tasks of the Party and the State. . . . In many cases,
> particularly where public schools are available, private schools can
> only be regarded as superfluous, especially those which cannot be
> regarded as ideologically objective. The pupils should be put in the
> public school system and the private schools closed.[7]

Of course, the proponents of the ideology that defends compulsory attendance at common schools do not bluntly favor domination of the weak by the politically strong. Their argument can be made more plausible and seductive if one draws a distinction between democracy as the balancing of competing private interests and democracy as the agreement on transcendent goals of a society as a whole. Politics based on interests is regarded by many Americans as undignified and corrupt, an activity carried out by venal power brokers; politics based on values is identified with high moral principles. By classifying their goals as universal and egalitarian, the assimilationists, who control the education system, portray themselves as being devoted solely to the common good. From the perspective of those who value distinctive communities, however, the government-school managers are hiding their political and economic interests behind pious words about children.

Another important question in a democracy is the extent to which unpopular views will receive protection. Critics of vouchers fear that schools with unorthodox philosophies will flourish. But it is a mistake to imagine that morally repugnant ideas can be prohibited by compelling students to attend public schools that officially repudiate those concepts. Some teachers in government schools quietly promote racism and sexism with impunity. They are not answerable to anyone as long as they are not too blatant. Is that deceitfulness preferable to a situation in which the issue would be brought into the open and challenged? Under a system of choice among schools with distinctive ideologies, parents would at least be able to decide if they wanted their children exposed to ideas they regard as pernicious or hateful. Fundamentally, the question for schools in a democracy is whether dissenting communities within the national community should receive support. Those who see the national community as frail and brittle fear that aiding diverse points of view by funding distinctive schools will shatter our society. They imagine that extremist ideologies will threaten society if they are widely disseminated. By contrast, those who see the national community as thriving on competing ideas believe that diverse schools will strengthen society. They regard extremist ideologies as dangerous only if they are suppressed and allowed to thrive on secrecy, paranoia, and a sense of being unjustly treated. More importantly, bad ideas are dangerous only if a group has the power to coerce everyone to follow them. We should therefore be more fearful of state-imposed ideology than of independent voices, however much we may disagree with them.

The Urgency of Strengthening Communities

The debate over uniform schooling is ultimately about whether the state should try to exercise beneficent control over people's private lives. On the subject of abortion, conservatives say yes. On the subject of education, liberals say yes. A society filled with moralists who want to run others' lives and make their moral decisions for them is bound to be miserable. In the case of both education and abortion, the question finally boils down to whether society ought to allow parents (or potential parents) to weigh the moral consequences of a decision themselves.

The alternative to state control is not necessarily pure individualism. Historically, people made important life decisions in the context of a community of personal affiliations that imposed moral expectations and sanctions on its members. That tradition can be revived by shifting from devotion to an abstract national community to reliance on particular, local communities. In other words, rather than expecting the state to resolve our disagreements with each other on moral issues, we should learn to rely on participatory communities to guide the behavior of individuals.

If we cannot at present trust our fellow community members to make sound decisions, we as a society need to develop better mechanisms to make collective judgments. The heavy hand of the law is less effective in dealing with many social problems than the older traditions of community sanctions.

Communities of shared values have the potential to deal with a range of conditions facing kids and their parents. For example, sex among teenagers leads to hundreds of thousands of pregnancies each year. The sex education classes in government schools have no apparent impact on either sexual activity or contraception, presumably because they present sexual issues in a purely neutral, amoral fashion, as if there were no social or moral implications. In the absence of a moral community, teenagers are largely on their own. The problem is compounded because the school where they spend much of the day is probably not offering any moral leadership. Nor do kids in most schools feel any sense of moral responsibility to the school or any expectations from its faculty and students.

In public schools, the only clear value message is that all fundamental values are purely subjective and weighted equally. No text, no

The Lone Ranger Doesn't Bring Community

The American heroic myth is that the problems of society can be solved by the strong individual with no ties to community. This is not only the story of the Lone Ranger; it also describes the activity of David Toma, a former New York City detective who now devotes himself to visiting high schools for two or three days per school, talking to kids about drug and alcohol abuse. The message is another "Just say no," but it is packaged in a highly emotional presentation that is modeled on a religious revival meeting, complete with testimonials and a request for those who repent to come forward at the end.

I witnessed his impressive performance when Toma came to the high school where I was teaching. To my surprise, dozens of kids stood up, crying, in front of the whole school and confessed they were drug or alcohol abusers and wanted help. The second day, hundreds of kids sat for hours inter-acting with Toma as he told stories of kids in trouble. Classes were effectively suspended while Toma met with groups in the auditorium, but students also wanted to talk about the same issues in the classroom. It was an emotionally intense time at the school.

Listening to the emotional stresses that kids face alone, with little adult guidance, I finally understood why they felt so intensely the lack of community on campus. Despite the existence of school clubs, athletic teams, and other groups based on common interests, most kids seemed to feel like strangers at school. Toma's impact revealed the absence of the support structures that young people need to deal with status competition, loneliness, and shame.

Unlike the Lone Ranger, however, Toma does not solve problems. He stirs them up, and then rides off into the sunset. Schools are left to follow up with more collective remedies, and some probably start programs on campus. But public schools are particularly individualistic in orientation. The average kid at school may stay sober for a few weeks or even months, but the underlying conditions remain in place.

What is required is a restructuring of schools to overcome the anonymity students experience. Officials are unlikely to contemplate that sort of radical change because it would dis-rupt the routines by which their schools operate. Thus the responsibility for creating community is left to the kids them-selves, and they lack the power to do much to bring it about.

set of ideas, no tradition is treated as normative. A few teachers may offer their personal views about how to make value judgments, but the school itself is formally neutral. That amounts to a subtle indoctrination about values. In addition, the curriculum teaches the importance of independence, of not sharing ideas with others. Students are responsible for their own work. Children are not encouraged to feel any responsibility for each other's lives and well-being. There are no group expectations or standards to which kids can hold each other. "No man is an island," but kids in school are surely treated as if they were. They are left in an existential morass, because they have been asked to figure out every aspect of life on their own. When adults abdicate the duty to provide boundaries, kids find themselves in trouble with sex or drugs, and they may have no adult from whom to seek advice if they are afraid of talking to their parents. We should not be surprised if a girl becomes pregnant or a boy becomes a weekend alcoholic in this atmosphere of vague acceptance of any action.

The structure of modern schools teaches children to think of morality as a purely individual issue. With the exception of being taught not to steal and to avoid violence toward each other, children are provided with no sense of responsibility to a tangible community. In other words, they learn that their actions are governed or limited only by the laws of the state.

By contrast, children who grow up in the midst of a community learn to feel answerable to the expectations of a concerned group of peers and adults. This helps them to consider the consequences of action in advance. The child or young adult imagines the other people in his or her life who will be hurt by an omission or commission. No amount of abstract discussion of moral issues or dialogue with therapeutic professionals can substitute for the sense of being imbedded in a group of people who care and who demand responsibility in return.

What Constitutes Community?

I have spoken about creating community, but it is surely a mistake to imagine that communities can be wished into existence. In fact, that is precisely what is wrong with public schools, at least in urban areas. They are artificial communities, like diverse clans or tribes thrown together as nations by European diplomats who determined territorial boundaries in the nineteenth century. In government schools, coerced attendance, not loyalty to a common ideal, keeps the various communities under one roof. There are presumably still some rural areas where schools function as an integrated part of a genuine community, where

parents of all social classes rub shoulders and talk with each other about
the life of the school as well as other community institutions. But the
pseudo-community remains the norm of school life in America.

The pseudo-community arises in urban areas as a result of what
Robert Bellah and his coauthors have called "lifestyle enclaves."[8] With
that term they are referring to people banding together to mingle with
others of their social class and to protect their private interests against
the rest of society. They have in mind primarily upper-middle-class
residential areas that are designed to allow people to enjoy themselves
while ignoring the decline of the rest of society.

In a school based on a lifestyle enclave instead of a genuine
community, parents unite only with those who are similar socially and
racially. They view their connection to the school entirely in contractual
terms: a relationship between an individual and a bureaucratic
institution. They view the purpose of the school solely in terms of
preparing children to engage in status competition by achieving high
scores on national tests. The parents regard the school as nothing more
than a collection of students being provided with the technical skills
necessary for success in American society.

Undoubtedly, some of the schools that would be formed as a result
of vouchers will also constitute pseudo-communities or lifestyle enclaves.
Since the dominant commercial culture continues systematically to
undermine community life for the sake of mobility and efficiency, it
would be naive to imagine that any institution could completely
withstand the current. But if inner-city Catholic schools and ethnic
schools are any indication, schools can survive against the tide of self-
centered, individualistic achievement by serving as the catalyst for the
formation or sustenance of a community.

A true community exists through its common memories and
anticipations, in other words, the stories it tells about itself. These
traditions are the binding forces that create group loyalty. Collective
memory gives an identity to the community and to each of its members.
Thus it is important for ethnic and religious groups to have the
opportunity to present American and world history in their own terms.

The family is the first layer of community. It passes on both
idiosyncratic traditions and larger cultural traditions. Neighborhoods,
linguistic communities, religious bodies, and other intermediate
institutions form—or should form—the next layer of community. The
national community is the next layer of community or group loyalty,
and for many people the most inclusive level. Others profess allegiance
to an international community.

Historically, people were born into a community or multiple communities. To some extent that is still true. One is born into a particular

family and in a particular nation. However, intermediate levels of community are in need of renewal. Without assigned membership in any enduring community, individuals are thus burdened with status anxiety and the need to strive to establish an identity.

The teenage years are the beginning of the quest for identity and thus the quest for belonging to some meaningful community. That is why it is important for a school to have a clear, though not rigid, identity that it can offer to students.

In that respect, schools based on religion have an advantage over other schools because they draw on a history that transcends the life of the individual school. If a child wants to know who "we" are, there is either a book or an oral history that provides guidance. A school that explicitly defines itself in religious terms offers to children a chance to participate in a tradition that is larger than the immediate community present within the school.

Ethnic schools have a similar advantage because they can draw on histories of nations or linguistic groups. Immigrants from Korea or Laos or El Salvador may fear that their children will entirely lose touch with their roots in a school that reflects the dominant culture and that gives only lip service to "multicultural awareness." Some families find that an afternoon or Saturday program in the history of their people is sufficient. Others want to establish day schools in which their ethnic heritage influences the way in which every subject is taught.

The need for independent ownership of schools and of the curriculum is especially important for many African Americans. The harsh regimens of slavery were intended to obliterate their past. Subsequent historiography has denied the value of African history and of the contributions of African Americans. Their search for identity and community cannot simply be tacked on to the Euro-American view of the world as an afterthought. When public schools in African-American neighborhoods continue to ignore black history, those schools are actively suppressing the development of community and committing cultural genocide.

To some extent, schools can begin to fashion their own traditions. The fact that not every school will have deep roots in preexisting traditions should not discourage experimentation. Our society has been so fragmented by individualism that a demand for instant realization of community cannot be fulfilled. Nevertheless, incipient communities could establish schools as inheritors of specific traditions.

Pluralism and the Liberal Ideal

What I have written thus far will have little bearing on the substantive fears voiced by some liberals: the prospect that socially conservative ideologies may be taught in the classroom. Those critics are anxious that a whole group of kids would pass through school believing in a literal interpretation of the Bible, the subordination of women, and the absolute truth of a particular brand of Christian thought. Yet one need not subscribe to conservative Christian views to accept the right of parents with those beliefs to state support in the education of their children.

Opposition to particularistic traditions is inherent in the modern belief that science alone imparts truth and that its truth is universal. From that perspective, competing claims to truth from other philosophical or religious traditions are simply naive heresies that will eventually be banished.

Yet the scientific method itself amounts to faith that statistical significance supersedes existential or ethical significance. Science is but one tradition among many, a tradition that enhances prediction and control but does little to aid apprehension of ultimate meanings. Many of those who believe in this one true faith contend, however, that everyone should be forced to adopt it. That this view is antidemocratic appears to be irrelevant to those who hold it. As a social institution, science gives legitimacy to those who continue to limit the freedom of religious or intellectual minorities to pass on their traditions to their children.

Although modern science and conservative Christian doctrines seem at complete odds, they are similar in their literal-minded understanding of truth and their view of themselves as the ultimate and final answer. In debates over what students should learn, extreme positions are often treated as the only possible perspectives. Yet there are alternatives to both a literal interpretation of Genesis and a theory of evolution that explains change in terms of purely mechanistic and purposeless processes. In a unitary school system, only one perspective can be presented as truth. A pluralistic array of schools under a voucher system would open the door to competing views of the nature and purpose of humans.

The Future of Pluralism

Pluralism is of utmost importance in a society where we have strong disagreements about foundational issues. A genuinely pluralistic society is colorful, not merely from a variety of skin tones, but because of competing ideas. The First Amendment's prohibition of a national church might be read as a warning against any official orthodoxy. Pluralism involves competing ideologies, no one of which gains enough support to dominate all others. Our society can endure competing absolute ideologies as long as the adherents of each are willing to accept limits to their power over others.

The irony of liberals who defend pluralism and critical self-reflection is that they are now defending a system of schools that is decidedly illiberal in its construction. Genuine liberalism should not seek to impose the same vision of truth on every child. It should instead promote policies that allow diverse communities to pass on diverse truths.

Conclusion

There is never likely to be a definitive response to those who fear the dissolution of the bonds that form the national community if smaller communities are strengthened. The specter of Sri Lanka or Northern Ireland will haunt those who choose to see the potential for those divisions emanating from our society.

The contest over vouchers puts our national capacity for pluralism and toleration of differences to the test. It directly challenges those who would have us inculcate certain ideas as universally true. It is threatening to those who have a vested psychological interest in trying to guarantee the ideological uniformity of all children.

Yet if we continue to insist on institutions that blot out the distinctive features of subgroups within the United States, we will destroy an important source of national strength. Without communities that keep alive traditions and beliefs, we are leaving children in a barren cultural wasteland with no sense of place in the world. Even if supporting community poses a risk of too much diversity, that is a risk worth taking.

14

Measures of Success:
Accountability in
School and Work

Any reform of the education system will pale in importance if decent employment remains out of reach for millions of young adults. Young teenagers begin learning informally about their prospects for future employment by observing the behavior of older teenagers and people in their twenties. If high school completion does not increase the chances of finding work outside the low-wage service sector, intelligent young people from low-status backgrounds will drop out of high school to work or to engage in illegal activities with high risks and high payoffs. A teenager from a family that cannot provide a financial safety net does not have the luxury of staying in a school program that has a low payoff.

Leaving school early is a crude accountability system that tells schools and employers how students perceive the financial advantages of academic effort. While businesses accuse schools of failing to maintain standards, and schools blame businesses for failing to specify what skills are necessary for employment, students are caught in the middle.

In this chapter, I will consider two separate measures of success: the accountability of schools and the accountability of employers. In both cases, the guidelines for evaluating accountability for performance and responsiveness to changing needs are ambiguous. To whom and how should schools and employers be accountable? At present, the consequences of failure are borne most intensively by students. If schools fail, the staff continues to be paid, but students lose out on an education.

If employment shifts from skilled manufacturing jobs to low-skilled service jobs, prospective employees, particularly from impoverished areas, feel betrayed.

In the long run, economic changes that alter the nature of employment may have a greater impact on education than direct reform of schooling. No exhortation to ghetto teenagers to stay in school will have as much effect as clear signals from the job market that demonstrate the concrete value of academic work.

One way to make schools more responsive to changing economic conditions is to increase their accountability to the people who are affected by school performance. But, as the following section demonstrates, accountability has several possible meanings.

Accountability of the Education System

Calling the education system unaccountable would be inaccurate. It is currently accountable—to the people who run it: teachers' unions, state legislators, school boards, school administrators, national testing services, textbook publishers, and other special-interest groups that vie with one another over particular policies. In many states and districts, the schools are ultimately answerable to the teachers' unions that dominate key elections with campaign contributions and strategically focused political attention.

Schools have also been made accountable to businesses since around 1910 by reforms that have sought to impose the corporate image of efficiency on school management. Earlier, urban schools had been accountable to politicians who handed out teaching jobs on the basis of patronage rather than competence. During the Progressive era, business leaders insisted on the introduction of "scientific management" to government schools. Since business was responsible for the reforms that bureaucratized the education system and made schools responsive to rules and centralized authority, there is considerable irony that business became the most vocal critic of schools in the 1980s. The reforms that saved schools at the beginning of the century had resulted in rigidity and unresponsiveness by the end of the century.

Education reform in this century has been accompanied by a decline in the accountability of schools to parents and communities and by an increase in accountability to education professionals. As in so many other domains of modern life, citizens have been taught to distrust their own experience and to rely on experts instead.

The voucher concept involves a direct assault on a bastion of professional control. Teachers and administrators would retain their professional authority, as they now do in nongovernment schools. Under a voucher system, however, parents, not self-appointed experts, would become the final arbiters of the best interests of children. People's right to choose lawyers and doctors does not reduce the authority of those professions, but it does enable clients to retain ultimate control over the duration of the relationship.

Accountability to Parents

Parents have learned through frustrating experience that complex state laws and union rules do not make schools accountable. Instead those layers of supposed protection for children have taken control of government schools out of the hands of concerned parents.

A voucher system, combined with greater autonomy of public schools, offers the most effective form of accountability: parental oversight. The management of an autonomous school that is chosen by parents must answer directly for its decisions. As few as 5 percent to 10 percent of the parents in an independent school can effectively monitor it for all families, if there is agreement about the purposes of the school.

Accountability to parents can maintain the quality of schools, but taxpayers may be skeptical. Citizens are willing to support higher school taxes if the schools are effective. Yet there is now no generally accepted method of evaluating school performance. Taxpayers have been asked to accept on faith the word of professional educators. Vouchers would require taxpayers to accept parental judgment as a supplement to or even a replacement for professional judgments.

Vouchers will therefore be successful only if taxpayers understand that accountability to parents is as legitimate as accountability to regulations administered by professionals. Sooner or later, however, some taxpayer is going to object to the "misuse" of public funds by irresponsible parents. Our society will then reveal whether it is mature enough to weather that sort of complaint. It is an act of faith to trust the judgment of neighbors when they choose schools for their children. Those who want to run their neighbors' lives will never be satisfied with this form of accountability. But accountability to parents is the most rigorous method of making schools responsible, because no state official can ever monitor the progress of a school as carefully as the parents of the children in it.

Accountability to Standards

There is growing pressure to develop uniform national standards to judge the performance of schools. Already there are calls for national tests that every student would take. In theory, the purpose is merely to allow comparisons between states and between schools. The concept of a national test is hard to resist in principle. Who can oppose the collection of more knowledge about where we stand?

Most of the people who promote testing envisage, however, that it will be used to hold schools accountable. That is a fancy way of saying they want test results to control what happens in schools. The most obvious method is by determining the flow of funds to schools according to test results. This would directly contradict the aim of a voucher system by taking power away from parents. In all probability it would also be inequitable. Suburban schools serving the upper middle class would benefit, while urban schools serving the children of the poor would lose.

Those who propose to use standardized criteria to hold schools accountable are part of a longstanding tradition that seeks to rationalize and standardize schools based on scientific management. Around the turn of the century, administrators began trying to reform schools by applying the management principles that had been developed for industry, such as Frederick W. Taylor's time and motion studies.[1] Others made efforts to carry over economic efficiency criteria from cost accounting to education.

Although the concepts may have been sound in business, their translation into the educational arena was artificial and contrived. Raymond Callahan cites one Massachusetts school superintendent at the early part of this century who proposed to eliminate Greek from the curriculum because it produced only 5.9 pupil-recitations per dollar compared with 23.8 pupil-recitations per dollar in French, 12.0 in science and 19.2 in English.[2] It is not clear why he did not propose that only French be taught since it was the most cost-effective subject.

Although the crudeness of early proponents of efficiency in education might appear humorous today, Arthur Wise explains that the "new" proposals for educational reform of the past three decades are little more than a repetition of the ideas documented by Callahan.

> The model of a successful factory is persistent although less explicit today. Callahan's account gives the reader a sense of how small a distance we have come in this century with regard both to the rationales invoked and the techniques employed. The most tragic aspect of the contemporary effort to rationalize education is the near total ignorance of history which each wave of reform displays.[3]

The idea of a national exam overlooks the ways in which business leaders have been trying for decades to mold schools in the image of industry, with various performance standards. One writer in 1913 observed "A school system can no more find standards of performance within itself than a steel mill can find the proper height or weight per yard for steel rails from the activities within the plant."[4] The author goes on to argue that society in general, and business in particular, needs to dictate the outputs of schools. This call for accountability has been repeated in every generation.

Wise observes that these efforts to increase the productivity of schools by setting goals and assessing progress with measurable criteria (such as tests) have led to a displacement of goals.

> In education there is no more highly developed technology than that of testing. Consequently, tests have come to define the goals of education, and schooling has come to be evaluated by changes in test scores. The generalized goal that schools should teach children to read and do arithmetic is transformed into the objective that children should be able to prove their ability to read and to do arithmetic by taking an examination. The technology of testing forces the belief that there is a cutoff score which reveals a level of performance which is adequate.[5]

The demand for a national system of tests may thus contribute further to the narrowing and distortion of goals within schools.

Accountability to Authority and Rules

As an alternative to accountability to parents or to measurable criteria, there is a third form—bureaucratic accountability—which is the one schools pursue today. Staff members are accountable to their superiors and to the rules of the system. Success is measured not by satisfying parents nor by producing good test scores, but by keeping the wheels of the system well oiled. Those who follow rules and minimize conflict (the main goals of bureaucratic governance) are rewarded. Those who bend the rules to improve student learning may be punished.

When educators claim that a voucher system would lack accountability, what they really mean is that it would involve a form of accountability that is different from what they are used to. Instead of accountability to rules and policies, parental choice defines accountability in terms of satisfaction with what children are learning. Public-school officials intuitively recognize that rule-governed schools do not provide the best educational environment for children and that accountability to parents will undermine the legitimacy of a system based on accountability to authority and rules.

A Business Funds Vouchers

Tired of waiting for government to take positive action on the education of children from poor families, J. Patrick Rooney, chairman of the Golden Rule Insurance Company, took the initiative. In the fall of 1991 his company, along with Eli Lilly and Company, began providing vouchers to pay for 50 percent of private-school tuition for over 700 students from low-income families in Indianapolis. The ceiling on vouchers is $800, and the program includes parochial schools.

Like many other voucher proponents, Rooney sees his program as challenging public schools to do a better job rather than destroying them. But he also thinks that public funds should be provided to parents to determine the best schools, public or private, for their children. In the meantime, he is setting a powerful example that the public-school monopoly will have to heed.

Opposition to the program emerged almost immediately from the Indianapolis chapter of the NAACP and from the local superintendent of schools. Parents, however, seem to like the program. With little publicity and on short notice, 10 percent of the parents in the affected districts with children in public elementary schools obtained applications. As a state legislator for a mostly black Indianapolis district says, "The parents see choice as empowering them to give their children a chance at upward mobility."*

The Educational CHOICE Charitable Trust, which has been set up to administer the voucher funds, has made a three-year commitment to the program. It will continue beyond that time if it raises funds.

As an interesting precedent to this action in behalf of the educationally underserved, the Golden Rule Insurance Company fought to make employment testing more equitable in the 1970s. After winning a suit to force the development of less culturally biased tests, Golden Rule went on to help form FairTest in Cambridge, Massachusetts, the leading testing-reform organization in the United States. Its aim is to make standardized tests less discriminatory and more educationally sound. Since equality of employment is one ultimate purpose of school reform, this direct attack on workplace discrimination is of great importance to the education reform movement.

---

* *Wall Street Journal,* September 6, 1991.

Accountability to the Job Market

When parents demand high-quality education for their children, many of them are operating on the assumption that better education will translate into better jobs. This is a particularly important issue for parents whose own hopes have been denied and who are themselves stuck in low-wage jobs or on welfare. If parents were given a chance to hold schools accountable, preparation of their children for the job market would be uppermost in the minds of many.

When business leaders demand greater accountability from schools, they are overlooking the ways in which employers already exercise a final form of accountability. Instead of blaming schools, business leaders should be asking themselves how they could increase the clarity and precision of the signals they are sending to high school students about future employment prospects. If those signals indicated which skills have a market value, more students would strive to acquire them.

Diplomas as Faulty Measures

One of the main ways that employers hold teenagers or young adults accountable for their educational attainments is by requiring that employees have a high school diploma. Employers rely on diplomas as a basis for screening potential employees: often they do not consider high school dropouts or even those who have completed the GED (general equivalency diploma) test. Few employers take the trouble to determine the achievement level of a student, in part because schools are not set up to respond quickly to requests for high school transcripts. Employers may recognize that graduation from high school is not related to the ability to perform a particular job, but they use diplomas as a device to reduce the total number of applicants.

Credentials are not a good indication of ability, but as John Bishop of Cornell University's Center for Advanced Human Resource Studies has shown, people are paid not according to their ability but according to their credentials.[6] In a study of high school graduates in the workforce, those with higher math and reading scores (by one standard deviation) were actually paid 3.5 percent *less* in the first job than graduates with average scores.[7] Learning is displaced by "diplomaism."

Employers sometimes justify the use of credentials as a measure of employability by arguing that a student who graduated from high school shows perseverance. In other words, they understand that completing a degree does not guarantee that the applicant's ability is greater than that of a dropout. The diploma merely signals that its holder was willing to endure school for twelve years. Secretary of

Education Lamar Alexander implicitly appealed to this understanding of credentials in a televised debate with Senator John Danforth over the Civil Rights Act of 1991. Part of Alexander's rationale was that disconnecting the link between graduation and employment would send the wrong signal to youth who are considering dropping out of school. Danforth argued that excluding potential employees simply because they lack a high school diploma is unfair, as long as they have acquired the relevant skills from some source. In effect, Alexander was proposing that credentials or diplomas have value in and of themselves, regardless of the skills or knowledge they actually represent.

Unless the link between diplomas and employment is broken, hiring policies will continue to place pressure on students to attend standard high schools in order to obtain a degree. Nonformal education, tutoring, apprenticeships, computer-based instruction, and various other alternatives will be neglected if the employment system favors the acquisition of diplomas. The potential freedom that is offered to students under a voucher system may be closed off if "diplomaism" forces all of them through the bottleneck of traditional high schools.

Testing the Skills Required by Employers

Diplomas are an imperfect guide to the ability of youth to meet the demands of the workplace. But are the alternatives—the subjective judgment of employers, and performance or aptitude testing—any better? From the perspective of employers, personal judgment is important in evaluating applicants for hiring and promotion. From the perspective of women and ethnic minorities who have historically been denied jobs because of prejudice, however, subjectivity allows employers to discriminate unfairly on the basis of unconscious biases. Subjective evaluation can never be eliminated from the hiring process entirely, but it can be tempered with more objective factors.

Tests appear on their face to be the least biased form of determining employment. Are they? One of the key equity issues of the past two decades has been the adequacy or inadequacy of standardized tests in revealing the capacity of an employee to perform a particular job.

In response to the Supreme Court's 1971 decision in *Griggs v. Duke Power Company*,[8] the Equal Employment Opportunity Commission (EEOC) issued Guidelines on Employment Testing Procedures prohibiting the use of any test on which minorities or women score lower than white males, unless the employer can prove that the test is a valid predictor of job performance.[9] To avoid the potential for lawsuits in which they would have to prove that their hiring procedures were racially and sexually neutral, some companies hired increased numbers of women and minorities. This practice became the basis of so-called quotas in hiring. Other companies continued to rely on tests, subjective evaluations, and credentials, and they were prepared to defend their criteria as job related. In practice, since most complaints to the EEOC dealt with dismissals rather than hiring, companies were relatively free to hire on the basis of race and gender rather than job-related criteria. The distinction between mandatory and voluntary affirmative-action policies has always been ambiguous. Consequently, the practical importance of the Supreme Court's recent reversal of *Griggs* is unclear. In *Ward's Cove Packing Company v. Atonio* in 1989, the Court shifted the burden of proving that hiring criteria are discriminatory from employers to employees.[10] Symbolically, this represents an end to affirmative action in overcoming discrimination. Symbols are undoubtedly important in shaping the behavior of employers, but the actual impact on hiring remains to be seen.

Whatever effect these court rulings and the Civil Rights Act of 1991 (which partially reversed some court decisions) have on hiring practices, employers need to invest in the development of tests that more accurately measure the complex skills actually needed on the job. Better tests of work skills could help minorities and women in the job market by reducing subjective judgment in evaluations.

Developing better tests would help overcome two decades of uncertainty about equity in hiring criteria. It would also provide students and teachers with a clear guide to the skills, concepts, attitudes, and behaviors that must be mastered to be successful in particular jobs. American College Testing, a company that designs standardized tests, is already engaged in research on "Work Keys," a study of the categories and levels of skill required to perform specific jobs. The objective is to devise both paper-and-pencil tests and performance tests that can be generalized across occupations and ascertain the ability to perform work more reliably than existing tests.

A voucher system would increase the pressure to improve test procedures used in hiring. With more diversity in educational institutions, employers would be forced to rely increasingly on tests. If employers indicated with precision which skills were required for particular jobs, some schools would choose to provide classes to help students pass those tests, just as there are now private classes to teach adults how to pass the test for a contractor's license or a license to sell insurance. Unless businesses devise tests that evaluate necessary job skills, however, the school-to-work transition will remain problematic, even under a voucher system. Neither government nor nongovernment schools can be expected to prepare students for the hiring process unless tests are more carefully designed.

The Changing Nature of Work

Improving tests alone will not suffice to increase the responsiveness of schools to the job market. The changing nature of work also demands an increasingly flexible education system. There has been a rapid shift away from jobs involving concrete, mechanical application of simple procedures to jobs involving increasingly complex reasoning. A voucher system would impel schools to adapt to these new requirements of the job market by rewarding innovative schools that promote creative approaches to learning.

Millions of students are preparing for jobs that either no longer exist or that have been radically transformed. With more and more production work under the control of computers, the task of operators is to understand the software and to know how to access information and use it. Sue Berryman, a Columbia University professor who has been researching this process, explains that work is even more automated than before, but instead of the "hard" automation involved in an assembly line, "soft" automation permits more customized work. Service is important, but it is no longer standardized.[11]

All of the changes in work composition add up to a blurring of the lines between production and management. Almost all employees must now have a capacity for critical thinking. As a result of changes in the speed of response times, workers are now expected to make decisions that would formerly have been left to management. The characteristics of blue-collar workers are increasingly similar to those required of white-collar workers: initiative, capacity to work as a team, ability to solve problems as they arise, and ability to work without detailed supervision. Schools designed to place graduates in an assembly-line work environment are now completely out of step.

In the textile industry, for example, the previously routine job of machine operator is being altered by technological innovation. Operators must understand the functioning of programmable machines, prevent down time, carry out a wide variety of activities, and respond to constant change in demands. As one personnel manager observed, "Our operations change too fast to be able to spell everything out. Operators have to be better able to figure things out for themselves."[12]

This transformation is also occurring in industries that do not manufacture physical products. The job of insurance claims adjuster has combined the previous jobs of messenger, file clerk, customer assistance clerk, claims adjuster, and policy writer into a single position more responsible than any of the previous ones. The new job is not routine. According to Berryman:

The person needs less specific and splintered knowledge and more systematic and abstract knowledge—the ability to understand multiple arrays of information, the rules governing them, and the relationships between arrays. He or she also needs to be able to frame answers to less standardized requests. Insurance companies used to hire high school dropouts or graduates for the five jobs. They now hire individuals with at least two years of college for the restructured claims adjuster job.[13]

The issue is not, however, the years of schooling required, but whether abstract reasoning and higher-order thinking are taught.

The New Curriculum

Changes in the demands of the workplace must be translated into changes in schools. To the extent that the education system has diverse centers of authority and is responsive to outside influence, it will be able to adapt the mode and content of teaching to new requirements. Those conditions can come about only if vouchers, or some other choice mechanism, enable clients (students and parents) to hold schools accountable.

If students are to succeed in the new economic paradigm, they need to learn higher-order cognitive thinking, defined by Lauren Resnick as non-algorithmic, which means that future actions cannot be foreseen in detail; complex, which means the total set of relations is not comprehensible from any single vantage point; and involving uncertainty, multiple and conflicting criteria, nuanced judgment, interpretation, and self-regulated thought rather than imposed meaning.[14]

Students in "average" classes are rarely asked to engage in that kind of thinking in school. Instead, they are rewarded for individually finding predetermined "right" answers. As Resnick points out, schooling has too often been shaped by the false assumption that higher-order thinking must follow years of routine work on "basics," devoid of concepts and open-ended problem solving. Even when teachers are aware of this fundamental problem, there is little they can do since they are required to cover the material in the prescribed curriculum.

School restructuring should aim at enhancing and evaluating the general competency of all students to deal with novel situations, not merely to learn content or specific skills of limited value. According to Berryman:

> Increasingly, non-school settings demand that we cope with the unprecedented and with information that is neither limited nor orderly. . . . School should include learning situations where

students are evaluated, not for having the "right" answer, but for figuring out how to obtain and structure the knowledge needed to create an orderly basis for action.[15]

Measuring school improvement *merely* on the basis of standardized proficiency tests may have the effect of stifling the learning of general concepts or skills that will enable children to become lifelong learners. In contrast to previous efforts to impose order on schools through hyper-rationalization, the task now is to devise a more integrated set of educational processes that will meet the demands of the emerging economy and teach thinking skills that can generalize to all aspects of life.

In the past, schools had no incentive to pay attention to the success of their students in the job market. With a virtual monopoly on the supply of education services, government schools could afford to ignore the signs of failure when their graduates could not find work. That was excusable perhaps in an era when factory jobs required little beyond a willingness to work. Job requirements have been changing rapidly, however, and schools have not responded. There is a growing barrier between low-paying, unskilled work and high-paying, skilled work. That barrier cannot be crossed as easily as before by acquiring skills on the job. Those who receive a poor education are consigned permanently to menial jobs. When schools fail, there are lifelong consequences.

Vouchers offer a new opportunity for public-school students who are now channeled into classes that fail to teach the higher-order thinking skills that Resnick and Berryman describe. Government schools are not designed to adapt to the needs of clients under conditions of rapid change. They continue to track students into mind-dulling classes and cut off possibilities of future employment. Independent schools, by contrast, have never tracked students so rigidly, and they can quickly modify their programs and structures in response to changing external conditions. Schools with a reputation for teaching skills that lead to both social responsibility and productive employment will outlast schools that teach specific skills of limited use in a time of constant technological change. The advantage will lie with schools that aid students in the pursuit of that elusive capacity known as "critical thinking," now more essential than ever in the competitive job market.

Accountability of Employers to Employees

Even if vouchers could succeed in transforming the nature of education, that would not be a sufficient response to the massive economic dislocations that are occurring. Although increasing the flexibility of schools will help them overcome their inertia and help students acquire necessary job-related skills, school reform should not be confused with economic reform.

Political leaders of both major parties contribute to the naive American belief in the power of education to transform society. Their proposals for reviving the American economy in recent years have assumed that better schools can miraculously solve problems that are actually caused by inept management of corporations and of the national government. Faith in school reform blinds them to the fact that worsening economic conditions must be addressed at the level of tax and trade policies, not at the level of education policy. No amount of school reform could compensate for allowing the Japanese to dump below-cost products in the United States in return for support of American Cold War policies or for allowing American corporations to move to low-wage countries while continuing to sell their products in domestic markets.

Instead of asking only how schools might be used to aid the economy, we should also be asking how to transform the economy to give hope to children in school. The expectations that students have about their opportunities for future employment profoundly affect their motivations while they are in school. Youth in inner-city ghettos who have watched jobs relocate from their neighborhoods to suburban business parks or to foreign countries have little reason to believe that hard work in school will help them find work. Unless businesses can show inner-city kids in concrete terms that education pays off, many will give up at an early age.

The final section of this chapter might be understood as a discussion of the limitations of vouchers, not in relation to school reform, but in relation to the larger issue of renewing community life. Education cannot carry the full burden of making modern societies more humane. As we demand that schools be more responsive to the job market, we also need to consider how to make employers more accountable to citizens, particularly those being left behind by the new information technologies.

Racism

An area in which businesses have long been remiss in fulfilling their social obligations is that of hiring practices that discriminate against ethnic minorities. The issue is that structural hiring patterns are discriminatory, not that employers have personal feelings of animosity toward certain ethnic groups. Those structures are deeply engrained in the way businesses operate—just as inflexibility is engrained in public schools.

Structural racism is largely invisible. Consequently, many whites assume that racism has disappeared. There are no longer signs in public places that say, "Whites only." Open discrimination has largely vanished from public view.

In fact, many whites are convinced that the situation has been reversed. They regard affirmative action and other visible symbols of relief of racism as saying, "This job is being reserved for a member of a minority group." In a zero-sum economy, whites competing for those jobs have become resistant to anything that smacks of favoritism. Nevertheless, the resentment that has fueled white backlash against affirmative action has been based on anecdotes rather than comprehensive evidence. Actual hiring patterns do not favor minorities. Discrimination against them still far outweighs whatever small improvements in equity have been brought about by affirmative action.

The Urban Institute recently conducted a study in which they sent ten pairs of men—one black and one white—with equal qualifications to apply for a total of 476 advertised entry-level jobs in Chicago and Washington, D.C.[16] The jobs mostly required only a high school education. All of the pairs were extensively trained to be as similar as possible in demeanor, openness, articulateness, and energy level.

The results should shock anyone who imagines that racial quotas have tilted the balance of power in the marketplace toward blacks. Whereas in 15 percent of the cases the white man was offered a job that was not offered the black man, only 5 percent of the black men received offers not made to their white counterparts. White applicants were more often favored than black applicants in terms of waiting time, length of interview, and encouraging comments received. In a number of cases, whites were steered toward more favorable jobs than the advertised position, whereas blacks were offered less desirable jobs. Overall, a white male is likely to receive preferential treatment in a job search at least 3 times as often as a black competitor with identical characteristics.

Approximately the same 3-to-1 ratio of favoritism was found in an earlier study in Chicago and San Diego comparing hiring of Anglos and Hispanics. In that study Anglos were preferentially offered a job 22 percent of the time, compared to preferential offers to Hispanics in just 8 percent of cases.[17]

With the odds stacked against them, is it any surprise that young black and Hispanic men lose enthusiasm for the search for employment? The most troubling feature of the evidence from these experiments is that this discrimination occurs in entry-level jobs. Those who cannot find work at this level are denied access to future advancement through work. Labor force participation of young black males remains especially low because so many have given up trying to find work.

The problem of employment discrimination leads directly to the failure of children in school. The young learn by fourth or fifth grade from watching adults around them what their life chances are. If racism in employment is not reduced, the advancement of minority children in school will be permanently handicapped.

Structural Economic Changes

Even if there were no racism, structural changes in the economy would be undermining the perceived value of education among lower-class youth of all races. Although the number of skilled jobs has been increasing, the low-skill service sector has been growing at a faster rate. Average real wages have been falling. A twenty- to twenty-four-year-old male *college* graduate in 1986 earned less in inflation-adjusted dollars than a similar male *high school* graduate in 1973, and one with some college education in 1986 earned less than a high school dropout in 1973.[18] Among black high school graduates in that age range, earnings were almost cut in half (a decline of 43.8 percent).[19] Although businesses may be desperate for more skilled workers, a young person from a poverty background is likely to see the world differently: the probability of obtaining a job with the potential for upward mobility is declining. For example, the proportion of black males ages twenty to twenty-four holding blue-collar jobs capable of supporting a family fell from 46 percent in 1974 to 25 percent in 1986.[20]

A tremendous number of high-wage manufacturing jobs have been lost as companies have closed or moved overseas in the past two decades. As a result, most job growth in the 1980s was in the service sector.

> To be sure, millions of new jobs have been created in recent years, predominantly in the retail trade and service sectors. The jury is still out, however, on whether careers in these growing fields can ever equal the earning power of the jobs that were lost in our declining basic industries. Currently, it takes two retail sector jobs to equal the wages of one lost manufacturing job. In April 1987, construction workers (all ages, both sexes) earned an average weekly wage of $473; manufacturing workers, $399; and retail trade positions, only $178. For young male high school graduates, employment in the retail trades and services now provides 48 percent of their jobs, up from only 30 percent in 1968.[21]

All of this portends the development of a dual labor market, divided according to level of educational attainment. Individuals with middle-class family backgrounds or with perseverance will rise to the top. Others will be relegated to the secondary labor market, with little hope of moving beyond it.

In fact, millions of people are already regarded as "surplus" or "expendable" because they cannot meet rising standards of productivity demanded in an impersonal global economy.[22] As economic changes stifle opportunities for some and relegate other people to oblivion, the social basis for democracy is being eroded. The frustration level is rising among those who feel they have been denied a reasonable chance of success. This leads to higher levels of violence, particularly of whites against minorities who are perceived incorrectly as the source of declining employment opportunities. Already these phenomena were beginning to emerge in the 1980s in the form of white-supremacist groups and in the early 1990s in the form of Japan bashing. Declining economic security is likely to lead to the growing popularity of these forms of racism among displaced white workers.

American ideology places all responsibility for economic success upon individuals. Yet individuals cannot overcome the damage caused by structural changes in the economy. The transfer of industry outside the United States, combined with continued imports of finished products, has led to trade deficits, the loss of high-wage jobs, and a general decline in manufacturing capacity.[23] The declining productivity of the American workforce has little to do with educational decline, since deteriorating schools in the 1970s could not have caused the stagnation of productivity among thirty- to sixty-five-year-old workers in the 1980s. The major factors that have caused America to lose its competitive edge have been high interest rates (which led to a deemphasis of long-term productive investment), low energy prices (which forestalled American investment in efficiency improvements), leasing of high-technology licenses at low rates, high levels of offshore investment at the expense of domestic investment, structural factors related to nations' different stages of industrial development, and the arrogance of American corporate managers (which blinded them to the importance of continuous innovation through quality control).[24]

As in the case of school reform, most proposals to remedy economic ills involve either more top-down control (a national industrial policy) or intensification of existing processes (increasing exports by following an aggressive trade strategy). Both types of policies are implicitly founded upon the economic benefits of free trade, regardless of its human cost in terms of unemployment among low-skilled workers. Neither approach considers the destruction of human dignity as increasing numbers of people feel unable to make a meaningful contribution to society.

Corporate managers who cajole workers and schoolchildren to become more productive implicitly define the purpose of human life in terms of people's contributions to economic growth. But we do not have to accept that inversion of values. Do we want a society in which all people serve a high-powered economy from which an elite benefits or a society in which a less dynamic economy serves all people? Do we want a super-competitive society in which the young, the old, and those who cannot keep up with the pace set by technology are treated as super-fluous? In the reform of both school and work, the ultimate question we should be raising is how to preserve the conditions that enhance personal dignity and local initiative when those values conflict with the demand for efficiency.

Renewing the bonds of community is hindered by the intensification of trade and the geographic mobility that have been tearing away at social cohesion. Rebuilding networks of solidarity will entail greater local self-reliance and new patterns of work and consumption that utilize the abilities of everyone, not just those who fit within the mold imposed by outside corporate or governmental institutions.

Vouchers can foster those networks by providing a basis for social experimentation. By defining education broadly enough to encompass the full range of activities of a community, including its economic survival, self-governing schools could eventually become centers of collective enterprise.

Conclusion

Accountability, like choice, is an appealing concept in the abstract. Yet neither term has any meaning until given some concrete form.

Typically, accountability in education is taken to mean either the observance of rules or the achievement of specific measurable out-puts. Bureaucrats prefer the former; businesses generally prefer the latter. Both follow the same precept that accountability involves top-down control.

Vouchers and other genuine choice plans offer an opposite form of accountability. The logic of choice is based on the belief that parents can monitor the quality of education for their children as well as or better than government officials. Parental oversight may be imperfect, but it is superior to a system that rewards seniority over competence or one that places undue emphasis on standardized tests that measure only a narrow range of skills.

Regardless of how a school is held accountable, students are ulti-mately held accountable when they look for work. The present methods by which employers hold applicants accountable are crude, however. In general, they rely on the degrees and credentials earned rather than the skills and knowledge acquired. The changing characteristics of work have created the need for better measures of competence. Above all, better tests need to be developed, and information about job skills must be transmitted more clearly to teachers and students.

School managers will be able to respond to those signals only if they have the flexibility to modify their curricula and teaching methods. Currently, schools are responsible to powerful political interests, not the people they serve. Vouchers would create an incentive to respond to new work requirements because students and their parents would prefer schools that prepared them well for employment.

Changes in the job market are destroying the future of those young adults who do not have the skills necessary to compete in the new economic order. Society is accountable for those who are being left behind in dead-end, low-skill jobs. Remedying the suffering caused by these dislocations in the economy will require a thorough transformation of the economy in order to strengthen local communities. At a minimum, we need a reevaluation of the policies that have led the United States to become a net importer of many manufactured goods and a net exporter of skilled jobs.

Education policy must make schools more flexible, more supportive, and more helpful in preparing children to participate in the world at large. This does not mean that schools should simply make students more technically proficient and ready to serve the needs of industry. Self-governing schools could be the nuclei around which communities could begin the process of developing local enterprises and other institutions of self-reliance.

Schools need to be diverse and to experiment with various approaches to the task of education. If school managers are free to innovate and learn from mistakes rather than being forced to follow a uniform plan, methods that are most useful will be copied and methods that do not work will be rejected. Vouchers and the deregulation of government schools are an important step in bringing about a new and effective system of education.

15

Prospects and Politics

The battle over our schools is fundamentally a battle over the future of our culture. Those who control the schools control one of the main methods of transmitting culture to the young.

A key question that faces our society today is whether we hold any ideals other than the pursuit of narrow self-interest. Those who are concerned about preserving civic virtue and concern for the public good fear that education vouchers will lead to the commercialization of the one institution that continues to symbolize the dream of unity. The talk of competition among schools in a marketplace has created a fear that schools will go the way of every other institution in American society.

Specifically, the vociferous defenders of the public-school monopoly seem to fear that vouchers will disrupt the common-school spirit and lead to the creation of "lifestyle enclaves" or exclusive groups. But this anxiety ignores history. It is not clear whether government schools have ever served the unifying purpose attributed to them. Exclusion and tracking of racial and ethnic minorities and lower-class whites in urban schools and the flight to the suburbs have been occurring for decades. The common school has remained a convenient fiction to maintain control over the lives of the poor. While the upper middle class has lived in protected enclaves, it has run the schools that everyone else attended.

Individualism, efficiency, and technical achievement, rather than contribution to the common good, are the guiding principles of the government schools. If these schools stood for any of the ideals their proponents claim for them, then ending their monopolistic control might indeed be unwise. Yet there is not a shred of evidence that government schools produce more public-spirited citizens than nongovernment schools.

One of the clearest signs of the moral vacuity of government schools is the cafeteria-style approach to curriculum in high school. The school says, in effect, "Each course is of equal importance. Choose the ones you prefer. Your taste is the ultimate arbiter of value." The curriculum is so designed, however, that all of the choices are grounded on the same philosophical, religious, class, and racial premises. Herein lies the ultimate irony of the debate over choice: public schools currently offer many choices, but the choices are empty. Those who favor choice among schools want to enable families to exercise choice among distinctive alternatives, not simply within a single value-neutral framework.

In order to achieve the original aims of the common school and move beyond the individualism inherent in mass education, it will be necessary to enable people with passionate commitments to create schools. At the same time, individual government schools should be granted the autonomy to define their own missions more clearly in terms of a specific understanding of the civic faith. To the extent that families have the option of leaving a government school, that school should be permitted to take a strong stance on controversial matters (as long as it remains nonsectarian). Choice and distinctiveness go hand in hand in both the public and the private sectors.

Vouchers do not threaten to break down the civic culture or national community; they offer a slim hope of restoring the fading sense of a common good. Loyalty to limited communities can carry over into loyalty to larger communities. One does not learn about responsibility to others except in the context of caring about those immediately at hand.

The critics of vouchers, by representing the status quo, are in the privileged position of being allowed to define the public debate about educational governance. From that privileged position they have held proponents to an impossible standard of evidence.

Critics who have demanded that proponents prove the wisdom of adopting vouchers are saying, in effect, "Show us where it has worked already, and we will believe you." Yet at the same time, the critics (specifically the unions and the school administrators) have used their political influence to block efforts to test the voucher model on a limited basis. They do not want to see the proof.

Moreover, when confronted with evidence from related programs, the critics deny its relevance. In Vermont, choice among nongovernment schools at public expense has quietly succeeded for one hundred years, but that is not *precisely* a voucher system. Tax funds are used for sectarian and independent schools in Europe, Canada, Australia, New Zealand, and Japan, all without calamitous effects. The social fabric has not come unraveled, not even in the Netherlands where almost three-fourths of the student population attend sectarian schools. Catholic schools have operated on a large scale for over a century in this country, often as an act of charity for poor non-Catholic children. They have provided a good education despite the need to charge low tuition and function with large classes. Other independent schools have provided distinctive forms of education for millions of children, yet those schools have not promoted the strange cults or extremist political ideologies predicted by opponents of vouchers.[1] Vouchers for higher education, daycare, job training, housing, and food assistance have all functioned successfully either in full-scale programs or in experiments.

Nevertheless, in the face of all of the evidence that vouchers could make a positive impact on education, strengthen communities, and return a sense of ownership of schools to parents, the idea of vouchers continues to create a lingering uneasiness even among people who have lost confidence in government schools.

Not a Laboratory Experiment

State legislatures may find preliminary tests of vouchers on a limited scale prudent for political reasons. But a full-fledged test of anything more than the administrative issues (how to distribute vouchers, how to provide information, how to regulate fraud) is not really feasible. Testing vouchers is similar to experimenting with democracy. Neither can be tested under laboratory conditions.

The voucher issue is thus similar to the question faced by the citizens of the United States in the 1780s: should we adopt a new constitution? The question could not have been resolved by a controlled experiment. Either the country was going to be a loosely knit confederation of sovereign states, or the states were going to give up some of their power to participate in a more centralized federation. No one knew with any certainty what the outcome of either option would be. No amount of social science research would have aided Americans in making a decision that still profoundly affects us today.

Who could have foretold which, if either, system of governance could carry the burden of two hundred years of conflict and compromise? Who could have foreseen that the Constitution, which made no mention of political parties, would give rise to a two-party system? Who could have imagined that the Constitution, with all of its serious flaws (especially the acceptance of slavery), would have the flexiblity to sustain a diverse nation for so long? No one could have predicted the resilience of the institutions that would arise under the auspices of that brief document. The drafters had to rely on their faith that the necessary institutions would arise that would give body to the skeleton they had created.

In our own time, we face some equally foundational issues. The contest between centralized and community authority in education is vital because the future of democracy hangs on the capacity of each of us as citizens to reclaim a sense of mastery or closure in relation to our own immediate surroundings. The declining authority of institutions based on personal bonds opens the door to all of the dangers of a mass society: demagoguery, tyranny of the majority over dissenting groups, and a general indifference to public life.

The effects of vouchers on the future of democracy cannot be predicted with complete confidence. Community-based education experiences can contribute far more than mass schooling to the kinds of social intelligence needed to sustain open debate and compromise. In ghettos, where the damaging effects of externally imposed schools are felt most keenly, new educational institutions could convert some of the self-destructive rage of youth into constructive political action and economic development.

Broadening Our Choices

The significance of vouchers lies not so much in the choices they offer among existing schools but in the potential they provide for new schools and other educational institutions to form.

Again, there is a similarity to one of the key issues of democracy. There is a tendency to see elections, the choice among candidates, as the central drama of democratic government. Yet few believe that elections in one-party nations have much significance, even if there is a superficial contest among candidates. The issue of choice among candidates is only the most visible element in a vast structure that makes democracy possible. Other important issues include whether political parties are internally democratic, whether interest groups representing ordinary citizens can influence public policy, and whether journalists provide enough information for the public to make intelligent decisions.

In education, the most important question is whether a method can be devised that will release the energies of creativity and caring that will motivate kids to aim high and work hard. Only a system that allows new institutions to come into existence and outworn institutions to die a natural death can tap the strength and determination of the people who are willing to take risks and invest themselves on behalf of children.

The rhetoric of choice masks the most crucial feature of a voucher system: the opportunity for innovators to devise new ways to bring children together for the purpose of learning. In other words, only expanded supply (new schools or learning networks) makes possible expanded demand (choice). Just as political choice relies on small-group associations to create a supply of people who are adept in bargaining, compromising, and gathering support for ideas, so choice in education relies on small groups of people with a vision of how to work with children and help them learn.

There is general agreement that vouchers will expand the supply of schools for middle-class children who are compliant and easy to teach. Yet many fear that no one will want to work with tough kids who have grown up amid drugs, violence, and hopelessness or kids who are belligerent because they cannot read at the age of sixteen and are ashamed of themselves. Who will teach in neighborhoods where gangs control the streets? Who will teach the kids from the "projects"?

The most obvious response to the supply problem is that there are currently people teaching "undesirable" kids or at least going through the motions of teaching them. In government schools, many of the staff in inner-city schools are there because they have no other place to go. In nongovernment schools, the teachers are in a school because they want to be there. Finding people willing to play the role of teacher in difficult situations is thus not the issue. Instead the question is whether government and nongovernment schools can attract to ghetto neighborhoods teachers who are motivated by a calling rather than by security and a pension. That can happen only if a school has a distinctive purpose that will attract dedicated teachers.

There are people who feel called to work with students who have been treated as social outcasts. Some are already teaching in government schools, struggling on behalf of the children against the indifference of the schools in which they work. Some work in inner-city nongovernment schools that parents have chosen. Some work for social service agencies or community organizations such as youth centers. Some work in unrelated fields because the existing system gives them no opportunity to make a contribution. Some are unemployed, perhaps living in a ghetto themselves. Some are mothers and fathers who have watched helplessly as their own children were devoured by "the street."

There are, thus, many people who will work with low-achieving, bitter, alienated students if institutions exist in which the kids are taken seriously and if diverse forms of competence among adults are honored. The supply problem can be solved if we accept that many people without certificates or other formally recognized training are qualified to teach, given the right setting. The capacity to teach also extends to teenagers, who often make the best teachers of younger children who have been turned off by school.

There are tens of millions of children and youths who desperately need to know that there are people who want them to succeed and who will stand by them and encourage them. There are hundreds of thousands, perhaps millions, of adults who would be willing to make that effort in a context where their dedication was valued. Many people choose to become teachers because of that idealism, but they are beaten down by a system that is oriented more toward empire building than learning.

Vouchers would enable concerned adults to form schools that would be appropriate for the needs and interests of the children and youth who are now treated with indifference and contempt. Nongovernment schools will take the lead in creating innovative schools, as they have done in the past. Government schools will need to follow suit by deregulating certification, hiring, and tenure practices. The example set by the private sector and the need to satisfy the demands of families will force changes that will enable government schools to serve the oppressed as well as nongovernment schools.

The Primacy of Economic Factors

All of these efforts will fall short, however, if investment in America, particularly in its cities, declines as capital flows overseas where labor is cheaper. The despair of the ghetto will expand in ever-widening circles to encompass a larger and larger proportion of society if improvement in education is shadowed by shrinking economic opportunities. We appear to be moving already toward a dual economy based on differential skill levels, and the globalization of trade merely exacerbates that condition. The Social Darwinians can applaud this turn of events because they ignore the suffering involved.

Those who oppose vouchers on the grounds that they will leave the less clever behind in the race for economic gain are fighting the wrong battle. The larger question of economic justice depends on designing policies and institutions that can at least partially offset the socially disruptive effects of plant closures, disinvestment in urban centers, and the import of goods produced by cheap labor.

No change in education can substitute for sound investment, trade, and employment policies. Allowing the market to determine international capital flows and wage rates may maximize profits and total consumption worldwide, but it will also destroy the community ethos that forms the social basis of democracy. Market forces can be prevented from undermining community connections. The Japanese have long understood that protecting cultural practices that are socially equalizing may be worth the price of some loss of productivity. There is no reason that we cannot follow the same path in our country.

The rationale for limiting the scope of market activity when it interferes with community and destroys local autonomy is the same as the basis for supporting vouchers. Although there might appear to be a contradiction between these two positions because vouchers represent competition, the more fundamental issue is one of scale. The issue in both educational and economic reform should be: how will a decision affect the ability of people to directly influence the factors that shape their daily lives? Any policy that subjects individuals and small communities to the whims of people who are beyond reach is a step back from democracy.

The Ideology of Social Control

For over a hundred years, school reformers have imagined that education was the engine of social change, when in fact it was an instrument of social control. Horace Mann and other reformers in the 1840s believed that the common schools would impose moral order on the massive influx of immigrants who threatened Anglo-Saxon Protestant purity with poverty, popery, disease, and above all, foreignness. The Progressive reformers at the turn of this century were likewise interested in using the education system to assimilate a new wave of immigrants, but they formulated the additional aim of making the work force more efficient. In both cases, school reform was viewed as hygienic, a condescending effort to cleanse the masses of bad habits, as viewed from the perspective of middle-class normality. Helping the poor by channeling them into suitable education programs, like the process of channeling African Americans into manual work in the Jim Crow era, was a powerful method of social control. It benefitted the dominant groups in society, but not those who were supposedly the beneficiaries of this help.

In a very important sense, then, vouchers do not represent one more step in the reform of education. They are a break with the past century and a half. The rationale for vouchers runs directly counter to the belief in the need to control some segment of the population. Instead, vouchers offer the possibility of empowering people and the communities they form.

The assault on the ideology of control is the feature that causes the concept of vouchers to be so vulnerable to counterattack. For many Americans mistrust of their neighbors outweighs any other consideration. "But how can we control what people will do with vouchers? How can we guarantee good schooling? How can the state protect people from their own stupidity by preventing parents from sending their children to schools where they won't learn anything?" Those are some of the first issues to arise when people are introduced to the idea of vouchers. The people who raise these questions are as often conservative Republicans as liberal Democrats.

The ideology of control is prevalent in attitudes toward child rearing that swing between authoritarian control and permissiveness, which are two sides of the same coin rather than genuine opposites. A child who is misbehaving and one who is simply acting autonomously but not causing any problems are both defined as out of control. An alternative ideology involves teaching children self-discipline, the regulation of their own behavior. From this perspective, adults can give up trying to control children and instead help them pay attention to the consequences of their behavior.

Similarly, when we think of government, the ideology of control posits extreme alternatives: control or no control. According to this world view, if the government does not manage an activity, chaos will result. In the case of education, this assumption leads to the conclusion that if the state legislature or the school board does not decide in great detail what will happen in classrooms, no teaching will occur.

To move away from the ideology of control requires us to look for ways in which a system is self-regulating and to strengthen those features of the system. The opposite of control is not a "do your own thing" philosophy. Freedom requires a framework in which individual decisions can reinforce the social good.

In education, teachers need the freedom to try alternative methods of instruction. They need respect and a sense of professional integrity. Simply granting power to teachers, however, does not solve the problem of overcoming the ideology of control. If teachers are given power in autonomous schools, a balance must be built in by empowering parents to choose among alternative schools. Parental choice creates a feedback system that tells teachers if they are performing satisfactorily. It avoids the need for heavy direct control with administrative rules and procedures.

Self-regulating systems sacrifice some short-term stability for the flexibility that permits greater long-term resilience. In the case of education, bureaucratic control is stable and orderly in the sense of guaranteeing some form of schooling for every child. But within the larger social system, the stability of bureaucratic control is a liability: it amounts to rigidity. Government schools lack a mechanism to respond to changing economic and social conditions. On the other hand, a flexible, self-regulating system that is responsive to changing conditions can never be as stable on a year-to-year basis as a rigid system.

The Opponents of Vouchers

Since innovation reduces job security for the people working in a previously stable system, opposition is inevitable to changes that promote flexibility and choice. Those who have a vested interest in protecting the status quo are concentrated and politically organized, giving them an advantage over those who want change. The huge teachers' unions and the smaller, but still powerful, associations of principals, district superintendents, and school boards differ on how the education budget should be divided, but the groups agree about the need to protect government schools from competition.

Most teachers are sincere and well intentioned. The public imagines, understandably, that the teachers' unions, the National Education Association (NEA) and the American Federation of Teachers (AFT), are as concerned for the well-being of children as individual teachers are. But union leaders are not paid to represent the interests of children. They are paid to gain benefits for teachers. Since they must defend their actions to the tax-paying public, they disguise their motives by claiming that what is good for teachers is good for children. But the unions do not even represent what is good for teachers. As two former state NEA executive directors, Bill Boyton of Nebraska and John Lloyd of Kansas, describe the situation: "Many classroom teachers want to be on the side of change. But their union does not. In fact, the NEA has been the single biggest obstacle to educational reform in this country. We know because we worked for the NEA."[2] Although the NEA and the AFT talk a great deal about educational reform, they should be judged by their actions, not their public relations campaigns.

According to one statistical study of why SAT scores declined, the most significant variable predicting the decline was the percentage of school-district employees covered by collective bargaining. (The study takes account of the changing pool of test takers, which was another major factor in declining scores.)[3] The negative effects of collective bargaining are not surprising: the hostility and conflicts between teachers and administrators in union-dominated districts can hardly be beneficial to students caught in the cross fire. If teachers were able to operate in a collegial atmosphere rather than one marked by conflict, at least part of the energy that is now focused on fighting battles with administrators could be turned toward constructive purposes in the classroom.

But the unions are not interested in improving the educational climate in schools by reducing the level of tension. The unions benefit by stirring up conflict. Under these strained conditions, teachers feel the union is necessary to defend their interests. Likewise, the unions have no desire to raise the standards and prestige of the teaching profession by allowing individual teachers to be judged. By contrast, as Boyton and Lloyd point out: "Most classroom teachers support efforts to improve teaching quality, even at the expense of their own job security. A 1984 Lou Harris poll of teachers found that 84 percent of the respondents favor changes that would make it easier to fire incompetent teachers."[4] This is only one of the ways in which the unions are at sharp variance with teachers. Above all, unions do not want to make schools less bureaucratic because that would mean teachers would work in less union-dependent settings.

The AFT and NEA do not represent the interests of their members because they are not democratically governed. Members (that is, teachers) do not have equal power within the organization. Instead, as is true of almost every large organization, unions function as oligarchies, which means that a small number of insiders set policy for everyone. The staff dominates decision making, including the nomination of elected officers. As Boyton and Lloyd explain: "In its present state, teachers don't run the NEA. The staff does—as much to serve its own interests as the aspirations of teachers and the cause of educational reform."[5] Presumably the same applies to the AFT as well.

The union leadership controls the information available to members just as surely as the controlling interests of a company control the information seen by stockholders. Boyton and Lloyd describe a meeting of western states directors at which they discussed how to avoid providing information to the elected teachers who were nominally their superiors. One even apologized to the other directors for having provided too much information to the state NEA president.[6]

The staff of the NEA control huge revenues, $400 million as of 1984.[7] Since the NEA budget is in direct proportion to teachers' salaries, the budget is presumably $600 to $700 million in 1992. That money represents a massive power base, against which any single teacher or small group of teachers is powerless. As a result, members could not mount an effective campaign against the leadership if they chose. Boyton and Lloyd describe the case of the newly elected president of the state NEA in Nebraska. As a teacher, she felt that teachers should be appointed to the policy-making committees that are now controlled by NEA professional staff. Feeling threatened, the staff kept her in the dark about important events and meetings and ensured her defeat at the next state convention by spreading rumors about her.[8] If the top elected official is unable to influence union policy and control the staff, the average teacher is even more powerless. In fact, without being able to express dissent in the newsletters and journals controlled by the staff, a teacher is less able to shape union policy than a citizen is to influence the foreign policy of the United States.

The powerlessness of individual teachers is best illustrated by the manner in which union dues (the "agency fee") are collected and used. In many districts, dues of $30 to $40 per month are deducted from a teacher's salary by the payroll department. In other words, the agency fee is not a voluntary contribution. Yet an undetermined portion is used to pay for state and federal union offices and to finance state and federal campaigns to which many of the members would not choose to contribute. In theory, teachers can withdraw from the union and designate to charity the portion of their dues that would be used for political purposes.[9] Legally, a teacher is required to pay only that portion of the fee that will be used for local collective bargaining purposes. In practice, the unions have not been willing to provide an accounting to teachers that would reveal how union dues are divided between collective bargaining and political work. In addition, district administrators and unions have failed to notify teachers of their rights, so few are aware that they have the option of not paying the full agency fee.

The policy of keeping teachers in the dark about the activities of their unions has considerable significance to the politics of vouchers. Although the NEA is on record as being in opposition to vouchers, the manner in which the decision was reached shows that the membership was not kept informed about the issues involved. At the annual national meeting in 1970, the Representative Assembly of the NEA adopted by voice vote and with only limited discussion a resolution urging the enactment of federal and state legislation prohibiting the establishment of any voucher plans. As David Kirkpatrick, the leader of the Pennsylvania delegation to that convention, reveals, the NEA leadership had not carefully read the proposal by Christopher Jencks and the Office of Economic Opportunity which they so readily condemned.[10]

Perhaps the staff forced the negative resolution through the convention in a hurry because they were not sure how teachers would react if given a chance to reflect on the opportunities that vouchers would open for them. In fact, in 1971, when the education journal *Phi Delta Kappan* polled its readers on the issue of vouchers, 45 percent of teachers favored vouchers.[11] As David Kirkpatrick observes, "Since the NEA is a very vocal defender of teachers' rights to professional participation and autonomy, it is strange that they would oppose the desire of so many teachers to be empowered to make their own decisions and to work directly with students and parents."[12] If the NEA truly represented the best interests of teachers, its opposition to vouchers would indeed be puzzling.

When there is a conflict between the interests of an organization and the interests of its members, the true significance of an oligarchic structure becomes manifest. In the case of vouchers, the many teachers who are dedicated and good at their jobs would benefit from the increased flexibility of the education system. But unions would be harmed. Teachers would have less incentive to act collectively because they would no longer be so closely tied to an employer with a near monopoly on hiring. Teachers can move from district to district now, but schools are very similar in their hiring criteria. With more options under a voucher system, teachers would be able to rely on their own personal bargaining power. Some would thus withdraw support from their unions.

The unions have fought vouchers with a complex patronage system and disinformation campaign. By funneling money into state and local political campaigns and certain minority-run organizations, the unions have gained tremendous political leverage. They have used that leverage to create the illusion that only conservatives support vouchers, even though polls show support across the political spectrum. The politicians who do the work of the unions in state legislatures have supported academic research and policy analysis that ignores vouchers. Research costs money, but state legislatures will not fund research on vouchers because the unions want to limit the flow of information available to the public on this subject. This is an insidious form of power because the public does not even know how it is being manipulated by the control of ideas.

For the NEA, which is several times larger than the AFT, the voucher issue is one on which no compromise is possible. It hopes to kill the issue by silence if possible, even opposing the proposed experiments by the Office of Economic Opportunity in the early 1970s. Since the staff members are directly threatened by vouchers, their efforts to ensure that the issue is never given a fair hearing are perfectly understandable, but we should be wary of their vested interests being represented to us as the public interest.

AFT president Albert Shanker has taken a seemingly more moderate position on vouchers. In his column in the *New York Times* and in a public debate with John Coons at Stanford, he has endorsed the concept of vouchers for students who are failing in the public schools. As he said in the debate:

> I think the issue of whether we give poor kids an opportunity, the same opportunity that rich kids have, I think I agree with Jack [Coons] on that. I have a proposal on that. There's no point in spending tax dollars and giving it to a kid who's already doing well in public school and saying, "Here you are, here's your $4,000 and you're doing great in public school, but if you don't like it, go to private school."
>
> We ought to do something else. I think we ought to try an experiment with vouchers. We ought to take the 5% of the kids in this country who are illiterate and who also don't attend school very much and when they do attend school they tend to be violent. I think those kids have been failed by the public schools. They are not making it. And the kid who's been in the public schools five, six, seven, eight, nine years and is still absent most of the time, illiterate and violent, is unlikely to change that behavior in another year or so. I think we ought to provide vouchers for these kids as an

experiment. We ought to give them the opportunities to go to private schools because these are the kids with the greatest needs. These are also the kids that the private schools will not accept.[13]

Interestingly, however, when a California group called Parents for Educational Choice drafted a proposed state constitutional amendment based on the concepts put forward by Shanker and asked for his endorsement, he never responded. Apparently Shanker's motive was to sound moderate and flexible in public debate, but he never intended to give serious support to any type of voucher plan.

Constituencies for Change

At present, the groups supporting vouchers in most states are small, isolated, and not well organized. Nevertheless, the growing number of parents, community leaders, and business executives who are fed up with government schools could form the base of support for statewide movements to enact legislation.

Ironically, the difficulty of organizing to promote vouchers points to one of the reasons why vouchers are of such importance. Political life in the sense of public dialogue has declined in this country for two reasons: local political organization has lost power, and television has created a system of one-way mass communication. Both of those factors have made public life flat and uninteresting, for much the same reason that government schools are purposeless. In politics and in education, the winners are those who avoid saying anything of substance that could offend anyone. Schools and legislatures are incapable of responding to growing crises for the same reason. They are victims of the desire to place public life in a realm beyond controversy.

A voucher system represents a method of funding not merely diverse forms of education but diverse political interests as well. The communities that are formed in the context of creating a school may not be explicitly political in the sense of seeking legislation. But the relationships among people that are established in community-based schools could potentially serve as the basis for group action.

No doubt this image of schools as the seedbed of political activity will disturb some people. They cling to an idea of childhood as a time of complete innocence, separate from the world of crime and pollution and war and economic crises. Schools do address all of those topics, but in a way guaranteed to keep kids in a fog. Yet children are already affected, if only by the barrage of images from the media. Children are not innocent; they are simply not offered ways of looking at events that could give them a coherent framework. Not surprisingly, most end up feeling apathetic, cynical, and powerless, just as most of their parents do.

Political organizing for the sake of vouchers is stymied because the kinds of groups that vouchers might ultimately bring into existence do not exist now. There are a handful of public interest groups that advocate for children, but they do not represent any political constituency. There are, here and there, some parent groups concerned about schools, but they have little continuity and no basis for contacting one another.

The most important work to be done to bring vouchers into existence, therefore, is to create groups with common interests, precisely the kinds of groups that are likely to form schools when voucher money is available. At the state level, an organization, existing or new, would need to serve as a clearinghouse to enable groups to contact each other. Perhaps a group could establish a national computer network and electronic bulletin board to enable groups to communicate with one another. Simply overcoming the sense of isolation experienced by individuals seriously concerned about education and tired of the timidity of the education establishment would be an enormous achievement.

The first and most obvious constituency for change is the parents of young children. One way to start organizing them into a network would be to contact daycare centers. Some daycare operators are already politically organized at the state level. Of course, since they do not benefit from the largesse of state and federal support on a level comparable to government schools, they do not have the power of the education establishment. Nevertheless, they have contact with millions of parents who will soon face the prospect of putting their children in school and who are fearful of the consequences. Moreover, daycare operators themselves have an incentive to create a voucher system because they could expand into lower elementary classes, if they have not already done so.

A second source for developing support for vouchers would be community-based organizations that are already providing services in low-income areas. Many of them receive state or federal funds to teach adult classes or provide youth programs. Some actively lobby on behalf of programs. These organizations may be reluctant to endorse vouchers openly, however, for fear that the teachers' unions will use their political clout to have their funds cut off. (This is not a hypothetical possibility. I know directly of two cases like this.) Nevertheless, they may be able to organize groups of parents from among their clients and constituents.

A large number of these organizations are ethnic in orientation. Despite overwhelming support for vouchers among African Americans and Hispanics in every poll, many of the social and political organizations that supposedly represent these minorities have either opposed or been neutral toward vouchers. In part this is due to co-optation of the middle-class members of any ethnic group. Added to that is a deep-seated mistrust of the market as a means of distributing resources, so that all of the rhetoric about competition in education almost invites resistance.

A third potential source of local organizers is the body of teachers, both in government and in nongovernment schools. Both have a lot to gain from a system of education based on choice rather than coercion. The former will gain the possibility of teaching in a more collegial, less depressing atmosphere, while the latter stand to gain security and a well-deserved salary increase. Public-school teachers who openly take on a pro-vouchers role, however, will likely face ostracism within their faculties. Since the teachers' unions control the means of communication within schools (limiting what can be put in teachers' boxes), the debate among teachers will be severely restricted. Nevertheless, it is important that some teachers speak out on this issue and explain why vouchers would improve their lives.

Fourth, churches could play a tremendous role in a pro-voucher consortium at the local and state level. Catholics have been fighting a losing battle for over a century to gain recognition for the contribution their schools have made. Although historic prejudices against them have waned, they must still contend with a legacy of suspicion. Evangelical and conservative Protestants also want the chance to operate their own schools without having to pay twice for the privilege, but many of them are distrustful of even the remotest interference in their activities. Some resist providing information to state officials because of their fear of how the information will be used. African-American churches, many of whose members have been subjected to the worst schools in the nation, have shown themselves less reticent to support vouchers.

The most important political shift that could make vouchers a reality would be support from predominantly white, liberal Protestant denominations. This would mark a major departure from more than a century of support for common schools, support which was originally based on blatant anti-Catholicism. A more ecumenical spirit since Vatican II, plus a growing recognition of the failure of public schools, might result in more Protestants following the lead of Ephraim Radner, an Episcopal priest in Stamford, Connecticut. He has argued that liberal Protestant churches should again become involved in education by providing "what inner-city public schools cannot: communal, cultural, and moral formation to children cast adrift in violence and hopelessness."[14] He further argues that churches should support voucher systems that include sectarian schools. Since liberal Protestantism forms the primary cultural source of support for the status quo in education, an endorsement from several denominations would effectively neutralize the propaganda of the NEA and the AFT.

Fifth, predominantly white liberal organizations, such as the League of Women Voters, might eventually become persuaded to support vouchers or at least remain neutral. These organizations, however, are the ones most likely to demand impossible levels of proof that vouchers will work. They tend to give the term "public" the meaning of government-produced rather than oriented to accomplishing a common purpose. All private interests are thereby suspect, although logically this position would taint their own work since it is private in the sense of not being produced by government. Given their subtle bias toward the centralization of power in the hands of professionals, it is not surprising that they implicitly define democracy either as governance by abstract principles of justice or as majority rule. Both of these definitions give short shrift to the need to protect dissenting points of view. Finally, liberal groups have chosen to interpret the term "equality" as an entitlement to a standardized quantity of government patronage rather than as the creation of empowering intermediate institutions. Either could serve as a counterbalance to the excesses of the impersonal forces of the market, but strengthening intermediate institutions places less trust in the benevolence of the state than traditional liberal remedies. In theory, liberals can support in good conscience the kind of transformations of power represented by vouchers. In practice, however, the faith in rational state power will probably outweigh other considerations.

Sixth, businesses comprise potentially the most important group that could join a coalition favoring a voucher system. They are of special importance because they alone have the financial resources necessary to launch a public information campaign on a scale to match that of the unions. (The NEA alone has hundreds of millions of dollars per year in income.) Moreover, no one has a more immediate interest than employers in raising the level of basic skills of high school graduates. Many corporate executives believe strongly in the power of market-based policies to bring about positive ends. Yet there are two reasons that major corporations have been reluctant to endorse vouchers or to fight for them at the state level.

One reason for the lukewarm response is the long tradition among businesses of paternalism toward workers. That includes providing them with little freedom of action on the job and believing that the best way to induce workers (or students) to produce more is to push them harder. Choice in education does not fit this model; it presupposes a willingness to let people make their own mistakes. Even though many business leaders may believe ideologically in some form of choice in education, in practice, what this seems to mean is: "Choice is good for people as long as the choices are regulated by what I (and others in power) think is best for them." Those who unconsciously act on the basis of this fundamental contradiction are supporters of vouchers only until they understand that freedom of choice means what it says. There are other corporate leaders who fully understand that choice is incompatible with paternalism, and they continue to support vouchers. But for many businesspeople this issue remains a fundamental source of tension.

Another reason for weak support among business leaders lies in their desire to avoid political controversy. Until there is a ground-swell of public opinion favoring vouchers, most businesses would prefer to keep a low profile on the subject. Unless vouchers can shake the negative image of being an elitist attack on public education, the short-term threat of bad publicity will outweigh the long-term benefits to the economy. In extreme cases, businesses might fear that publicly favoring vouchers could lead to a national campaign attacking them, organized by the NEA and the AFT. I have been told that some local affiliates have made threats of this nature, and both unions are adept at political street-fighting. When journalist Debra Saunders published the salaries of teachers in Los Angeles, the local union, United Teachers of Los Angeles, sent Saunders's home phone number to its members, some of whom subsequently harassed her and threatened her until she was forced to change her phone number. As she put it, "I felt that these people sounded like thugs."[15] If the unions are willing to engage in tactics of personal intimidation against a newspaper colum-nist, businesses are understandably reluctant to risk similar attacks on their reputations.

Nevertheless, there are increasing signs that business leaders are beginning to realize the inadequacy of previous top-down efforts to reform education. In part the change may be due to shifts in the work-place environment. American corporations have recognized in recent years that the Japanese management system induces greater produc-tivity because it is not so rigidly authoritarian as the old assembly-line model. There is more accountability within the work team and less to external authority. The comparable shift in education would be toward schools that are more flexible and more likely to win the trust and loyalty of participants. Some business executives have recognized vouchers as a means of accomplishing the same managerial revolution in education that has begun to take place in industry.

Seventh, political parties could endorse and support vouchers. Libertarians are already the leading proponents of the concept, but they lack credibility. Two Republican presidents, Ronald Reagan and George Bush, have supported vouchers, but there has been little visible Republican support at the state level (where it really counts), outside of Wisconsin and Illinois. Currently the Democratic party appears staunchly opposed to vouchers because it is so heavily dominated by money from the teachers' unions and their allies, but the first voucher system for low-income students was initiated by a Democrat (Polly Williams) in Wisconsin. Thus, change is possible.

The fundamental question is what kind of changes the two major parties will make in order to increase their power. Both parties are increasingly perceived by voters as representative of special interests rather than the ordinary middle-class voter. As a result, the intensity of party loyalty has declined. That leaves open the possibility of a realignment of political forces if the leadership of either party can capitalize on the widespread disaffection with existing choices.

Vouchers could be one of several issues that cut across traditional liberal or conservative lines and provide a new framework for thinking about public life. In order to be politically significant, the new framework will need to provide answers to other problems as well: rising welfare costs, declining productivity, health care anxieties, and environmental crises. I propose that vouchers can form one element of a communitarian perspective that rejects both big government and market-oriented individualism as solutions.

Regardless of the precise form that the realignment of political forces takes, the party that simply hangs on to its old base of support will lose ground, while whichever party takes the risk of responding to the demand for change by embracing policies such as vouchers will gain increasing support.

Lingering Problems

Even if all of the groups that might potentially support vouchers could agree in principle on the concept, they will still have to overcome their differences on some key elements.

One issue is whether voucher plans should include religiously based schools. The mistrust in American thought of any source of faith other than rationalism can be traced to the "natural religion" of Deists such as Thomas Jefferson and Benjamin Franklin. It was the basis of the nineteenth-century triumph of common schools based on generic Protestantism over schools tied to denominations that emphasized revelation and authority. It continues today in the contempt of liberal Protestants for conservative, evangelical Protestantism. But if a voucher system excludes sectarian schools, it will be crippled by that limitation. At present, about 90 percent of nongovernment schools are sectarian in origin or purpose. In terms of starting new schools, the energy that drives people to unite behind a common purpose is going to be either a material interest or a philosophy. The latter motivation is more likely to lead to enduring and caring communities than the former. Moreover, excluding schools from eligibility because their foundations are explicitly theistic would amount to an unwarranted interference in freedom of religion. (Since Buddhism, for example, is nontheistic, a Buddhist school might qualify to redeem vouchers when a Christian school would not.)

A second and related issue is the extent to which schools eligible to redeem vouchers should be regulated. Some voucher supporters want schools to have absolute freedom, limited only by the constraints of parental oversight. Most would accept the idea that the state could require financial accounts of the schools to be audited in order to prevent fraud (such as phantom students) and kickbacks. Thus, conflict over regulation primarily concerns whether the state would have veto power over curriculum, instructional methods, or the type of facilities used. Some believe that parental oversight will not guarantee an adequate education and that the state must insist on minimum standards. If they are truly minimal ("Children shall learn to read, write, and do arithmetic."), few would object. If the standards begin to take on the appearance of existing curriculum guidelines or required tests, however, then the point of the voucher system is lost. Autonomy and choice would lose most of their meaning if every school were to adopt the same curriculum or teach toward the same set of exams. Although exams might appear neutral, they will have a tremendous impact in determining whether schools emphasize accumulation of facts, synthesis of ideas, or analytic skills.

A third question is how to treat home schooling. The simplest way to deal with this group (less than 2 percent of the existing school-aged population) would be to allow home schools to participate on an equal footing with others. In other words, a parent teaching three children at home would receive around $12,000 to $15,000 to teach them. This, however, would create tremendous potential for fraud and abuse (for example, if parents simply pocketed the money without teaching their children anything). A variety of alternatives could avoid that problem. Reimbursable expenses could be limited to books and equipment, explicitly excluding salaries. A school could be defined as having at least four or five unrelated children, so that home schooling parents could become eligible to redeem vouchers, but only by forming a consortium that would keep financial records. Some fraud might still be possible, but it would now require collusion on the part of several parents, all willing to deprive their own children of an education. No doubt other mechanisms could be devised that would minimize fraud and be acceptable to home schoolers. If home schoolers could accumulate or "bank" voucher funds for college education, then denial of funds to them in the early years would not be so inequitable.

The fourth and perhaps most important issue is whether and how a voucher plan should seek to help students from low-income families. The division here is between those who believe the poor need an even playing field and those who think the poor should be given compensatory advantages. Since low-income families have been badly treated by the existing paternalistic school system, giving them the opportunity to start new schools in conjunction with community organizations would be a significant step forward. On the other hand, since one ultimate test of an education system is whether it has provided equal opportunity in the job market, fairness might call for additional compensatory measures. One obvious method would be assigning higher voucher amounts to those with low incomes. Another possibility would be setting aside a number of spaces in each school that can only be filled by children from low-income families. A third idea would be to set aside a portion of each voucher to be used by schools only for scholarships for the poor, thus giving an incentive to attract such students. Still another method would be to establish a voucher system exclusively for low-income families as has been done in Milwaukee. Each of these options will gain some supporters and lose others. Obviously vouchers cannot be enacted into law without a winning coalition able to agree on this issue. What is perhaps less obvious is that the compromise reached will only work in practice if it encourages the creation of new schools. If the record-keeping and reporting requirements for complying with the provisions to aid low-income students are too stringent, some potential school operators may decide not to make the effort.

A fifth unresolved issue involves dealing with handicapped students. It will need to be decided how much to set aside for special education and how to divide that money among students with varying disabilities. The additional amounts of money available to disabled students will have to be sufficient to induce schools to accept them. Both separate classes and integrated (mainstream) classes need to be provided in independent schools. Unless these issues can be resolved, severely handicapped students will not be able to benefit from alternatives. They will likely remain in government schools, neither harmed nor helped. Since many handicapped students could benefit from options (and the pressure this would place on government schools to take their needs seriously), it is important to find ways to include the disabled.

The sixth, and most complicated, issue is whether and how to modify the regulations under which government schools operate. One approach would be to leave them as they are and allow them to change in response to the pressure of competition and loss of students. But given the tremendous power of teachers' unions to block substantive change in government-school personnel policies (which is the heart of the issue), it may be naive to believe that competition alone will suffice. A second approach would permit new "charter" schools to be established in the public sector, free of most regulations. This is a policy which Minnesota is following in the absence of vouchers, but the two policies could be adopted in conjunction with each other. A third approach would be to reverse a set of mistakes made in the past few decades in government schools. The state could create incentives for large urban schools and districts to split apart into smaller units, each unit with the power to hire and fire. The state might also require creation of new districts, limits on the scope of collective bargaining, elimination of provisions that require all teachers to join the designated union, simplification of the due process requirements for removing incompetent teachers (or elimination of tenure altogether), and removal of state credentialing requirements. As part of a general voucher package, the charter-schools approach probably makes the most sense, but the political conditions will vary from state to state.

A New Educational Order

The battle over vouchers promises to be intense. Many citizens are angry at the failure to achieve effective reform of the existing educational order and increasingly ready to try fundamental change. On the other hand, those who regard public education as a sacred institution have an emotional investment in blocking tax funds from being used in schools not under direct government control.

The voucher debate is divisive because it extends beyond the usual controversies over textbooks or teacher qualifications. Vouchers are exciting to some and threatening to others because they represent a challenge to a paternalistic way of providing education.

Despite the claims of opponents, vouchers do not represent a retreat into privatization. They simply entail a redistribution of power, a democratization of education. In fact, those who refuse to acknowledge the public's declining faith in schools are inadvertently fomenting the conditions for genuine privatization—the loss of public support for government spending on education. As the population ages and as the number of childless adults increases, the constituency willing to pay for schools is likely to decline. This will be even more true if schools are perceived by the public to be ineffective institutions. If the leaders of government schools allow support for education to erode by clinging to a dying form of social organization, an increasing burden will be thrown on the students' families, regardless of their ability to pay. By contrast, providing every family with the financial means to obtain an education for their children is one way to promote vital schools that will continue to attract public support.

What is at stake is more than the quality of education that will be received by the next generation, although that is of great importance. The contest over vouchers is, at its root, a struggle over the future of democracy. Almost every institution in American life has grown beyond the reach of ordinary people. Education is the most visible example of that phenomenon because the damage to children's lives caused by forcing them to participate in impersonal institutions is particularly painful. Millions of Americans recognize the need to remedy this situation.

The most important step is to restrict government control of key institutions in American society to a level at which ordinary people can become personally involved and make a difference. For too long Americans have accepted paternalism—the idea that some expert knows what is best for us. As a result, we have accepted a range of policies that have stripped each of us of power. The consequences for democracy have been devastating.

Vouchers represent a reversal of this process by promoting community-based organizations in which individuals would not be so powerless. The capacity for self-governance is the basic principle of democracy, and education in a democracy could once again embody that principle by establishing the means to form voluntary communities. The question before us is whether we shall put our faith in institutions that operate "by the people" or ones that are "for the people." That is the fundamental choice in education.

Notes

Introduction

1. Alexis de Tocqueville, *Democracy in America* (New York: Vintage Books, 1945), p. 109. (Originally published in 1840.)

2. Seymour Martin Lipset, Martin Trow, and James Coleman, *Union Democracy* (Garden City, N.Y.: Doubleday, 1956).

3. Thus the teachers' unions contribute to national democracy by serving as intermediate institutions. But this democratizing influence is undermined in two ways. First, these organizations apply political pressure to increase the scope of state and national government involvement in education instead of encouraging local self-governance. Second, the internal structure of the unions is oligarchic. They are controlled by small cliques who manage information and resources. The relationship between teachers and their unions is like that between individual citizens and the state. In both cases, the individual is effectively powerless.

4. Lipset, Trow, and Coleman, *Union Democracy,* p. 89.

5. Peter Berger, Brigitte Berger, and Hansfried Kellner, *The Homeless Mind: Modernization and Consciousness* (New York: Random House, 1973).

6. See Robert Nisbet, *The Quest for Community: A Study in the Ethics of Freedom and Order* (San Francisco: ICS Press, 1990; originally Oxford University Press, 1953), pp. 33–38, on the dangers that war will serve as the primary source of social solidarity in an atomized society that lacks diverse centers of loyalty.

7. Donald Oliver, "Utilitarian Perfectionism and Education: A Critique of Underlying Forces of Innovative Education," in *Social Forces and Schooling: An Anthropological and Sociological Perspective,* ed. Nobuo Kenneth Shimahara and Adam Scrupski (New York: David McKay Company, 1975), pp. 272, 276, 274. This article is also reprinted as chapter 2 of Donald Oliver, *Education and Community: A Radical Critique of Innovative Schooling* (Berkeley, Calif.: McCuthan, 1976). In the latter book, Oliver examines the importance of

affiliative groups and shows how they have functioned in community-based schools such as the Highlander Folk School and those run by Hutterites, kibbutzim, and Synanon.

8. Oliver, *Education and Community,* pp. 8–9.

Chapter 1

1. Theodore Sizer, *Horace's Compromise: The Dilemma of the American High School* (Boston: Houghton Mifflin, 1984) introduces the idea of compromises with students, or "treaties." John I. Goodlad, *A Place Called School: Prospects for the Future* (New York: McGraw Hill, 1984) describes the "passivity among students and emotional flatness in classrooms"; Arthur G. Powell, Eleanor Farrar, and David K. Cohen, *The Shopping Mall High School: Winners and Losers in the Educational Marketplace* (Boston: Houghton Mifflin, 1985) discuss the absence of focused purpose in public schools.

2. Richard Louv, *Childhood's Future* (Boston: Houghton Mifflin, 1990), p. 165.

3. The first and third estimates are cited in Louv, *Childhood's Future,* pp. 154 and 166. The statistic on young black men is frequently cited without any source by civil rights leaders. I have no reason to doubt it.

4. Ibid., p. 166. The author cites a Johns Hopkins University study.

5. Myron Lieberman, *Privatization and Educational Choice* (New York: St. Martin's Press, 1989), table 5.3, p. 136. The author cites the Heritage Foundation's *Education Update* 9 (Fall 1986), p. 7.

6. This number is based on comments made by various business leaders during roundtable discussions of education. See, for example, Jerry Hume, in Jeanne Allen, ed., *Can Business Save Education? Strategies for the 1990s* (Washington, D.C.: Heritage Foundation, 1989), ERIC microfiche ED 311 528.

7. National Center for Education Statistics, *Young Adult Literacy and Schooling* (Washington, D.C.: U.S. Department of Education, 1986), cited in National Center for Education Statistics, *Digest of Education Statistics, 1989* (Washington, D.C.: U.S. Department of Education, 1990), table 334, p. 376.

8. For a discussion of the community-control movement, see George La Noue and Bruce L. R. Smith, *The Politics of School Decentralization* (Lexington, Mass.: D.C. Heath, 1973).

9. Michael Timpane, "Systemic Approaches to Reducing Dropouts," in *Promising Practices: Reducing Dropouts* (Los Angeles: Center for the Study of Evaluation, University of California, 1987), ERIC microfiche ED 294 951.

10. Joseph Schumpeter, *Capitalism, Socialism, and Democracy,* 3d ed. (New York: Harper and Bros., 1950) p. 83. Cited by Denis Doyle, speaking at a Heritage Foundation forum, "Can Business Save Education?" (1988), ERIC microfiche ED 311 528.

11. In my description, I use the film as a parable about the value of publicly acknowledging failure, without regard to the real Joe Clark's behavior as principal. Apparently the film is only loosely based on actual events.

12. Louv, *Childhood's Future,* p. 333.

13. Alfred North Whitehead, *The Aims of Education and Other Essays* (New York: Free Press, 1967), p. 14.

14. Ibid., p. 44.

15. Quoted in Carolyn Lochhead, "The ABC's of Reform: Give Parents a Choice," *Insight*, September 24, 1990, p. 13.

16. Ibid.

Chapter 2

1. According to a 1991 Gallup poll of attitudes on education, 50 percent favored vouchers, 39 percent opposed them, and 11 percent were undecided. Among nonwhites and among inner-city residents, vouchers were favored by 57 percent. A Times-Mirror poll in 1988 generally confirmed these results. It showed 49 percent preferring candidates who supported vouchers and 27 percent preferring those opposed. See *Phi Delta Kappan* (September 1991), p. 47; "Voters Like Vouchers," *Newsweek*, May 16, 1988, p. 8.

Age-group differences in attitudes toward vouchers are not available. The poll data do reveal, however, that support for choice among public schools declines rapidly with the respondents' age. Although the general population supports public school choice by a margin of 62 percent to 33 percent, those fifty and over (the group with the greatest political influence) favor it by a margin of only 50 percent to 42 percent. Presumably support for vouchers also declines with age.

2. See Charles Glenn, *The Myth of the Common School* (Amherst: University of Massachusetts Press, 1987), chapter 4.

3. See Glenn, *Myth of the Common School*, p. 220. Also see Michael Katz, *Reconstructing American Education* (Cambridge, Mass.: Harvard University Press, 1987). Katz describes the perceived options in the early 19th century as democratic localism, paternalistic voluntarism, and bureaucratic centralization.

4. Derrick Bell, *"Brown* and the Interest-Convergence Dilemma," in *Shades of Brown: New Perspectives on School Desegregation,* ed. Derrick Bell (New York: Teachers College Press, 1980), pp. 91–106.

5. Joel Spring, "Dare Educators Build a New School System?" in *Family Choice in Schooling: Issues and Dilemmas,* ed. Michael E. Manley-Casimir (Lexington, Mass.: Lexington Books, 1982), p. 39. See also William J. Wilson, *The Declining Significance of Race: Blacks and Changing American Institutions* (Chicago: University of Chicago Press, 1978), pp. 122–44.

Chapter 3

1. Educational Research Service, *Effects of Open Enrollment in Minnesota* (Arlington, Va., 1990). This booklet summarizes Minnesota House of Representatives Research Department, *Open Enrollment Study: Student and District Participation, 1989–90.*

2. Donald R. Moore and Suzanne Davenport, "High School Choice and Students at Risk," *Equity and Choice* (Februrary 1989), p. 6. This article is derived from the authors' study entitled *The New Improved Sorting Machine,* available from Designs for Change, Suite 1900, 220 S. State Street, Chicago, IL 60604, phone (312) 922-0317.

3. Mary Anne Raywid, "The Mounting Case for Schools of Choice," in *Public Schools by Choice: Expanding Opportunities for Parents, Students, and*

Teachers, ed. Joe Nathan (St. Paul, Minn.: Institute for Learning and Teaching, 1989), p. 26.

4. See Eliot Levinson et al., *The Politics and Implementation of the Alum Rock Multiple Option System: The Second Year, 1973–1974* (Santa Monica, Calif.: Rand Corporation, 1976).

5. Pierce Barker, T.K. Bikson, and J. Kimbrough, *A Study of Alternatives in American Education,* vol. 5, *Diversity in the Classroom* (Santa Monica, Calif.: Rand Corporation, 1978), ERIC microfiche ED 206 058.

6. R. Gary Bridge and Julie Blackman, *A Study of Alternatives in American Education,* vol. 4, *Family Choice in Schooling* (Santa Monica, Calif.: Rand Corporation, 1978), ERIC microfiche ED 206 058, p. 47.

7. F. J. Capell, *A Study of Alternatives in American Education,* vol. 6, *Student Outcomes at Alum Rock* (Santa Monica, Calif.: Rand Corporation, 1979) ERIC microfiche ED 216 426.

8. Information about District 4 is taken largely from two sources. One is Sy Fliegel, "Parental Choice in East Harlem Schools," in *Public Schools by Choice,* ed. Joe Nathan, chapter 5. The other source is Myron Lieberman, *Public School Choice: Current Issues/Future Prospects* (Lancaster, Pa.: Technomic Publishing Company, 1990).

9. These figures, cited in Lieberman, *Public School Choice,* pp. 58–59, are derived from Center for Educational Innovation, *Model for Choice: A Report on District 4,* Educational Policy Paper no. 1 (New York: Manhattan Institute for Policy Research, June 1989), pp. 10–19.

10. Sy Fliegel, "Creative Non-compliance," in *Choice and Control in American Education,* vol. 2, *The Practice of Choice, Decentralization, and Restructuring,* ed. William H. Clune and John F. Witte (Bristol, Pa.: The Falmer Press, 1990), p. 201.

11. Howard L. Hurwitz, *The Last Angry Principal* (Portland, Oreg.: Halcyon House, 1988), pp. 166–67, cited in Lieberman, *Public School Choice,* p. 60.

12. Sy Fliegel, "Creative Non-compliance," p. 207. Actually Fliegel says that 49.4 percent of transfers were reading below grade level.

13. "Known for Choice, New York's District 4 Offers a Complex Tale for Urban Reformers," *Education Week,* November 1, 1989, pp. 1, 13, cited in Lieberman, *Public School Choice,* p. 61.

14. Rolf K. Blank, "Educational Effects of Magnet High Schools," in *Choice and Control,* vol. 2, ed. Clune and Witte, p. 99.

15. Lieberman, *Public School Choice,* p. 61.

16. Quoted by John Merrow, "Schools of Choice: More Talk than Action," in *Public Schools by Choice,* ed. Nathan, p. 119.

17. Sy Fliegel, "Parental Choice in East Harlem Schools," in *Public Schools by Choice,* ed. Nathan, p. 99.

18. John E. Chubb and Terry M. Moe, *Politics, Markets, and America's Schools* (Washington, D.C.: Brookings Institution, 1990), pp. 214–15.

19. Blank, "Educational Effects of Magnet High Schools," p. 102.

20. Ibid.

21. Polly Williams, interviewed by John H. Fund, "Champion of Choice: Shaking up Milwaukee's Schools," *Reason*, October 1990, p. 39.

Chapter 4

1. *Mueller et al. v. Allen et al.*, 463 U.S. 388 (1983).

2. Estelle James, "Public Subsidies for Private and Public Education: The Dutch Case," in *Private Education: Studies in Choice and Public Policy*, ed. Daniel C. Levy (New York: Oxford University Press, 1986), p. 130.

3. See, for example, James S. Catterall, *Tuition Tax Credits: Fact and Fiction* (Bloomington, Ind.: Phi Delta Kappa Educational Foundation, 1983).

4. For an extensive treatment of how education vouchers might overcome inequities and of legal and administrative issues related to voucher plans, see John Coons and Stephen Sugarman, *Education by Choice: The Case for Family Control* (Berkeley: University of California Press, 1978). Also see Coons and Sugarman, *Scholarships for Children* (1992) for a detailed discussion of how their proposed voucher plan would work. The latter book is available for $6 plus postage from the Institute of Governmental Studies, University of California, Berkeley, California 94720.

5. Technically, government schools will benefit if the voucher amount exceeds the cost of an additional student or, in economic terms, the marginal cost. Since marginal-cost estimates are not available, we must rely on average costs.

6. Coons and Sugarman, *Education by Choice*, chapter 11.

7. This idea was proposed to me by Roger Magyar, staff member of the Assembly Republican Caucus, California Legislature, in a personal conversation, April 1991.

8. The 10- to 12-percent approximation is derived from Education Commission of the States, *Special Education Finance: The Interaction Between State and Federal Support Systems*, Report F79-3 (Denver, 1979). The 2:1 ratio of expenditures is from Ellen S. Raphael, Judith D. Singer, and Deborah Klein Walker, "Per Pupil Expenditures on Special Education in Three Metropolitan School Districts," *Journal of Education Finance* 11, no. 1 (Summer 1985), pp. 69–88.

Chapter 5

1. Rona Wilensky and D. M. Kline, *Renewing Urban Schools: The Community Connection* (Denver: The Education Commission of the States, 1988), ERIC microfiche ED 309 218, p. 13. Within the quote, the authors cite Michele Fine and Pearl Rosenberg, "Dropping Out of High Schools: The Ideology of School and Work," *Journal of Education* 165 (1983), pp. 257–72.

2. Quoted in Bernard Lefkowitz, *Tough Change: Growing Up on Your Own in America* (New York: Free Press, 1987), pp. 109–10.

3. Anthony S. Bryk and Yeow Meng Thum, "The Effects of High School Organization on Dropping Out: An Exploratory Investigation," *American Educational Research Journal* 26, no. 3 (Fall 1989), pp. 370–71.

4. Jeannie Oakes, *Keeping Track: How Schools Structure Inequality* (New Haven, Conn.: Yale University Press, 1985), p. 7.

5. Marshall Smith, "Equality of Educational Opportunity: The Basic Findings Reconsidered," in *On Equality of Educational Opportunity,* ed. F. Mosteller and Daniel Moynihan, p. 263, cited in David Kirp, "Schools as Sorters: The Constitutional and Policy Implications of Student Classification," *University of Pennsylvania Law Review* 123, no. 4 (April 1973), p. 730.

6. *Elementary and Secondary School Civil Rights Survey, 1986,* National Summaries (Arlington, Va.: DBS Corporation, and Washington, D.C.: Opportunity Systems, December 1987), table 1, ERIC microfiche ED 304 485.

7. J. McPartland, "The Relative Influence of School and of Classroom Desegregation on the Academic Achievement of Ninth Grade Negro Students," *Journal of Social Issues* (Summer 1969), p. 93, cited in Kirp, "Schools as Sorters," p. 760.

8. U.S. Commission on Civil Rights, *Racial Isolation in the Public Schools* (Washington, D.C., 1967), pp. 86–87, cited in Kirp, "Schools as Sorters," p. 762.

9. Oakes, *Keeping Track,* cites several studies that demonstrate the negative effects of tracking on students' attitudes about themselves. More important, the research conducted by Oakes and others in an in-depth observational study of 38 schools, revealed the same devastating effect on low-track students.

10. Oakes, *Keeping Track,* pp. 12–13.

11. Ibid., pp. 76–77.

12. Joel Spring, *Education and the Rise of the Corporate State* (Boston: Beacon Press, 1972), pp. 105–7. Also see Martin Carnoy, "Educational Reform and Social Control in the United States: 1830–1970," in *The Limits of Educational Reform,* ed. Martin Carnoy and Henry M. Levin (New York: David McKay Company, 1976), pp. 133–40.

13. This discussion derives from National Catholic Education Association, *Catholic High Schools: Their Impact on Low-Income Students* (Washington, D.C., 1986), p. 20.

14. Kenneth Clark, *Dark Ghetto* (New York: Harper and Row, 1965), pp. 131 and 139.

15. U.S. Commission on Civil Rights, *Teachers and Students* (Washington, D.C., 1973), p. 43, cited in Alvin Y. So, *Hispanic Education in the 1980s: Issues and Analyses* (Honolulu: University of Hawaii, 1985), ERIC microfiche ED 270 239, p. 138.

16. Jim Cummins, "Empowering Minority Students: A Framework for Intervention," *Harvard Educational Review* 56, no. 1 (February 1986).

17. Quoted in Joan Davis Ratteray and Mwalimu Shujaa, "Defining a Tradition: Parental Choice in Independent Neighborhood Schools," in *Visible Now: Blacks in Private Schools,* ed. Diana T. Slaughter and Deborah J. Johnson (Westport, Conn.: Greenwood Press, 1988), p. 187. (parentheses in original)

18. Ratteray and Shujaa, "Defining a Tradition," in *Visible Now,* ed. Slaughter and Johnson, pp. 190–91.

Chapter 6

1. *Brown v. Board of Education,* 347 U.S. 483 (1954).

2. Mary Ellen Goodman, *Sanctuaries for Tradition: Virginia's New Private Schools* (Atlanta: Southern Regional Council, 1961), ERIC microfiche ED 029 075. Supreme Court decisions prohibiting the closure of Southern schools to avoid integration include: *Allen,* 207 F. Supp. 349; *Griffin,* 322 F. 2nd 332 (4th Circ.); *Griffin,* 377 U.S. 218; *Lee,* 243 F. Supp. 743; and *Wallace,* 389 U.S. 215.

3. Vouchers were available, but only for whites, in Alabama, Mississippi, Louisiana, Virginia, and South Carolina. See Jim Leeson, "Private Schools Continue to Increase in the South," *Southern Education Report* (November 1966), p. 22.

4. See Vagn K. Hansen, "Desegregation, Resegregation, and the Southern Courts," paper presented to the annual meeting of the Southern Political Association, Atlanta, Georgia (November 1972), ERIC microfiche ED 083 349. He cites *Griffin v. County School Board,* 377 U.S. 218; *Coffey* 296 F. Supp. 1389; *Poindexter v. Louisiana Financial Assistance Commission,* 275 F. Supp. 833; *Louisiana Education Commission,* 393 U.S. 17; *Brown v. South Carolina,* 296 F. Supp. 199.

5. Alabama Council on Human Relations, *The First Year of Desegregation Under Title VI in Alabama* (September 1965), ERIC microfiche ED 031 547.

6. *Green v. County School Board of New Kent County,* 391 U.S. 430 (1968).

7. CORE filed an amicus brief in the case of *Swann v. Charlotte-Mecklenburg Board of Education,* 402 U.S. 1 (1971), arguing that the assumption that black children could not be well educated in predominantly black schools was racist.

8. James M. Palmer, Sr., "Unitary School Systems: One Race or Two," paper presented at the annual meeting of the Association of Southern Agricultural Workers, Jacksonville, Florida (February 1971), ERIC microfiche ED 048 402.

9. Thomas Vitullo-Martin, *Catholic Inner-City Schools: the Future* (Washington, D.C.: United States Catholic Conference, 1979), ERIC microfiche ED 179 646, p. 53.

10. David Tyack, *The One Best System* (Cambridge: Harvard University Press, 1974), p. 110.

11. This is a paraphrase of Walker's position by Tyack, *One Best System,* p. 113.

12. U.S. Immigration Commission, *Children of Immigrants,* I, 8–13, 129–33, cited in Tyack, *One Best System,* p. 117.

13. Joan Davis Ratteray, *Freedom of the Mind* (Washington, D.C.: Institute for Independent Education, 1988), pp. 5–6.

14. Anthony S. Bryk, Valerie Lee, and Julia Smith, "High School Organization and its Effects on Teachers and Students: An Interpretive Summary of the Research," in *Choice and Control in American Education,* vol. 1, *The Theory of Choice and Control in American Education,* ed. William H. Clune and John F. Witte (Bristol, Pa.: Falmer Press, 1990), pp. 148–49.

15. Ibid., p. 148. Also see R. E. Mahard and R. L. Crain, "Research on Minority Achievement in Desegregated Schools," in *The Consequences of School Desegregation,* ed. Christine H. Rossell and Willis D. Hawley, (Philadelphia: Temple University Press, 1983), pp. 103–25.

16. James Coleman et al., *Equality of Educational Opportunity* (Washington, D.C.: U.S. Government Printing Office, 1966). This report argued that most of the variation in achievement that seemed to be due to integration could in fact be accounted for by variations in the social class of students. But David K. Cohen, Thomas F. Pettigrew, and Robert T. Riley, "Race and the Outcomes of Schooling," in *On Equality of Educational Opportunity,* ed. Frederick Mosteller and Daniel P. Moynihan (New York: Random House, 1972), p. 347, contend that the effects of the race and social class of peers cannot be statistically disentangled.

17. *Milliken v. Bradley,* 418 U.S. 717 (1974).

18. Office of Intergroup Relations, *Desegregation and Bilingual Education: Partners in Quality Education* (Sacramento: Calif. Department of Education, 1983). Benjamin Williams was a speaker at a conference with the same title as the booklet, in San Diego, California, April 2–3, 1981.

19. J. Michael Ross, *Effectiveness of Alternative Desegregation Strategies: The Issue of Voluntary vs. Mandatory Policies in Los Angeles* (Boston: Aggregate Data Analysis, Inc., 1983), ERIC microfiche ED 240 185.

20. Ibid., pp. 20–26.

21. See Carl A. Grant, "Desegregation, Racial Attitudes, and Intergroup Contact: A Discussion of Change," *Phi Delta Kappan* (September 1990), pp. 25–32.

22. Derrick Bell, "Learning from Our Losses: Is School Desegregation Still Feasible in the 1980s?" *Phi Delta Kappan* (April 1983), pp. 574–75.

23. Patricia M. Lines, "The Denial of Choice and *Brown v. Board of Education,*" *Metropolitan Education* (Spring 1987), p. 108.

24. Ibid., p. 114.

25. Lines cites as a precedent for this the court's remedy in *Pennsylvania Association for Retarded Children v. Pennsylvania,* 343 F. Supp. 279 (E.D. Pa. 1972). In that decision, the parents of handicapped children were allowed to choose a private school for their children at public expense if the public school was unable to meet the mandated requirements.

26. See the "Amicus Brief Supporting Court-Ordered Voluntary Integration Plan in *Crawford v. Los Angeles Unified School District* (1977)," reprinted in *Parents, Teachers, and Children* (San Francisco: Institute for Contemporary Studies, 1977), Appendix A.

27. William Snider, "Voucher Plan for Disadvantaged Pursued in Kansas City Lawsuit," *Education Week,* August 2, 1989, pp. 1, 28. Also, see Patricia King, "When Desegregation Backfires," *Newsweek,* July 31, 1989, p. 56.

28. Reported in John E. Coons, "Parable from the Prairie," unpublished manuscript, 1989.

29. Derrick Bell quoted in John H. Ralph, "Vouchers Revisited: The Prospects for Education Vouchers in the Eighties," paper presented at the annual meeting of the American Educational Research Association, New York (March 1982), ERIC microfiche ED 216 447.

30. "A 'Free Choice' Plan for Boston Schools," *Newsweek*, April 5, 1982, p. 13, cited in John Ralph, "Vouchers Revisited."

31. Joan Davis Ratteray and Mwalimu Shujaa, *Dare to Choose: Parental Choice at Independent Neighborhood Schools* (Washington, D.C.: Institute for Independent Education, 1987). See also Joan Davis Ratteray: *Freedom of the Mind; Access to Quality: Private Schools in Chicago's Inner City* (Chicago: Heartland Institute, 1986); *Alternative Education Options for Minorities and the Poor* (Washington, D.C.: National Center for Neighborhood Enterprise, 1983); and "Public and Private Choices for African-American Parents," in *Liberating Schools: Education in the Inner City*, ed. David Boaz (Washington, D.C.: Cato Institute, 1991).

32. Robert L. Woodson, "Educational Options for the Disadvantaged," in *Content, Character and Choice in Schooling: Public Policy and Research Implications* (Washington, D.C.: National Council on Educational Research, 1986), p. 125.

33. Kenneth B. Clark, "Alternative Public School Systems," in *Equal Educational Opportunity, Harvard Educational Review* (Cambridge: Harvard University Press, 1969), p. 184.

34. From H. Manuel, *The Education of Mexican and Spanish-speaking Children in Texas* (Austin: University of Texas Fund for Research in the Social Sciences, 1930), cited in Colman Brez Stein, "Hispanic Students in the Sink or Swim Era, 1900–1960," *Urban Education* 20, no. 2 (July 1985), p. 190.

35. See *Mendez et al. v. Westminster School District of Orange County et al.*, Civil Action No. 4292, District Court, San Diego, California, Central Division, February 18, 1946, cited in Mario T. Garcia, *Mexican-Americans: Leadership, Ideology, and Identity* (New Haven: Yale University Press, 1989), p. 56.

36. *Minerva Delgado v. Bastrop Independent School District of Bastrop County, Texas, et al.*, Civil Action No. 388, United States District Court of Texas, Western District of Texas, Austin, Texas, June 15, 1948. Cited in Garcia, *Mexican-Americans*, p. 57, from which the quote in the text comes.

37. Stein, "Hispanic Students," p. 191.

38. G. San Miguel, "Endless Pursuits: the Chicano Educational Experience in Corpus Christi, Texas." Ph.D. diss., Stanford University, 1978. Cited in Stein, "Hispanic Students," p. 191.

39. Stephan Cole, *Attitudes towards Bilingual Education among Hispanics and a Nationwide Sample* (New York: Center for the Social Sciences, 1980), ERIC microfiche ED 235 295, pp. 14–15.

40. Mary Frase Williams, Kimberley Small Hancher, and Amy Hutner, *Parents and School Choice: A Household Survey*, School Finance Project Working Paper (Washington, D.C.: Office of Educational Research and Improvement, U.S. Dept. of Education, 1983), ERIC microfiche ED 240 739, table 3-4, p. 52.

41. See Robert Bezdek and Ray Cross, "Tax Breaks for Parents of Private School Students: Who Favors Them and Who Would Take Advantage of Them?" *Integrated Education* 21, no. 1–6, (1983).

42. This poll was conducted for "a state legislator" according to a February 1979 article in *United Teacher*, the newspaper of the United Teachers of Los Angeles.

43. A paraphrase of Jesse Jackson's comment in his television broadcast of April 29, 1991.

44. James Reusswig, "The National Hispanic University Story," in *The State of Hispanic America* (National Hispanic Center for Advanced Studies and Policy Analysis, n.d.), vol. 3, p. 6.

45. Derrick Bell, "The Moral Dilemma of Middle Class Educational Reformers" (Speech delivered at the Citizens Education Center Northwest Annual Membership Meeting, June 7, 1980).

46. Quoted by Russ Tershey in *Undereducation of Minorities and the Impact on California's Economy,* hearing of the Joint Committee on the State's Economy and the Assembly Standing Committee on Education, California State Legislature, December 9, 1985.

47. Nathan Glazer and Daniel P. Moynihan, *Beyond the Melting Pot* (Cambridge, Mass.: MIT Press, 1970).

Chapter 7

1. Chubb and Moe, *Politics, Markets, and America's Schools,* table 3-2, p. 74.

2. Ibid., table 4-9, p. 129.

3. See, for example, Educational Research Service, "A Summary of Research on Class Size," *Education Digest* (December 1978), pp. 26–28.

4. Gene V. Glass and Mary Lee Smith, *Meta-Analysis of Research on the Relationship of Class-Size and Achievement* (San Francisco: Far West Lab for Educational Research and Development, 1978), ERIC microfiche ED 168 129.

5. Educational Research Service, "Summary of Research," p. 27.

6. James B. Conant, *The American High School Today* (New York: McGraw Hill, 1959). Goodlad, *A Place Called School,* p. 310, concurred in 1984, saying that he would not want to have to justify enrollment of more than five hundred or six hundred students in a high school.

7. Roger G. Barker and Paul V. Gump, *Big School, Small School: High School Size and Student Behavior* (Stanford, Calif.: Stanford University Press, 1964).

8. Mary Anne Raywid, *The Current Status of Choice in Public Education* (Hempstead, N.Y.: Project on Alternatives in Education, Hofstra University, 1982).

9. Robert B. Pittman and Perri Haughwout, "Influence of High School Size on Dropout Rate," *Educational Evaluation and Policy Analysis* 9, no. 4 (Winter 1987), p. 343; Randall W. Eberts, E. Kehoe, and J. Stone, *The Effect of School Size on Student Outcomes: Final Report* (Eugene, Oreg.: Center for Educational Policy and Management, 1984), ERIC microfiche 245 382; and Robert W. Jewell, "School and District Size Relationships: Costs, Results, Minorities, and Private School Enrollments," *Education and Urban Society* (February 1989), p. 152.

10. Noah E. Friedkin and Juan Necochea, "School System Size and Performance: A Contingency Perspective," *Educational Evaluation and Policy Analysis* 10, no. 3, (1988), pp. 237–49. Friedkin and Necochea conclude that "the

negative association among low SES [socio-economic status] school systems is much stronger than the positive association among high SES school systems." See also H. Walberg and W. Fowler, "Expenditure and Size Efficiencies of Public School Districts," *Educational Researcher* 16, no. 7, (1987), pp. 5–13.

11. Valerie Lee and Anthony Bryk, "A Multilevel Model of the Social Distribution of High School Achievement," *Sociology of Education* 62, pp. 172–92.

12. James Coleman et al., *Equality of Educational Opportunity.* See also Irwin Katz, "Academic Motivation and Equal Educational Opportunity," *Equal Educational Opportunity, Harvard Educational Review* (Cambridge: Harvard University Press, 1969), p. 68.

13. Allan C. Ornstein, "Private and Public School Comparisons: Size, Organization, and Effectiveness," *Education and Urban Society* 21, no. 2 (February 1989).

14. National Center for Education Statistics, *Digest of Education Statistics, 1990* (Washington, D.C., 1991), tables 53 and 90. Since median estimates are not provided, I have estimated them from statistics of enrollment by school size.

15. James S. Coleman and Thomas Hoffer, *Public and Private High Schools: The Impact of Communities* (New York: Basic Books, 1987).

16. Powell, Farrar, and Cohen, *The Shopping Mall High School.*

17. Ibid., p. 196.

18. Ibid., p. 197.

19. James Coleman, "Choice, Community, and Future Schools," in *Choice and Control in American Education,* vol. 1, ed. Clune and Witte, p. xvii. Coleman cites the following references:

1. E. Jimenez and M. Lockheed, *The Relative Effectiveness of Single-Sex and Co-educational Schools in Thailand,* Working Paper 27 (Washington, D.C.: The World Bank, 1988).

2. Valerie Lee and Anthony Bryk, "Effects of Single-Sex Secondary Schools on Student Achievement and Attitudes," *Journal of Educational Psychology* 78 (1988), pp. 381–95.

3. Cornelius Riordan, *Boys and Girls in School: Together or Separate* (New York: Teachers College Press, 1990).

20. Sara Lawrence Lightfoot, "Families as Educators: The Forgotten People of *Brown,*" in *Shades of Brown: New Perspectives on School Desegregation,* ed. Derrick Bell (New York: Teachers College Press, 1980), p. 9.

21. Ibid., p. 15.

22. Ibid., p. 16.

23. Mary Anne Raywid, "Community and Schools: A Prolegomenon," *Teachers College Record* 90, no. 2, (Winter 1988), pp. 203–4.

24. Ibid., p. 206.

25. Alan Gartner, Mary Kohler, and Frank Riessman, *Children Teach Children: Learning by Teaching* (New York: Harper and Row, 1971).

26. Ibid., pp. 29–30.

27. Representatives Ember Reichgott and Becky Kelso sponsored the legislation. Ted Kolderie of the Center for Policy Studies in Minneapolis is also knowledgeable about the concepts on which the legislation is based.

28. Denis P. Doyle, Bruce S. Cooper, and Roberta Trachtman, *Taking Charge: State Action on School Reform in the 1980s* (Indianapolis: Hudson Institute, 1991), pp. 123–24.

29. David Brooks, "British Schools Declare Independence," *Wall Street Journal,* July 26, 1990, p. A 11, cited in Doyle, Cooper, and Trachtman, *Taking Charge,* p. 124.

30. Doyle, Cooper, and Trachtman, *Taking Charge,* p. 124.

Chapter 8

1. U.S. Bureau of the Census, *School Enrollment—Social and Economic Characteristics of Students: October 1988 and 1987,* Current Population Reports, Series P-20, no. 443 (Washington, D.C., 1990), table 25.

2. From a *Times-Mirror* survey conducted by Gallup poll, appearing as an advertisement in the *New York Times,* May 8, 1988, p. E 29. Respondents were asked if they would be likely to vote for a candidate who supported vouchers. Forty-nine percent responded "yes," and 27 percent responded "no."

3. Williams, Hancher, and Hutner, *Parents and School Choice: A Household Survey,* table 3-4, p. 52.

4. Ibid.

5. Cibulka, O'Brien, and Zewe, *Inner-City Private Elementary Schools,* table 47.

6. National Catholic Education Association, *Catholic High Schools,* exhibit 13.3, p. 159.

7. Summarized from remarks of Sy Fliegel, "Parental Choice in East Harlem Schools," *Public Schools by Choice,* ed. Joe Nathan (St. Paul, Minn.: The Institute for Learning and Teaching, 1989), p. 96.

8. Coleman and Hoffer, *Public and Private High Schools,* chapter 3.

9. Ibid., p. 132.

10. Jonathan Kozol, *Free Schools* (New York: Bantam Books, 1972), p. 38.

11. This account is derived from a transcript of the television show "60 Minutes," segment entitled "Marva," produced by Suzanne St. Pierre, broadcast November 11, 1979.

12. Information on St. Leo derives from Virgil C. Blum, "Minority Families Sacrifice for Quality Education" (Presented to the American Educational Research Association, 1984), ERIC microfiche ED 249 332.

13. Monroe Saunders, Jr., quoted in John Hood, "Strength in Diversity," *Reason* (January 1991), p. 29. I have relied on this article for information about the Monroe Saunders School.

14. Hood, "Strength in Diversity," p. 31. I have relied on this article and on information provided by the Sheenway School.

15. This account is derived from Barbara Taylor, "The St. Thomas Community School: A Harlem Success Story," in *Private Schools and the Public Good: Policy Alternatives for the Eighties,* ed. Edward McGlynn Gaffney, Jr. (Notre Dame, Ind.: University of Notre Dame Press, 1981), chapter 4.

16. See Ratteray, *Access to Quality.*

17. See Charles Lawrence et al., "Highland Park Free School," in *Education by, for, and about African-Americans: A Profile of Several Black Community Schools*, ed. Deborah Daniels (Lincoln, Nebr.: Nebraska University Curriculum Development Center, 1972), ERIC microfiche ED 086 772, pp. 32–36.

18. This issue is raised by Bonnie Barrett Stretch, "The Rise of the Free School,'" in *Schooling in a Corporate Society: The Political Economy of Education in America*, 2d ed., ed. Martin Carnoy (New York: David McKay Company, 1975), p. 267.

19. Joan Davis Ratteray, "Reaching beyond Our Limitations," based on an interview with Rev. Floyd H. Flake, a member of the U.S. House of Representatives and founder of the Allen Christian School (Washington, D.C.: Institute for Independent Education, 1987), ERIC microfiche ED 286 982.

20. See Susan Dwyer-Schick, "The Islamic School of Seattle," *Ethnic Heritage and Language Schools in America* (Washington, D.C.: American Folk Life Center, Library of Congress, 1988).

21. Kozol, *Free Schools*, pp. 89–90.

22. The following information is derived from an evaluation report and supportive letters made available by Options for Youth, 1717 North Gramercy Place, Los Angeles, CA 90026.

23. Information derived from articles in the *Oakland Tribune* on March 19, 1989; September 2, 1988; October 23, 1980; December 2, 1977; and May 17, 1975 (primarily the 1989 article).

24. Kitty Kelly Epstein, *Oakland Tribune*, March 19, 1989, p. D 6.

25. Ibid.

26. The information on Prince George's County schools is derived from "Applied Anxiety: Forceful Educator Gets Teachers and Children to be More Productive," *Wall Street Journal*, June 5, 1991, pp. A 1, A 4.

Chapter 9

1. Diane Ravitch, *The Troubled Crusade* (New York: Basic Books, 1983), pp. 12–15.

2. Office of Educational Research and Improvement, *The Condition of Education: A Statistical Report, 1987* (Washington, D.C., U.S. Department of Education, 1988), table 2-15, p. 126. Reproduced in Lloyd D. Andrew and Rocco Russo, "Who Gets What? Impact of Financial Aid Policies," ERIC microfiche ED 309 717, p. 18.

3. Andrew and Russo, "Who Gets What?" p. 19.

4. David O'Neill and Sue Goetz Ross, *Voucher Funding of Training: A Study of the GI Bill* (Arlington, Va.: Public Research Institute, 1976), ERIC microfiche ED 141 506, p. 3.

5. Ibid., p. 39.

6. See Chester E. Finn, Jr., *Scholars, Dollars, and Bureaucrats* (Washington, D.C.: Brookings Institution, 1978), p. 63, for a discussion of this early shift from institutional payments to individual entitlements.

7. House Committee on Veterans' Affairs, *Report of Educational Testing Service, Princeton University, on Educational Assistance Programs for Veterans,* September 19, 1973. Cited by Scott E. Sterling, "The GI Bill: An Education Entitlement," in *Entitlement Studies,* ed. Norman D. Kurland (Washington, D.C.: National Institute of Education, 1977), ERIC microfiche ED 138 164, p. 129.

8. Elizabeth Becker, "Student GIs Bilk VA," *Washington Post,* May 28, 1975, p. C 1, cited in Sterling, "The GI Bill," p. 131.

9. The following discussion of proprietary schools is derived (except where noted) from two articles by Wellford W. Wilms: "Proprietary Schools," *Change* 19 (January/February 1987), pp. 10–22, and "Proprietary Schools and Student Financial Aid," *The Journal of Student Financial Aid* 13, no. 2 (Spring 1983), pp. 7–17.

10. "Career Schools: An Overview," *Change* 19 (January/February 1987), pp. 29–34.

11. O'Neill and Ross, *Voucher Funding of Training,* p. A-4, n. 1.

12. These figures are from SRI International, "The Outlook for the Proprietary School Industry," discussion draft of a final memorandum report, project no. 8354, Menlo Park, Calif., 1979. Cited in Wilms, "Proprietary Schools and Student Financial Aid," p. 12.

13. This is a paraphrase of Henry Herzing's words in Wilms, "Proprietary Schools," p. 17.

14. National Center for Education Statistics, *Enrollments and Programs in Noncollegiate Postsecondary Schools* (Washington, D.C.: U.S. Department of Education, 1979), cited in Wilms, "Proprietary Schools and Student Financial Aid," p. 13.

15. Keon S. Chi, *Fraud Control in State Human Services Programs: Innovations and New Strategies* (Lexington, Ky.: Council of State Governments, 1984).

16. Testimony of Rudolph Penner (Urban Institute) before the Senate Banking, Housing, and Urban Affairs Committee, *Hearings on the Abuse and Management of HUD,* Senate Hearing 101-868, vol. 1, 1990.

17. Stephen Bloom, "Richmond District Just Tip of Iceberg, Audit Says," *Sacramento Bee,* May 16, 1991, p. A 1.

Chapter 10

1. See Charles Glenn, *Choice of Schools in Six Nations* (Washington, D.C.: U.S. Government Printing Office, 1989), p. 22.

2. Glenn, *Choice of Schools,* p. 36, paraphrasing Robert Ballion.

3. Ibid., p. 37.

4. Ibid., p. 199.

5. Bundesverfassungsgericht, "In den Verfahren zur verfassungsrechtlichen Pruefung der . . . Privatschulgesetzes der Freien und Hansestadt Hamburg," April 8, 1987. Cited in Glenn, *Choice of Schools,* pp. 204–5.

6. Henry Barnes, "Facts Relevant to the History and Extent of the Worldwide Waldorf Educational Movement" (unpublished paper, 1991).

7. Information on Denmark's support for parental choice in private schools comes from Organization for Economic Cooperation and Development (OECD), *Adolescents and Comprehensive Schooling* (Paris: OECD, 1987), chapter 2; from Peter Mason, *Private Education in the EEC* (April 1983), pp. 7–9; and from Denis P. Doyle, *Family Choice in Education: The Case of Denmark, Holland, and Australia* (Washington, D.C.: American Enterprise Institute, 1984), pp. 9–12.

8. *Adolescents and Comprehensive Schooling*, p. 43.

9. Mason, *Private Education in the EEC*, p. 9.

10. John McClaughry, "Who Says Vouchers Wouldn't Work?" *Reason* (January 1984), citing an interview with Estelle James.

11. Glenn, *Choice of Schools*, pp. 55–78.

12. Ibid., p. 74.

13. Ibid., p. 76.

14. Peter Mason, *Private Education in Australia and New Zealand* (Peter Mason, 1987), p. 15.

15. Peter Mason, *Private Education in the United States and Canada* (Peter Mason, 1985), p. 35.

16. See Donald A. Erickson, "Disturbing Evidence about the 'One Best System,'" in *The Public School Monopoly: A Critical Analysis of Education and the State in American Society,* ed. Robert B. Everhart (San Francisco: Pacific Institute for Public Policy Research, 1982); and Donald A. Erickson, "Choice and Private Schools: Dynamics of Supply and Demand," in *Private Education: Studies in Choice and Public Policy,* ed. Daniel C. Levy (New York: Oxford University Press, 1986).

17. Daniel Patrick Moynihan, "Government and the Ruin of Education," *Harper's* (April 1978), pp. 32–33.

18. Henry Greenleaf Pearson, in *Commonwealth History of Massachusetts,* ed. Albert Bushnell Hart (New York: State History, 1930) vol. 4, pp. 488–91, cited in Charles Glenn, *The Myth of the Common School* (Amherst: University of Massachusetts Press, 1987), p. 72.

19. See Mark J. Hurley, *Church-State Relationships in Education in California* (Washington, D.C.: Catholic University of America, 1948).

20. Both the majority and the dissenting opinions in *Everson v. Board of Education,* 330 U.S. 1 (1947) held that any state aid for religious purposes was a violation of the Establishment Clause of the First Amendment. They cited a debate in the Virginia Assembly in 1785 as the authority for this judgment, ignoring the clear intent of James Madison and others. For an extended treatment of this subject, see "Vincent A. Crockenberg, "An Argument for the Constitutionality of Direct Aid to Religious Schools," *Journal of Law and Education* 13, no. 1, (1984), pp. 1–18.

21. *Mueller et al. v. Allen et al.,* 463 U.S. 388 (1983). See also *Witters v. Washington Department of Services for the Blind,* 474 U.S. 481 (1986), in which the Court held that a state subsidy to a blind man attending a Christian seminary for vocational rehabilitation did not violate the Establishment Clause because, under the state's program, aid that "flows to religious institutions does so only as a result of the genuinely independent and private choices of aid recipients."

22. Except where specified, information about Vermont comes from Joe Nathan, "The Rhetoric and Reality of Expanding Educational Choices," *Phi Delta Kappan* (March 1985), pp. 476–81, or from McClaughry, "Who Says Vouchers Wouldn't Work?" pp. 24–26.

23. Myron Lieberman, *Privatization and Educational Choice*, p. 245.

24. Richard Koehne, quoted in McClaughry, "Who Says Vouchers Wouldn't Work?" p. 26.

25. This section relies on information from Nathan, "Rhetoric and Reality," and Jessie Montano, "Choice Comes to Minnesota," in *Public Schools by Choice*, ed. Joe Nathan (St. Paul, Minn.: The Institute for Learning and Teaching, 1989), pp. 165–80.

26. *Mueller et al. v. Allen et al.*, 463 U.S. 388 (1983).

27. Minnesota Statute, Section 126.22, subdivision 3, clause d. Subdivision 3a includes sectarian schools; Section 126.23 specifies the amount of payment that follows the student.

28. Estimate provided by Mike Ricci, Minnesota Federation of Citizens for Educational Freedom, 350-S Griggs Midway Building, 1821 University Avenue W., St. Paul, MN 55104-2801, phone (612) 645-0373.

Chapter 11

1. Bridge and Blackman, *Study of Alternatives*, vol. 4, chapter 3.

2. Michael A. Olivas, "Information Inequities: A Fatal Flaw in Parochaid Plans," in *Private Schools and the Public Good: Policy Alternatives for the Eighties*, ed. Edward McGlynn Gaffney, Jr. (Notre Dame, Ind.: University of Notre Dame Press, 1981), chapter 12.

3. Melvin Seeman, "Alienation and Knowledge-Seeking: A Note on Attitude and Action," *Social Problems* 20, no. 1, (1972), pp. 3–17. Seeman shows that people who regard themselves as powerless do not invest in information because it will not help them gain mastery over their social environment.

4. Olivas, "Information Inequities," p. 139.

5. Ibid.

6. Ibid., p. 141.

7. Henry M. Levin, "Educational Vouchers and Educational Equality," in *Schooling in a Corporate Society: The Political Economy of Education in America*, ed. Martin Carnoy (New York: David McKay Company, 1972), p. 302.

8. National Center for Educational Statistics, *Digest of Education Statistics, 1990* (Washington, D.C.: U.S. Department of Education, 1991), table 35, p. 48.

9. Levin, "Educational Vouchers and Educational Equality," pp. 304–5.

10. Ibid., p. 306.

11. Patricia A. Bauch and Thomas W. Small, "Parents' Reasons for School Choice in Four Inner-City Catholic High Schools: Their Relationship to Education, Income, Child Aspirations, Religion, and Race," paper presented at the annual meeting of the American Educational Research Association, San Francisco (April 1986), ERIC microfiche ED 298 650, table 5.

12. Ellen Anderson Brantlinger, "Low-Income Parents' Opinions about the Social Class Composition of Schools," *American Journal of Education* (May 1985), pp. 389–408.

13. Henry M. Levin, "Educational Choice and the Pains of Democracy," in *Public Dollars for Private Schools: The Case for Tuition Tax Credits,* ed. Thomas James and Henry Levin (Philadelphia: Temple University Press, 1983), pp. 17–38.

14. Henry M. Levin, *Individual Entitlements for Recurrent Education,* Program Report No. 79-B14 (Palo Alto, Calif.: Center for Educational Research at Stanford, 1979), ERIC microfiche ED 176 370.

15. Henry M. Levin, "The Case for Community Control of Schools," in *New Models for American Education,* ed. James W. Guthrie and Edward Wynne (Englewood Cliffs, N.J.: Prentice-Hall, 1971).

Chapter 12

1. U.S. Bureau of the Census, *School Enrollment,* table 25.

2. For this and following estimates, see Office of Educational Research and Improvement, "Private School Tuition Patterns, 1985–86," *Bulletin* (Washington, D.C.: National Center for Education Statistics, U.S. Department of Education, September 1987). In the 1985–86 school year, when public school costs nationally were around $3,000 to $5,000, sectarian schools constituted around 88% of nongovernment schools, and their mean costs were $952 for Catholic schools and $1,484 for other sectarian schools. The mean cost for the other 12% of nongovernment schools was $3,326. I have inferred that fewer than 10% of all nongovernment schools charged tuition higher than government school costs. Probably fewer than 5% of private-school parents pay tuition higher than government school per-pupil costs.

3. Vitullo-Martin, *Catholic Inner City Schools,* p. 58.

4. See Glenn, *Myth of the Common School,* p. 220.

5. Sally B. Kilgore, "Educational Standards in Private and Public Schools," in *Education on Trial: Strategies for the Future,* ed., William J. Johnston (San Francisco: Institute for Contemporary Studies, 1985), p. 109.

6. For a discussion of the issues related to admissions and selectivity, see Coons and Sugarman, *Education by Choice,* pp. 135–45.

7. Abigail Thernstrom, *School Choice in Massachusetts: A Modest Proposal* (Boston: Pioneer Institute for Public Policy Research, 1991), pp. 78–79. See also Patrick Welsh, *Tales Out of School* (New York: Viking Penguin, 1986), chapter 4.

8. Thernstrom, *School Choice,* pp. 48–49. Thernstrom cites Paul T. Hill, Gail E. Foster, and Tamar Gendler, *High Schools with Character* (Santa Monica, Calif.: Rand Corporation, 1990).

9. The quote is from Carol Jouzaitis, "Top College's Edge a Myth, Book Claims," *Sacramento Bee,* May 23, 1991, p. A 19. Her article is based on Ernest Pascarella and Patrick Terenzini, *How College Affects Students* (San Francisco: Jossey-Bass Publishers, 1991).

10. Coons and Sugarman, *Education by Choice,* p. 139.

11. Kilgore, *Education Standards,* pp. 106–7.

12. Coleman, "Choice, Community, and Future Schools," p. xvi.

13. Fliegel, "Parental Choice in East Harlem Schools," p. 97.

14. Cornelius Riordan, "Public and Catholic Schooling: The Effects of Gender Context Policy," *American Journal of Education* (August 1985), pp. 518–40.

Chapter 13

1. John E. Coons, "As Arrows in the Hand," in *Choice and Control in American Education,* vol. 1, *The Theory of Choice and Control in American Education,* ed. William H. Clune and John F. Witte (Bristol, Pa.: Falmer Press, 1990), p. 323.

2. There is no set of universally accepted terms by which to describe the boundaries between ethnic groups. My definitions are intended to take account of the ambiguous ways they are used.

3. John Higham, "Ethnic Pluralism in Modern American Thought," in *Send These to Me: Jews and Other Immigrants in Urban America* (New York: Atheneum Publishers, 1975). Cited in Nathan Glazer, "Public Education and American Pluralism," in *Parents, Teachers, and Children: Prospects for Choice in American Education* (San Francisco: Institute for Contemporary Studies, 1977), p.108.

4. Glazer, "Public Education and American Pluralism," p. 108.

5. Michael Novak, "Conclusion: Social Trust," in *Parents, Teachers, and Children: Prospects for Choice in American Education* (San Francisco: Institute for Contemporary Studies, 1977), p. 273.

6. Oregon closed its private schools in 1922, nominally in order "to standardize its children" but actually in response to the Ku Klux Klan, which opposed the existence of Catholic schools. See *Pierce v. Society of Sisters,* 268 U.S. 510 (1925) and Stephen Arons, *Compelling Belief: The Culture of American Schooling* (Amherst: University of Massachusetts Press, 1986), p. 208.

7. Quoted in Glenn, *Choice of Schools,* p. 196.

8. Robert N. Bellah et al., *Habits of the Heart: Individualism and Commitment in American Life* (San Francisco: Harper and Row, 1986), pp. 71–75.

Chapter 14

1. Joel Spring, *Education and the Rise of the Corporate State* (Boston: Beacon Press, 1972), p. 32.

2. Raymond Callahan, *Education and the Cult of Efficiency* (Chicago: University of Chicago Press, 1962), p. 73. Cited in Arthur E. Wise, *Legislated Learning: The Bureaucratization of the American Classroom* (Berkeley: University of California Press, 1979), p. 18.

3. Wise, *Legislated Learning,* p. 82.

4. Bobbit, "The Supervision of City Schools," quoted in Callahan, *Education and the Cult of Efficiency,* p. 83, and cited in Wise, *Legislated Learning,* p. 84.

5. Wise, *Legislated Learning,* p. 60.

6. John Bishop, *Information Externalities and the Social Payoff to Academic Achievement* (Ithaca, N.Y.: Cornell University, Center for Advanced Human Resource Studies, 1988), ERIC microfiche ED 297 440.

7. Robert Willis and Sherwin Rosen, "Education and Self-Selection," *Journal of Political Economy* 87 (October 1979), pp. 517–36, cited in Bishop, *Information Externalities.*

8. *Griggs v. Duke Power Company,* 401 U.S. 424.

9. 29 CFR S607.5(b). These guidelines are cited in Bishop, *Information Externalities,* p. 8.

10. *Ward's Cove Packing Company v. Atonio,* 109 S.Ct. 2115 (1989).

11. Sue Berryman, "Education and the Economy: A Diagnostic Review and Implications for the Federal Role," Columbia University, Institute on Education and the Economy (July 1988), ERIC microfiche ED 314 530.

12. Ibid., p. 12.

13. Ibid., p. 9.

14. Lauren Resnick, *Education and Learning to Think* (Washington, D.C.: National Academy Press, 1987). Cited in Berryman, "Education and the Economy," p. 18.

15. Berryman, "Education and the Economy," pp. 25–27.

16. Margery Austin Turner, Michael Fix, and Raymond J. Struyk, *Opportunities Denied, Opportunities Diminished: Discrimination in Hiring* (Washington, D.C.: Urban Institute, 1991).

17. H. Cross, et al., *Employer Hiring Practices: Differential Treatment of Hispanic and Anglo Job Seekers* (Washington, D.C.: Urban Institute, 1990).

18. William T. Grant Foundation Commission on Work, Family, and Citizenship, *The Forgotten Half: Non-College Youth in America, An Interim Report on the School-to-Work Transition.* A copy can be obtained by writing to the foundation at 1001 Connecticut Avenue, N.W., Suite 301, Washington, D.C. 20036-5541. The estimates are derived from Current Population Survey (U.S. Bureau of the Census) Public Use Tapes (March 1974 and March 1987), and calculations were made by Prof. Andrew M. Sum and W. Neal Fogg of the Center for Labor Market Studies, Northeastern University.

19. *The Forgotten Half,* p. 21.

20. Ibid., p. 21.

21. Ibid., p. 19.

22. Charles Burgess, "Growing Up Blighted: Reflections on the Secret Power' in the American Experience," in *Public School Monopoly: A Critical Analysis of Education and the State in American Society,* ed. Robert B. Everhart (Pacific Institute for Public Policy Research, 1982), p. 68. Burgess cites Richard L. Rubenstein, *The Cunning of History* (New York: Harper and Row, 1975) as the source of this idea. He also refers to a number of other social commentators who have observed the way in which children have come to be regarded as excess baggage.

23. See Stephen S. Cohen and John Zysman, *Manufacturing Matters: The Myth of the Post-Industrial Economy* (New York: Basic Books, 1987). Their thesis

is that the kinds of services that can keep the American economy growing are those that are directly linked to manufacturing. If the United States allows its manufacturing capacity to move offshore, it will also lose the services that are internationally competitive. In short, high-tech or knowledge-based services are complements of manufacturing, not substitutes for them. Milton Friedman argues that when foreign governments subsidize production of their exports, the lower cost imports are a pure gift. Cohen and Zysman argue that the gift is a Trojan horse because it reduces the long-run productive capacity of the economy. "The costs of recapturing a lost market share will go up if the infrastructure, in the form of suppliers, and distribution networks, is undermined" (p. 217).

24. See, for example, Robert U. Ayres, *The Next Industrial Revolution: Reviving Industry Through Innovation* (Cambridge, Mass.: Ballinger, 1984). One structural factor that Ayres considers irreversible is the product life cycle that locks initial manufacturers into mass production equipment that soon becomes obsolete, allowing overseas competitors to surpass the home-country producers eventually. Ayres also cites the theory of group behavior proposed by Mancur Olson, *The Rise and Fall of Nations* (New Haven, Conn.: Yale University Press, 1982). Olson suggests that mature societies develop special-interest organizations that collude to protect themselves and end up causing sclerosis or inefficiency in society. This leads to stagflation—inflation and unemployment rising together. On the effects of failing to adopt the quality-control processes that have been largely responsible for Japanese productivity gains, see W. Edwards Deming, *Out of the Crisis* (Cambridge, Mass.: MIT Press, 1986). Deming took the idea of statistical quality control to Japan in the 1950s and is widely honored in that society for his contribution. He is barely known in this country.

Chapter 15

1. Bill Honig, superintendent of public instruction for California, argued in the *New York Times,* June 29, 1990, p. A 25, that vouchers would open the door to "cult schools," astrology, and racism. Typical of those who make hysterical charges against vouchers, he cites no evidence or basis for this claim.

2. Bill Boyton and John Lloyd, "Why the Largest Teachers Union Puts Its Staff First and Education Second," *Washington Monthly,* May 1985, p. 25.

3. Michael M. Kurth, "Teachers' Unions and Excellence in Education: An Analysis of the Decline in SAT Scores," *Journal of Labor Research,* 8, no. 4 (Fall 1987), pp. 351–67.

4. Boyton and Lloyd, "Largest Teachers Union," p. 30.

5. Ibid., p. 26.

6. Ibid., p. 29.

7. Ibid., p. 30.

8. Ibid., p. 29.

9. This is in accordance with the U.S. Supreme Court case *Chicago Teachers Union v. Annie Lee Hudson,* 475 U.S. 292 (1986).

10. David Kirkpatrick, *Choice in Schooling: A Case for Tuition Vouchers* (Chicago: Loyola University Press, 1990), p. 74.

11. *Phi Delta Kappan* (May 1971), p. 512.

12. Kirkpatrick, *Choice in Schooling,* p. 77.

13. From debate at Stanford University, January 18, 1989.

14. Ephraim Radner, "Religious Schooling as Inner-City Ministry," *The Christian Century,* March 6, 1991, pp. 261–62.

15. *Education Week,* January 23, 1991, p. 6.

Bibliography

Alabama Council on Human Relations. *The First Year of Desegregation under Title VI in Alabama*, 1965; ERIC microfiche ED 031 547.

Allen, Jeanne, ed., *Can Business Save Education? Strategies for the 1990s* (Washington, D.C.: Heritage Foundation, 1989).

"Amicus Brief Supporting Court-Ordered Voluntary Integration Plan in *Crawford v. Los Angeles Unified School District* (1977)." Reprinted in Appendix A of *Parents, Teachers, and Children*. San Francisco: Institute for Contemporary Studies, 1977.

Andrew, Lloyd D., and Rocco Russo. "Who Gets What? Impact of Financial Aid Policies." ERIC microfiche ED 309 717.

Appleton, Susan Frelich. "Alternative Schools for Minority Students: The Constitution, the Civil Rights Act, and the Berkeley Experiment." *California Law Review* 61 (May 1973), pp. 858ff.

"Applied Anxiety: Forceful Educator Gets Teachers and Children to be More Productive." *Wall Street Journal*, June 5, 1991, pp. A 1, A 4.

Arons, Stephen. *Compelling Belief: The Culture of American Schooling*. Amherst: University of Massachusetts Press, 1986.

Ayres, Robert U. *The Next Industrial Revolution: Reviving Industry Through Innovation*. Cambridge, Mass.: Ballinger, 1984.

Baratz-Snowden, Joan, Donald Rock, Judith Pollack, and Gita Wilder. *Parent Preference Study*. Princeton, N.J.: Educational Testing Service, 1988.

Barker, P., T. K. Bikson, and J. Kimbrough. *A Study of Alternatives in American Education*, vol. 5, *Diversity in the Classroom*. Santa Monica, Calif.: Rand Corporation, 1978.

Barker, Roger G., and Paul V. Gump. *Big School, Small School: High School Size and Student Behavior*. Stanford, Calif.: Stanford University Press, 1964.

Barnes, Henry. "Facts Relevant to the History and Extent of the Worldwide Waldorf Educational Movement." Unpublished paper, 1991.

271

Bauch, Patricia A., and Thomas W. Small. "Parents' Reasons for School Choice in Four Inner-City Catholic High Schools: Their Relationship to Education, Income, Child Aspirations, Religion, and Race." Paper presented at the annual meeting of the American Educational Research Association, San Francisco, April, 1986, ERIC microfiche ED 298 650.

Becker, Elizabeth. "Student GIs Bilk VA." *Washington Post,* May 28, 1975, p. C 1.

Bell, Derrick. "*Brown* and the Interest-Convergence Dilemma." In *Shades of Brown: New Perspectives on School Desegregation,* edited by Derrick Bell. New York: Teachers College Press, 1980.

———. "Learning from Our Losses: Is School Desegregation Still Feasible in the 1980s?" *Phi Delta Kappan* (April 1983), pp. 574–75.

———. "The Moral Dilemma of Middle Class Educational Reformers." Speech before the Citizens Education Center Northwest Annual Membership Meeting, June 7, 1980.

Bellah, Robert N., Richard Madsen, William M. Sullivan, Ann Swidler, and Steven Tipton. *Habits of the Heart: Individualism and Commitment in American Life.* San Francisco: Harper and Row, 1986.

Berger, Peter, Brigitte Berger, and Hansfried Kellner. *The Homeless Mind: Modernization and Consciousness.* New York: Random House, 1973.

Berryman, Sue. "Education and the Economy: A Diagnostic Review and Implications for the Federal Role." Columbia University, Institute on Education and the Economy, July 1988, ERIC microfiche ED 314 530.

Berube, Maurice R. "The Influence of Teacher Unions in Politics." 1988, ERIC microfiche ED 299 659.

Bezdek, Robert, and Ray Cross. "Tax Breaks for Parents of Private School Students: Who Favors Them and Who Would Take Advantage of Them?" *Integrated Education* 21, no. 1–6 (1983).

Bishop, John. *Information Externalities and the Social Payoff to Academic Achievement.* Ithaca, N.Y.: Cornell University, Center for Advanced Human Resource Studies, 1988.

Blank, Rolf K. "Educational Effects of Magnet High Schools." In *Choice and Control in American Education,* vol. 2, *The Practice of Choice, Decentralization, and Restructuring,* edited by William H. Clune and John F. Witte. Bristol, Pa.: Falmer Press, 1990.

Bloom, Stephen. "Richmond District Just Tip of Iceberg, Audit Says." *Sacramento Bee,* May 16, 1991, p. A 1.

Blum, Virgil C. "Minority Families Sacrifice for Quality Education." Presented to the American Educational Research Association, 1984, ERIC microfiche ED 249 332.

Boaz, David, ed. *Liberating Schools: Education in the Inner City.* Washington, D.C.: Cato Institute, 1991.

Boyton, Bill, and John Lloyd. "Why the Largest Teachers Union Puts its Staff First and Education Second." *Washington Monthly* (May 1985).

Brantlinger, Ellen Anderson. "Low-Income Parents' Opinions about the Social Class Composition of Schools." *American Journal of Education* (May 1985), pp. 389–408.

Bridge, R. Gary, and Julie Blackman. *A Study of Alternatives in American Education*, vol. 4, *Family Choice in Schooling*. Santa Monica, Calif.: Rand Corporation, 1978.

Brooks, David. "British Schools Declare Independence." *Wall Street Journal*, July 26, 1990, p. A 11.

Bryk, Anthony S., Valerie Lee, and Julia Smith. "High School Organization and its Effects on Teachers and Students: An Interpretive Summary of the Research." In *Choice and Control in American Education*, vol. 1, *The Theory of Choice and Control in American Education*, edited by William H. Clune and John F. Witte. Bristol, Pa.: Falmer Press, 1990.

Bryk, Anthony S., and Yeow Meng Thum. "The Effects of High School Organization on Dropping Out: An Exploratory Investigation." *American Educational Research Journal* 26, no. 3 (Fall 1989), pp. 370–71.

Burgess, Charles. "Growing Up Blighted: Reflections on the 'Secret Power' in the American Experience." In *The Public School Monopoly: A Critical Analysis of Education and the State in American Society*, edited by Robert B. Everhart. San Francisco: Pacific Institute for Public Policy Research, 1982.

Callahan, Raymond. *Education and the Cult of Efficiency*. Chicago: University of Chicago Press, 1962.

Capell, F. J. *A Study of Alternatives in American Education*, vol. 6, *Student Outcomes at Alum Rock*. Santa Monica, Calif.: Rand Corporation, 1979.

Carnoy, Martin, ed. *Schooling in a Corporate Society: The Political Economy of Education in America*. New York: David McKay Company, 1972.

"Career Schools: An Overview," *Change* 19 (January/February 1987), pp. 29–34.

Carter, Thomas P., and Michael L. Chatfield. "Effective Bilingual Schools: Implications for Policy and Practice." *American Journal of Education* 95, no. 1 (November 1986).

Casa de la Raza, Separatism or Segregation: Chicanos in Public Education (Hayward, Calif.: Southwest Network, n.d.).

Catterall, Barbara, and Carol Williams. *Voucher Subsidized Child Care: The Hudson County Project*. Trenton: New Jersey Department of Human Services, 1985.

Catterall, James S. *Tuition Tax Credits: Fact and Fiction*. Bloomington, Ind.: Phi Delta Kappa Educational Foundation, 1983.

Center for Educational Innovation. *Model for Choice: A Report on District 4*. Educational Policy Paper no. 1. New York: Manhattan Institute for Policy Research, June 1989.

Chi, Keon S. *Fraud Control in State Human Services Programs: Innovations and New Strategies*. Lexington, Ky.: Council of State Governments, 1984.

Chubb, John E., and Terry M. Moe. *Politics, Markets, and America's Schools*. Washington, D.C.: Brookings Institution, 1990.

Cibulka, James G., Timothy J. O'Brien, and Donald Zewe. *Inner-City Private Elementary Schools: A Study*. Milwaukee: Marquette University Press, 1982.

Clark, Kenneth. "Alternative Public School Systems." In *Equal Educational Opportunity. Harvard Educational Review.* Cambridge: Harvard University Press, 1969.

——. *Dark Ghetto.* New York: Harper and Row, 1965.

Clune, William H., and John F. Witte, eds. *Choice and Control in American Education,* vol. 1, *The Theory of Choice and Control in American Education.* Bristol, Pa.: Falmer Press, 1990.

——. *Choice and Control in American Education,* vol. 2, *The Practice of Choice, Decentralization, and Restructuring.* Bristol, Pa.: Falmer Press, 1990.

Cohen, David K., Thomas F. Pettigrew, and Robert T. Riley. "Race and the Outcomes of Schooling." In *On Equality of Educational Opportunity,* edited by Frederick Mosteller and Daniel P. Moynihan. New York: Random House, 1972.

Cohen, Stephen S., and John Zysman. *Manufacturing Matters: The Myth of the Post-Industrial Economy.* New York: Basic Books, 1987.

Cole, Stephan. *Attitudes towards Bilingual Education among Hispanics and a Nationwide Sample.* New York: Center for the Social Sciences, 1980, ERIC microfiche ED 235 295.

Coleman, James. "Choice, Community, and Future Schools." In *Choice and Control in American Education,* vol. 1, *The Theory of Choice and Control in American Education,* edited by William H. Clune and John F. Witte. Bristol, Pa.: Falmer Press, 1990.

Coleman, James, E. Campbell, C. Hobson, J. McPartland, A. Mood, F. Weinfeld, and R. York. *Equality of Educational Opportunity Report.* Washington, D.C.: U.S. Government Printing Office, 1966.

Coleman, James S., and Thomas Hoffer. *Public and Private High Schools: The Impact of Communities.* New York: Basic Books, 1987.

Conant, James B. *The American High School Today.* New York: McGraw Hill, 1959.

Coons, John E. "As Arrows in the Hand." In *Choice and Control in American Education,* vol. 1, *The Theory of Choice and Control in American Education,* edited by William H. Clune and John F. Witte. Bristol, Pa.: Falmer Press, 1990.

——. "Parable from the Prairie." Unpublished manuscript, 1989.

Coons, John E., and Stephen D. Sugarman. *Education by Choice: The Case for Family Control.* Berkeley: University of California Press, 1978.

——. *Scholarships for Children.* Berkeley, Calif: Institute for Governmental Studies, 1992

Crockenberg, Vincent A. "An Argument for the Constitutionality of Direct Aid to Religious Schools." *Journal of Law and Education* 13, no. 1 (1984), pp. 1–18.

Cross, H., G. Kenney, J. Mell, and W. Zimmermann. *Employer Hiring Practices: Differential Treatment of Hispanic and Anglo Job Seekers.* Washington, D.C.: Urban Institute, 1990.

Cummins, Jim. "Empowering Minority Students: A Framework for Intervention." *Harvard Educational Review* 56, no. 1 (February 1986).

Daniels, Deborah, ed. *Education by, for, and about African-Americans: A Profile of Several Black Community Schools.* Lincoln, Nebr.: Nebraska University Curriculum Development Center, 1972, ERIC microfiche ED 086 772.

Deming, W. Edwards. *Out of the Crisis.* Cambridge, Mass.: MIT Press, 1986.

Doyle, Denis P. *Family Choice in Education: The Case of Denmark, Holland, and Australia.* Washington, D.C.: American Enterprise Institute, 1984.

Doyle, Denis P., Bruce S. Cooper, and Roberta Trachtman. *Taking Charge: State Action on School Reform in the 1980s.* Indianapolis: Hudson Institute, 1991.

Dwyer-Schick, Susan. "The Islamic School of Seattle." in *Ethnic Heritage and Language Schools in America.* Washington, D.C.: American Folk Life Center, Library of Congress, 1988.

Eberts, Randall W., E. Kehoe, and J. Stone. *The Effect of School Size on Student Outcomes: Final Report.* Eugene, Oreg.: Center for Educational Policy and Management, 1984, ERIC microfiche ED 245 382.

Educational Research Service. *Effects of Open Enrollment in Minnesota.* (Arlington, Va., 1990). Summary of Minnesota House of Representatives Research Department. *Open Enrollment Study: Student and District Participation, 1989–90.*

———. "A Summary of Research on Class Size." *Education Digest* (December 1978), pp. 26–28.

Education Commission of the States. *Special Education Finance: The Interaction Between State and Federal Support Systems.* Report F79-3. Denver, 1979.

Elementary and Secondary School Civil Rights Survey. 1986 National Summaries. Arlington, Va.: DBS Corporation and Washington, D.C.: Opportunity Systems, December 1987, ERIC microfiche ED 304 485.

Erickson, Donald A. "Choice and Private Schools: Dynamics of Supply and Demand." In *Private Education: Studies in Choice and Public Policy,* edited by Daniel C. Levy. New York: Oxford University Press, 1986.

———. "Disturbing Evidence about the 'One Best System.'" In *The Public School Monopoly: A Critical Analysis of Education and the State in American Society,* edited by Robert B. Everhart. San Francisco: Pacific Institute for Public Policy Research, 1982.

Everhart, Robert B., ed. *The Public School Monopoly: A Critical Analysis of Education and the State in American Society.* San Francisco: Pacific Institute for Public Policy Research, 1982.

Fine, Michele, and Pearl Rosenberg. "Dropping Out of High Schools: The Ideology of School and Work." *Journal of Education* 165 (1983), pp. 257–72.

Finn, Chester E., Jr. *Scholars, Dollars, and Bureaucrats.* Washington, D.C.: Brookings Institution, 1978.

Fliegel, Sy. "Creative Non-Compliance." In *Choice and Control in American Education,* vol. 2, *The Practice of Choice, Decentralization, and Restructuring,* edited by William H. Clune and John F. Witte. Bristol, Pa.: Falmer Press, 1990.

———. "Parental Choice in East Harlem Schools." Chap. 5 in *Public Schools by Choice: Expanding Opportunities for Parents, Students, and Teachers,* edited by Joe Nathan. St. Paul, Minn.: Institute for Learning and Teaching, 1989.

Freund, Deborah, with Polly M. Ehrenhaft and Marie Hackbarth. *Medicaid Reform: Four Studies of Case Management.* Washington, D.C.: American Enterprise Institute, 1984.

Friedkin, Noah E., and Juan Necochea. "School System Size and Performance: A Contingency Perspective." *Educational Evaluation and Policy Analysis* 10, no. 3 (1988), pp. 237–49.

Friedman, Joseph, and Daniel H. Weinberg, eds. *The Great Housing Experiment.* Beverly Hills, Calif.: Sage Publications, 1983.

Fund, John H. "Champion of Choice: Shaking up Milwaukee's Schools." *Reason* (October 1990).

Gaffney, Edward McGlynn, Jr., ed. *Private Schools and the Public Good: Policy Alternatives for the Eighties* (Notre Dame, Ind.: University of Notre Dame Press, 1981).

Garcia, Mario T. *Mexican-Americans: Leadership, Ideology, and Identity.* New Haven: Yale University Press, 1989.

Gartner, Alan, Mary Kohler, and Frank Riessman. *Children Teach Children: Learning by Teaching.* New York: Harper and Row, 1971.

Gewirtz, Paul. "Choice in the Transition: School Desegregation and the Corrective Ideal." *Columbia Law Review* 86 (1986).

Glass, Gene V., and Mary Lee Smith. *Meta-Analysis of Research on the Relationship of Class-Size and Achievement.* San Francisco: Far West Lab for Educational Research and Development, 1978, ERIC microfiche ED 168 129.

Glazer, Nathan. "Public Education and American Pluralism." In *Parents, Teachers, and Children: Prospects for Choice in American Education.* San Francisco: Institute for Contemporary Studies, 1977.

Glazer, Nathan, and Daniel P. Moynihan. *Beyond the Melting Pot.* Rev. ed. Cambridge, Mass.: MIT Press, 1970.

Glenn, Charles Leslie, Jr., *Choice of Schools in Six Nations.* Washington, D.C.: U.S. Government Printing Office, 1989.

——— . *The Myth of the Common School.* Amherst: University of Massachusetts Press, 1987.

Goodlad, John I. *A Place Called School: Prospects for the Future.* New York: McGraw Hill, 1984.

Goodman, Mary Ellen. *Sanctuaries for Tradition: Virginia's New Private Schools.* Atlanta: Southern Regional Council, 1961, ERIC microfiche ED 029 075.

Grant, Carl A. "Desegregation, Racial Attitudes, and Intergroup Contact: A Discussion of Change." *Phi Delta Kappan* (September 1990), pp. 25–32.

William T. Grant Foundation Commission on Work, Family, and Citizenship. *The Forgotten Half: Non-College Youth in America, An Interim Report on the School-to-Work Transition.* A copy can be obtained from the foundation at 1001 Connecticut Avenue, N.W., Suite 301, Washington, DC 20036-5541.

Guthrie, James W., Michael W. Kirst, Gerald C. Hayward, Allen R. Odden, Julia E. Koppich, Jacob E. Adams, Jr., and Florence R. Webb. *The Condition of Education in California, 1989.* Berkeley: Policy Analysis for California Education, 1990.

Hansen, Vagn K. "Desegregation, Resegregation, and the Southern Courts," November 1972, ERIC microfiche ED 083 349.

Heritage Foundation, *Education Update* 9 (Fall 1986).

Higham, John. "Ethnic Pluralism in Modern American Thought." In *Send These to Me: Jews and Other Immigrants in Urban America.* New York: Atheneum Publishers, 1975.

Hill, Paul T., Gail E. Foster, and Tamar Gendler. *High Schools with Character.* Santa Monica, Calif.: Rand Corporation, 1990.

Holhouser, William L., Jr. "The Role of Supportive Services." In *The Great Housing Experiment,* edited by Joseph Friedman and Daniel Weinberg. Beverly Hills, Calif.: Sage Publications, 1983.

Honig, Bill. *New York Times,* June 29, 1990, p. A 25.

Hood, John. "Strength in Diversity." *Reason* (January 1991).

Hurley, Mark J. *Church-State Relationships in Education in California.* Washington, D.C.: Catholic University of America, 1948.

Hurwitz, Howard L. *The Last Angry Principal.* Portland, Oreg.: Halcyon House, 1988.

James, Thomas, and Henry Levin, eds. *Public Dollars for Private Schools: The Case for Tuition Tax Credits.* Philadelphia: Temple University Press, 1983.

James, Estelle. "Public Subsidies for Private and Public Education: The Dutch Case." In *Private Education: Studies in Choice and Public Policy,* edited by Daniel C. Levy. New York: Oxford University Press, 1986.

Jewell, Robert W. "School and District Size Relationships: Costs, Results, Minorities, and Private School Enrollments." *Education and Urban Society* (February 1989).

Jimenez, E. and M. Lockheed. *The Relative Effectiveness of Single-sex and Co-educational Schools in Thailand.* Working Paper 27. Washington, D.C.: The World Bank, 1988.

Johnston, William J., ed. *Education on Trial: Strategies for the Future.* San Francisco: Institute for Contemporary Studies, 1985.

Jouzaitis, Carol. "Top College's Edge a Myth, Book Claims." *Sacramento Bee,* May 23, 1991, p. A 19.

Katz, Irwin. "Academic Motivation and Equal Educational Opportunity." In *Equal Educational Opportunity. Harvard Educational Review.* Cambridge: Harvard University Press, 1969.

Katz, Michael. *Reconstructing American Education.* Cambridge, Mass.: Harvard University Press, 1987.

Katznelson, Ira, and Margaret Weir. *Schooling for All: Class, Race, and the Decline of the Democratic Ideal.* New York: Basic Books, 1985.

Kilgore, Sally B. "Educational Standards in Private and Public Schools." In *Education on Trial: Strategies for the Future,* edited by William J. Johnston. San Francisco: Institute for Contemporary Studies, 1985.

Kirkpatrick, David. *Choice in Schooling: A Case for Tuition Vouchers.* Chicago: Loyola University Press, 1990.

Kirp, David. "Schools as Sorters: The Constitutional and Policy Implications of Student Classification." *University of Pennsylvania Law Review* 123, no. 4 (April 1973).

"Known for Choice, New York's District 4 Offers a Complex Tale for Urban Reformers." *Education Week*, November 1, 1989, pp. 1, 13.

Kozol, Jonathan. *Free Schools*. New York: Bantam Books, 1972.

Kurth, Michael M. "Teachers' Unions and Excellence in Education: An Analysis of the Decline in SAT Scores." *Journal of Labor Research* 8, no. 4 (Fall 1987), pp. 351–67.

La Noue, George, and Bruce L. R. Smith. *The Politics of School Decentralization.* Lexington, Mass.: D.C. Heath, 1973.

Lawrence, Charles, et al. "Highland Park Free School." In *Education by, for, and about African-Americans: A Profile of Several Black Community Schools,* edited by Deborah Daniels. Lincoln, Nebr.: Nebraska University Curriculum Development Center, 1972, ERIC microfiche ED 086 772, pp. 32–36.

Leacock, Eleanor. "Education, Socialization, and the 'Culture of Poverty.'" In *Schools Against Children,* edited by Annette T. Rubinstein. New York: Monthly Review Press, 1970.

Lee, Valerie, and Anthony Bryk. "Effects of Single-Sex Secondary Schools on Student Achievement and Attitudes." *Journal of Educational Psychology* 78 (1988), pp. 381–95.

———. "A Multilevel Model of the Social Distribution of High School Achievement." *Sociology of Education* 62, pp. 172–92.

Leeson, Jim. "Private Schools Continue to Increase in the South." *Southern Education Report* (November 1966).

Lefkowitz, Bernard. *Tough Change: Growing Up on Your Own in America.* New York: Free Press, 1987.

Levin, Henry M. "The Case for Community Control of Schools." In *New Models for American Education,* edited by James W. Guthrie and Edward Wynne. Englewood Cliffs, N.J.: Prentice-Hall, 1971.

———. "Educational Choice and the Pains of Democracy." In *Public Dollars for Private Schools: The Case for Tuition Tax Credits,* edited by Thomas James and Henry Levin. Philadelphia: Temple University Press, 1983, pp. 17–38.

———. "Educational Vouchers and Educational Equality." In *Schooling in a Corporate Society: The Political Economy of Education in America,* edited by Martin Carnoy. New York: David McKay Company, 1972.

———. *Individual Entitlements for Recurrent Education.* Program Report No. 79-B14. Palo Alto, Calif.: Center for Educational Research at Stanford, 1979, ERIC microfiche ED 176 370.

Levinson, Eliot, S. Abramowitz, W. Furry, and D. Joseph. *The Politics and Implementation of the Alum Rock Multiple Option System: The Second Year, 1973–1974.* Santa Monica, Calif.: Rand Corporation, 1976.

Levy, Daniel C., ed. *Private Education: Choice and Public Policy.* New York: Oxford University Press, 1986.

Lieberman, Myron. *Privatization and Educational Choice.* New York: St. Martin's Press, 1989.

———. *Public School Choice: Current Issues/Future Prospects.* Lancaster, Pa.: Technomic Publishing Company, 1990.

Lightfoot, Sara Lawrence. "Families as Educators: The Forgotten People of *Brown.*" In *Shades of Brown: New Perspectives on School Desegregation,* edited by Derrick Bell. New York: Teachers College Press, 1980.

Lines, Patricia M. "The Denial of Choice and *Brown v. Board of Education.*" *Metropolitan Education* (Spring 1987).

Lipset, Seymour Martin, Martin Trow, and James Coleman. *Union Democracy.* Garden City, N.Y.: Doubleday, 1956.

Lochhead, Carolyn. "The ABC's of Reform: Give Parents a Choice." *Insight* (September 24, 1990).

Louv, Richard. *Childhood's Future.* Boston: Houghton Mifflin, 1990.

Mahard, R. E., and R. L. Crain. "Research on Minority Achievement in Desegregated Schools." In *The Consequences of School Desegregation,* edited by Christine H. Rossell and Willis D. Hawley. Philadelphia: Temple University Press, 1983.

Manley-Casimir, Michael E., ed. *Family Choice in Schooling: Issues and Dilemmas.* Lexington, Mass.: Lexington Books, 1982.

Manuel, H. *The Education of Mexican and Spanish-speaking Children in Texas.* Austin: University of Texas Fund for Research in the Social Sciences, 1930.

Mason, Peter. *Private Education in Australia and New Zealand.* Peter Mason, 1987.

———. *Private Education in the EEC.* Peter Mason, April 1983.

———. *Private Education in the United States and Canada.* Peter Mason, 1985.

McClaughry, John. "Who Says Vouchers Wouldn't Work?" *Reason* (January 1984).

McPartland, J. "The Relative Influence of School and of Classroom Desegregation on the Academic Achievement of Ninth Grade Negro Students." *Journal of Social Issues* (Summer 1969).

Merrow, John. "Schools of Choice: More Talk than Action." In *Public Schools by Choice: Expanding Opportunities for Parents, Students, and Teachers,* edited by Joe Nathan. St. Paul, Minn.: Institute for Learning and Teaching, 1989.

Montano, Jessie. "Choice Comes to Minnesota." In *Public Schools by Choice,* edited by Joe Nathan. St. Paul, Minn.: The Institute for Learning and Teaching, 1989, pp. 165–80.

Moore, Donald R., and Suzanne Davenport. "High School Choice and Students at Risk." *Equity and Choice* (Februrary 1989), pp. 5–10.

———. *The New Improved Sorting Machine.* Copies are available from Designs for Change, Suite 1900, 220 S. State Street, Chicago, IL 60604, phone (312)922-0317.

Mosher, Lottie. *Training Experiences and Early Employment Patterns: Experiences with the Portland WIN Voucher Training Program.* Washington, D.C.: Bureau of Social Science Research, Inc., 1977.

Moynihan, Daniel Patrick. "Government and the Ruin of Education." *Harper's* (April 1978), pp. 28–38.

Nathan, Joe, ed. *Public Schools by Choice.* St. Paul, Minn.: The Institute for Learning and Teaching, 1989.

———. "The Rhetoric and Reality of Expanding Educational Choices." *Phi Delta Kappan* (March 1985), pp. 476–81.

National Catholic Education Association. *Catholic High Schools: Their Impact on Low-Income Students.* Washington, D.C., 1986.

National Center for Education Statistics. *Digest of Education Statistics, 1989.* Washington, D.C.: U.S. Department of Education, 1990.

———. *Digest of Education Statistics, 1990.* Washington, D.C.: U.S. Department of Education, 1991.

———. *Enrollments and Programs in Noncollegiate Postsecondary Schools.* Washington, D.C.: U.S. Department of Education, 1979.

———. *Young Adult Literacy and Schooling.* Washington, D.C.: U.S. Department of Education, 1986.

New York Times. An advertisement showing a *Times-Mirror* survey conducted by Gallup, May 8, 1988, p. E 29.

Newsweek, May 16, 1988, "Voters like vouchers," p. 8.

Nisbet, Robert. *The Quest for Community: A Study in the Ethics of Freedom and Order.* San Francisco: ICS Press, 1990, originally Oxford University Press, 1953.

Novak, Michael. "Conclusion: Social Trust," in *Parents, Teachers, and Children: Prospects for Choice in American Education* (San Francisco: Institute for Contemporary Studies, 1977).

O'Neill, David, and Sue Goetz Ross. *Voucher Funding of Training: A Study of the GI Bill.* Arlington, Va.: Public Research Institute, 1976, ERIC microfiche ED 141 506.

Oakes, Jeannie. *Keeping Track: How Schools Structure Inequality.* New Haven, Conn.: Yale University Press, 1985.

Oakland Tribune, March 19, 1989, p. D 6.

Office of Educational Research and Improvement. *The Condition of Education: A Statistical Report, 1987.* Washington, D.C.: Department of Education, 1988.

———. "Private School Tuition Patterns, 1985–86." *Bulletin.* Center for Education Statistics, U.S. Department of Education (September 1987).

Olivas, Michael A. "Information Inequities: A Fatal Flaw in Parochaid Plans." In *Private Schools and the Public Good: Policy Alternatives for the Eighties,* edited by Edward McGlynn Gaffney, Jr. Notre Dame: University of Notre Dame Press, 1981.

Oliver, Donald. *Education and Community: A Radical Critique of Innovative Schooling.* Berkeley, Calif.: McCutchan, 1976.

———. "Utilitarian Perfectionism and Education: A Critique of Underlying Forces of Innovative Education." In *Social Forces and Schooling: An Anthropological and Sociological Perspective,* edited by Nobuo Kenneth Shimahara and Adam Scrupski. New York: David McKay Company, 1975.

Ols, John M., Jr. (director of housing and community development issues of the GAO). Testimony before the United States Senate Committee on

Banking, Housing, and Urban Affairs. *Hearings on the Abuse and Management of HUD.* Senate Hearing 101-868, vol.1, 1990.

Olson, Mancur. *The Rise and Fall of Nations.* New Haven, Conn.: Yale University Press, 1982.

Organization for Economic Cooperation and Development (OECD). *Adolescents and Comprehensive Schooling,* chap. 2. Paris, 1987.

Ornstein, Allan C. "Private and Public School Comparisons: Size, Organization, and Effectiveness." *Education and Urban Society* 21, no. 2 (February 1989).

Palmer, James M., Sr. "Unitary School Systems: One Race or Two," 1971, ERIC microfiche ED 048-402.

Parents, Teachers, and Children: Prospects for Choice in American Education (San Francisco: Institute for Contemporary Studies, 1977).

Pascarella, Ernest, and Patrick Terenzini. *How College Affects Students.* San Francisco: Jossey-Bass Publishers, 1991.

Pearson, Henry Greenleaf. In *Commonwealth History of Massachusetts,* edited by Albert Bushnell Hart, vol. 4, pp. 488–91. New York: State History, 1930.

Penner, Rudolph. Testimony before the United States Senate Committee on the Banking, Housing, and Urban Affairs Committee. *Hearings on the Abuse and Management of HUD.* Senate Hearing 101-868, vol. 1, 1990.

Phi Delta Kappan, Gallup poll, (September 1991), p. 47.

Phi Delta Kappan, (May 1971), p. 512.

Pittman, Robert B., and Perri Haughwout. "Influence of High School Size on Dropout Rate." *Educational Evaluation and Policy Analysis* 9, no. 4 (Winter 1987).

Powell, Arthur G., Eleanor Farrar, and David K. Cohen. *The Shopping Mall High School: Winners and Losers in the Educational Marketplace.* Boston: Houghton Mifflin, 1985.

Price, James, and Jan Ondrich. Unpublished manuscript, 1983. Cited by James Allen. "The Welfare Cost of the Underground Economy." *Economic Inquiry* 23, no. 2 (April 1985).

Promising Practices: Reducing Dropouts. 1987, ERIC microfiche ED 294 951.

Radner, Ephraim. "Religious Schooling as Inner-City Ministry." *The Christian Century* (March 6, 1991), pp. 261–62.

Ralph, John H. "Vouchers Revisited: The Prospects for Education Vouchers in the Eighties," 1982, ERIC microfiche ED 216 447.

Raphael, Ellen S. et al. "Per Pupil Expenditures on Special Education in Three Metropolitan School Districts." *Journal of Education Finance* 11, no. 1 (Summer 1985), pp. 69–88.

Ratteray, Joan Davis. *Access to Quality: Private Schools in Chicago's Inner City.* Chicago: Heartland Institute, 1986.

———. *Alternative Education Options for Minorities and the Poor.* Washington, D.C.: National Center for Neighborhood Enterprise, 1983.

———. *Freedom of the Mind.* Washington, D.C.: Institute for Independent Education, 1988.

——. "Public and Private Choices for African-American Parents." In *Liberating Schools: Education in the Inner City*, edited by David Boaz. Washington, D.C.: Cato Institute, 1991.

——. "Reaching Beyond Our Limitations." Washington, D.C.: Institute for Independent Education, 1987, ERIC microfiche ED 286 982.

Ratteray, Joan Davis, and Mwalimu Shujaa. *Dare to Choose: Parental Choice at Independent Neighborhood Schools.* Washington, D.C.: Institute for Independent Education, 1987.

——. "Defining a Tradition: Parental Choice in Independent Neighborhood Schools." In *Visible Now: Blacks in Private Schools,* edited by Diana T. Slaughter and Deborah J. Johnson. Westport, Conn.: Greenwood Press, 1988.

Ravitch, Diane. *The Troubled Crusade.* New York: Basic Books, 1983.

Raywid, Mary Anne. "Community and Schools: A Prolegomenon." *Teachers College Record* 90, no. 2 (Winter 1988).

——. *The Current Status of Choice in Public Education.* Hempstead, N.Y.: Project on Alternatives in Education, Hofstra University, 1982.

——. "The Mounting Case for Schools of Choice." In *Public Schools by Choice: Expanding Opportunities for Parents, Students, and Teachers,* edited by Joe Nathan. St. Paul, Minn.: Institute for Learning and Teaching, 1989.

Resnick, Lauren. *Education and Learning to Think.* Washington, D.C.: National Academy Press, 1987.

Reusswig, James. "The National Hispanic University Story." In vol. 3 of *The State of Hispanic America.* National Hispanic Center for Advanced Studies and Policy Analysis, n.d.

Richardson, Ann. *Vouchered Skill Training in WIN: Program Guidelines and Selected Empirical Findings.* Washington, D.C.: Bureau of Social Science Research, Inc., 1977, ERIC microfiche ED 139 915.

Riordan, Cornelius. *Boys and Girls in School: Together or Separate.* New York: Teachers College Press, 1990.

——. "Public and Catholic Schooling: The Effects of Gender Context Policy." *American Journal of Education* (August 1985), pp. 518–40.

Ross, J. Michael. *Effectiveness of Alternative Desegregation Strategies: The Issue of Voluntary vs. Mandatory Policies in Los Angeles.* Boston: Aggregate Data Analysis, 1983.

Rubinstein, Richard L. *The Cunning of History.* New York: Harper and Row, 1975.

Russ Tershey. In *Undereducation of Minorities and the Impact on California's Economy.* Hearing of the Joint Committee on the State's Economy and the Assembly Standing Committee on Education, California State Legislature, December 9, 1985.

San Miguel, G. "Endless Pursuits: the Chicano Educational Experience in Corpus Christi, Texas." Ph.D. diss., Stanford University, 1978.

School Enrollment—Social and Economic Characteristics of Students: October 1988 and 1987. Current Population Reports. Series P-20, no. 443, table 25.

Schumpeter, Joseph. *Capitalism, Socialism, and Democracy.* 3d ed. New York: Harper and Bros., 1950.

Scoll, Barbara, and Roger Engstrom. *Hennepin County Grant Purchase of Child Day Care Through a Voucher System: An Evaluation and Use of Technology.* Minneapolis, Minn.: Hennepin County Community Services Department, 1985.

Seeman, Melvin. "Alienation and Knowledge-Seeking: A Note on Attitude and Action." *Social Problems* 20, no. 1 (1972), pp. 3–17.

Sizer, Theodore. *Horace's Compromise: The Dilemma of the American High School.* Boston: Houghton Mifflin, 1984.

Slaughter, Diana T., and Deborah J. Johnson, eds. *Visible Now: Blacks in Private Schools.* Westport, Conn.: Greenwood Press, 1988.

Smith, Marshall. "Equality of Educational Opportunity: The Basic Findings Reconsidered." In *On Equality of Educational Opportunity,* edited by F. Mosteller and Daniel Moynihan. New York: Random House, 1972.

So, Alvin. *Hispanic Education in the 1980s: Issues and Analyses,* 1985, ERIC microfiche ED 270 239.

Spring, Joel. "Dare Educators Build a New School System?" In *Family Choice in Schooling: Issues and Dilemmas,* edited by Michael E. Manley-Casimir. Lexington, Mass.: Lexington Books, 1982.

———. *Education and the Rise of the Corporate State.* Boston: Beacon Press, 1972.

SRI International. "The Outlook for the Proprietary School Industry," a discussion draft of a final memorandum report, project #8354, Menlo Park, Calif., 1979.

Stein, Colman Brez. "Hispanic Students in the Sink or Swim Era, 1900–1960." *Urban Education* 20, no. 2 (July 1985).

Sterling, Scott E. "The GI Bill: An Education Entitlement." In *Entitlement Studies,* edited by Norman D. Kurland. Washington, D.C.: National Institute of Education, 1977, ERIC microfiche ED 138 164.

Stretch, Bonnie Barrett. "The Rise of the 'Free School.'" In *Schooling in a Corporate Society: The Political Economy of Education in America,* edited by Martin Carnoy. 2d ed. New York: David McKay Company, 1975.

Tanzi, Vito, ed. *The Underground Economy in the United States and Abroad.* Lexington, Mass.: Lexington Books, 1982.

Taylor, Barbara. "The St. Thomas Community School: A Harlem Success Story." Chap. 4 in *Private Schools and the Public Good: Policy Alternatives for the Eighties,* edited by Edward McGlynn Gaffney, Jr. Notre Dame, Ind.: University of Notre Dame Press, 1981.

Thernstrom, Abigail. *School Choice in Massachusetts: A Modest Proposal.* Boston: Pioneer Institute for Public Policy Research, 1991.

de Tocqueville, Alexis. *Democracy in America.* New York: Vintage Books, 1945. (Originally published in 1840.)

Turner, Margery Austin, Michael Fix, and Raymond J. Struyk. *Opportunities Denied, Opportunities Diminished: Discrimination in Hiring.* Washington, D.C.: Urban Institute, 1991.

Tyack, David. *The One Best System.* Cambridge: Harvard University Press, 1974.

United States Commission on Civil Rights. *Racial Isolation in the Public Schools.* Washington, D.C., 1967.

———. *Teachers and Students.* Washington, D.C., 1973.

United States Congress, House Committee on Veterans' Affairs. *Report of Educational Testing Service, Princeton University, on Educational Assistance Programs for Veterans,* September 19, 1973.

United States Senate Commitee on Finance. *New Approaches to Providing Health Care to the Poor: Medicaid Freedom of Choice Waiver Activities.* Washington, D.C., 1984.

Vitullo-Martin, Thomas. *Catholic Inner-City Schools: The Future.* Washington, D.C.: United States Catholic Conference, 1979, ERIC microfiche ED 179 646.

Walberg, H., and W. Fowler. "Expenditure and Size Efficiencies of Public School Districts." *Educational Researcher* 16, no. 7 (1987), pp. 5–13.

Wall Street Journal, March 15, 1991, p. A 11.

Welsh, Patrick. *Tales Out of School.* New York: Viking Penguin, Inc., 1986.

Whitehead, Alfred North. *The Aims of Education and Other Essays.* New York: Free Press, 1967.

Wilensky, Rona, and D. M. Kline. *Renewing Urban Schools: The Community Connection.* Denver: The Education Commission of the States, 1988, ERIC microfiche ED 309 218.

Williams, Mary Frase, Kimberley Small Hancher, and Amy Hutner. *Parents and School Choice: A Household Survey.* School Finance Project Working Paper. Washington, D.C.: Office of Educational Research and Improvement, U.S. Dept. of Education, 1983, ERIC microfiche ED 240 739.

Williams, Benjamin. In Education Commision of the States. *Desegregation and Bilingual Education: Partners in Quality Education.* Sacramento: California Department of Education, 1983.

Willis, Robert, and Sherwin Rosen. "Education and Self-Selection." *Journal of Political Economy* 87 (October 1979), pp. 517–36.

Wilms, Wellford W. "Proprietary Schools and Student Financial Aid." *The Journal of Student Financial Aid* 13, no. 2 (Spring 1983), pp. 7–17.

———. "Proprietary Schools." *Change* 19, (January/February 1987), pp. 10–22.

Wilson, William Julius. *The Declining Significance of Race: Blacks and Changing American Institutions.* Chicago: University of Chicago Press, 1978.

Wise, Arthur E. *Legislated Learning: The Bureaucratization of the American Classroom.* Berkeley, Calif.: University of California Press, 1979.

Woodson, Robert L. "Blacks Seeking Educational Quality." *The Clearinghouse on Educational Choice* 2, nos. 6 and 7 (June and July 1986), p. 1.

———. "Educational Options for the Disadvantaged." *Content, Character and Choice in Schooling: Public Policy and Research Implications.* Washington, D.C.: National Council on Educational Research, 1986.

Further Reading
and Activity

Perhaps the most important work that any citizen can do on education policy is to organize discussions within social, religious, and political organizations. If nothing else, Americans need to become clearer about the terms of the controversies. Can we simultaneously have more centralized guidance in the form of national standards and increased decentralization of power in the form of choice? Do critics of vouchers have any ideas about how to renew education that would encourage risk taking and innovation and break the stranglehold of bureaucracy and politics? How should schools be made accountable? These questions need to be addressed in a spirit of dialogue. We need to move beyond the question of education content to the question of context: How can we create conditions for effective and self-correcting programs?

The education establishment will generate round after round of pseudo-reforms if we sit by idly and wait for experts to solve problems. Thus, it is important for parents and other citizens to learn how schools actually operate and what can be done to improve them.

Readers who wish to continue their study or to become active in education reform can consult a number of resources, many of which can be found in the Bibliography. *Education by Choice* and *Scholarships for Children,* both by John Coons and Stephen Sugarman, offer a somewhat different perspective on vouchers from that found in this book. (*Scholarships for Children* is available for $6, plus postage, from the Institute for Governmental Studies, University of California, Berkeley, CA 94720.) Coons and Sugarman's books, particularly the second, analyze specific components that might be included in voucher legislation.

A summary of state legislative proposals ("Sample Educational Choice Legislation") is available for $7.50 from the Heartland Institute, 634 South Wabash Avenue, Second Floor, Chicago, IL 60605 (phone [312] 427-3060). For $45, the Heartland Institute will provide *Rebuilding America's Schools,* a compendium that contains the report just mentioned and seven others, including design guidelines for legislation, a marketing plan, and a bibliography.

Heartland's marketing plan (available separately for $7.50) is especially valuable for any group contemplating activism. It contains an evaluation of Oregon's failed attempt to enact a tuition tax credit through a citizens' initiative. The Oregon experience shows the importance of drafting legislation properly and building a coalition across the political spectrum in support of new options in education.

Among the groups that support genuine choice in education, Citizens for Educational Freedom, 927 S. Walter Reed Drive, Suite One, Arlington, VA 22204 (phone [703] 486-8311) is the only one devoted exclusively to this issue. Some states have active chapters. A list of other state-based organizations may be obtained from the Heartland Institute.

Index

About the Author

Clifford W. Cobb was born in Atlanta, Georgia, and now lives in Sacramento, California, where he is executive director of the Institute for Educational Choice. He holds a master's degree in public policy from the University of California, Berkeley, and has taught in government schools in the United States and at the Palmore Institute in Kobe, Japan.